SOUND AND SENSE

An Introduction to Poetry

THIRD EDITION

SOUND
AND
SENSE

An Introduction to Poetry

THIRD EDITION

LAURENCE PERRINE
Southern Methodist University

HARCOURT, BRACE & WORLD, INC.
New York   Chicago   San Francisco   Atlanta

COPYRIGHTS AND ACKNOWLEDGMENTS

Cover photograph by JUN ICHIURA

DONALD W. BAKER for "Formal Application," *Saturday Review*, May 11, 1963.

ROBERT BLY for "Driving to Town Late to Mail a Letter," copyright 1962 by Robert Bly. Reprinted from *Silence in the Snowy Fields* by Robert Bly (Wesleyan University Press, 1962) by permission of the author.

THE BODLEY HEAD, LTD. for "Cha Till Maccruimein" by E. A. Mackintosh.

WILLIAM BURFORD for "A Christmas Tree" from *Man Now* by William Burford.

JONATHAN CAPE LIMITED for "The Villain" from *The Collected Poems of W. H. Davies*; "Naming of Parts" and "Judging Distances" from *A Map of Verona* by Henry Reed.

CHATTO & WINDUS LTD. for "Dulce et Decorum Est" and "The Send-Off" from *Poems* by Wilfred Owen.

CHILMARK PRESS, INC. for "John Anderson" from *Collected Poems* by Keith Douglas.

COLLINS-KNOWLTON-WING for "The Troll's Nosegay" from *The Pier Glass* by Robert Graves. Reprinted by permission of Collins-Knowlton-Wing, Inc. Copyright © 1921 by Robert Graves.

MALCOLM COWLEY for "The Long Voyage" from *The Dry Season*, copyright 1941 by Malcolm Cowley.

THE CRESSET PRESS for "The Guitarist Tunes Up" from *On a Calm Shore* by Frances Cornford.

J. M. DENT & SONS LTD. for "The hand that signed the paper felled a city" from *Collected Poems* by Dylan Thomas. For "Poem in October" and "Do not go gentle into that good night" from *The Collected Poems of Dylan Thomas*. By permission of J. M. Dent and the Trustees for the copyrights of the late Dylan Thomas.

DOUBLEDAY & COMPANY, INC. for "The Waking," copyright 1953 by Theodore Roethke from *The Collected Poems of Theodore Roethke*. Reprinted by permission of Doubleday & Company, Inc. For "The Rich Man" from *Tobogganing on Parnassus* by Franklin P. Adams. Copyright 1911 by Doubleday & Company, Inc. Reprinted by permission of the publisher. For two haiku, "Fallen flowers rise" and "A lightning gleam," from *An Introduction to Haiku* by Harold G. Henderson. Copyright © 1958 by Harold G. Henderson. Reprinted by permission of Doubleday & Company, Inc. For "I Knew a Woman," copyright 1954 by Theodore Roethke from *Words for the Wind*, by Theodore Roethke. Reprinted by permission of Doubleday & Company, Inc.

GERALD DUCKWORTH & CO. LTD. for "The Changeling" from *Collected Poems* by Charlotte Mew.

ALAN DUGAN for "Love Song: I and Thou" from *Poems* by Alan Dugan (Yale University Press, 1961).

E. P. DUTTON & CO. for "The Hunt" from *Declensions of the Air* by Louis Kent. Copyright 1950, by E. P. Dutton & Co., Inc. Reprinted by permission of the publisher.

EDITIONS POETRY LONDON for "Vergissmeinicht" from *Collected Poems* by Keith Douglas.

NORMA MILLAY ELLIS for "Safe upon the solid rock" from *Collected Poems* (Harper & Row, 1956) by Edna St. Vincent Millay. Copyright 1922, 1950 by Edna St. Vincent Millay.

FABER & FABER LTD. for "John Anderson" from *Collected Poems* (1966) by Keith Douglas. For "View of a Pig" from *Lupercal* by Ted Hughes. For "Fugal-Chorus" from *For the Time Being* by W. H. Auden. For "A Study of Reading Habits" from *The Whitsun Weddings* by Philip Larkin. For "The Horses" from *One Foot in Eden* by Edwin Muir. For "The Love Song of J. Alfred Prufrock" from *Collected Poems, 1909–1935*, by T. S. Eliot. For "The Unknown Citizen" and "That night when joy began" from *The Collected Shorter Poems 1930–1944* by W. H. Auden. For "The Shield of Achilles" from *The Shield of Achilles* by W. H. Auden. For "Base Details" from *Collected Poems* by Siegfried Sassoon. Reprinted by permission of Faber & Faber Ltd.

PADRAIC FALLON for "Mary Hynes."

FARRAR, STRAUS & GIROUX for "The Drinker," reprinted with the permission of Farrar, Straus & Giroux, Inc., from *For the Union Dead* by Robert Lowell. Copyright © 1960 by Robert Lowell.

FUNK AND WAGNALLS for haiku by Moritake, "The falling flower." Reprinted from *Poetry Handbook; A Dictionary of Terms* by Babette Deutsch. By permission of the publishers, Funk & Wagnalls, New York.

VICTOR GOLLANCZ, LTD. for "A Bookshop Idyll" from *A Case of Samples* by Kingsley Amis.

GROVE PRESS, INC. for "The Horses" from *One Foot in Eden* by Edwin Muir.

HARCOURT, BRACE & WORLD, INC. for "Stop" from *Advice to a Prophet* by Richard Wilbur. © 1961 by Richard Wilbur. Reprinted from his volume *Advice to a Prophet and Other Poems* by permission of Harcourt, Brace & World, Inc. First published in *The New Yorker*. For "Children of Light" from *Lord Weary's Castle*, copyright 1944, 1946, by Robert Lowell. Reprinted by permission of Harcourt, Brace & World, Inc. For "when serpents bargain for the right to squirm" from *Poems 1923–1954* by E. E. Cummings. Copyright 1950 by E. E. Cummings. Reprinted from his volume *Poems 1923–1954* by permission of Harcourt, Brace & World, Inc. For "the greedy the people" from *73 Poems* by E. E. Cummings. © 1960 by E. E. Cummings. Reprinted from his volume *73 Poems* by permission of Harcourt, Brace & World, Inc. For "Naming of Parts" and "Judging Distances" from *A Map of Verona and Other Poems*, copyright 1947 by Henry Reed. Reprinted by permission of Harcourt, Brace & World, Inc. For "Splinter" from *Good Morning, America*, copyright 1928, 1956, by Carl Sandburg. Reprinted by permission of Harcourt, Brace & World, Inc. For "A Bookshop Idyll" from *A Case of Samples* © 1956 by Kingsley Amis. Reprinted by permission of Harcourt, Brace & World, Inc. For "A Baroque Wall-Fountain in the Villa Sciarra" from *Things of This World*, © 1956 by Richard Wilbur.

ix

True ease in writing comes from art, not chance,
As those move easiest who have learned to dance.
'Tis not enough no harshness gives offense,
The sound must seem an echo to the sense.

ALEXANDER POPE from *An Essay on Criticism*

Contents

Preface

The third edition of *Sound and Sense*, like the earlier editions, is written for the college student who is beginning a serious study of poetry. It seeks to give him a sufficient grasp of the nature and variety of poetry, some reasonable means for reading it with appreciative understanding, and a few primary ideas of how to evaluate it. The separate chapters gradually introduce the student to the elements of poetry, putting the emphasis always on *how* and *why*.

How can the reader use these elements to get at the meaning of the poem, to interpret it correctly and respond to it adequately?

Why does the poet use these elements? What values have they for the poet and the reader?

In matters of theory, some issues are undoubtedly oversimplified, but I hope none seriously. The purpose has always been to give the beginning student something he can understand and use. The first assumptions of *Sound and Sense* are that poetry needs to be read carefully and thought about considerably and that, when so read, poetry gives its readers continuing rewards in experience and understanding.

The third edition differs from the second chiefly in two respects: almost a third of the poems are new, and the number of poems by contemporary poets has been increased. As in the second edition, three poets—Frost, Housman, and Yeats—are represented by a sufficient number of poems to support study of them as individual artists.

A book of this kind inevitably owes something to all who have thought or written about poetry. It would be impossible to express all indebtedness, but for personal advice, criticism, and assistance I wish especially to thank my wife, Catherine Perrine; Professor Maynard Mack, Yale University; Charles S. Holmes, Pomona College; Donald Peet, Indiana University; James W. Byrd, East Texas State University; Calvin L. Skaggs, Drew University; Professor Willis Glover, Mercer University; and Margaret Morton Blum, Southern Methodist University.

L. P.

SOUND AND SENSE

An Introduction to Poetry

THIRD EDITION

The
Elements
of Poetry

What Is Poetry?

Poetry is as universal as language and almost as ancient. The most primitive peoples have used it, and the most civilized have cultivated it. In all ages, and in all countries, poetry has been written—and eagerly read or listened to—by all kinds and conditions of people, by soldiers, statesmen, lawyers, farmers, doctors, scientists, clergymen, philosophers, kings, and queens. In all ages it has been especially the concern of the educated, the intelligent, and the sensitive, and it has appealed, in its simpler forms, to the uneducated and to children. Why? First, because it has given pleasure. People have read it or listened to it or recited it because they liked it, because it gave them enjoyment. But this is not the whole answer. Poetry in all ages has been regarded as important, not simply as one of several alternative forms of amusement, as one man might choose bowling, another chess, and another poetry. Rather, it has been regarded as something central to each man's existence, something having unique value to the fully realized life, something that he is better off for having and spiritually impoverished without. To understand the reasons for this, we need to have at least a provisional understanding of what poetry is—provisional, because man has always been more successful at appreciating poetry than at defining it.

Initially, poetry might be defined as a kind of language that says more and says it more intensely than does ordinary language. In order to understand this fully, we need to understand what it is that poetry "says." For language is employed on different occasions to say quite different kinds of things; in other words, language has different uses.

Perhaps the commonest use of language is to communicate *information*. We say that it is nine o'clock, that there is a good movie downtown, that George Washington was the first president of the United States, that bromine and iodine are members of the halogen group of chemical elements. This we might call the *practical* use of language; it helps us with the ordinary business of living.

But it is not primarily to communicate information that novels and short stories and plays and poems are written. These exist to bring us a sense and a perception of life, to widen and sharpen our contacts with existence. Their concern is with *experience*. We all have an inner need to live more deeply and fully and with greater awareness, to know the experience of others and to know better our own experience. The poet, from his own store of felt, observed, or imagined experiences, selects, combines, and reorganizes. He creates significant new experiences for the reader—significant because focused and formed—in which the reader can participate and that he may use to give him a greater awareness and understanding of his world. Literature, in other words, can be used as a gear for stepping up the intensity and increasing the range of our experience and as a glass for clarifying it. This is the *literary* use of language, for literature is not only an aid to living but a means of living.*

Suppose, for instance, that we are interested in eagles. If we want simply to acquire information about eagles, we may turn to an encyclopedia or a book of natural history. There we find that the family Falconidae, to which eagles belong, is characterized by imperforate nostrils, legs of medium length, a hooked bill, the hind toe inserted on a level with the three front ones, and the claws roundly curved and sharp; that land eagles are feathered to the toes and sea-fishing eagles halfway to the toes; that their length is about three feet, the extent of wing seven feet; that the nest is usually placed on some inaccessible cliff; that

---

*A third use of language is as an instrument of persuasion. This is the use we find in advertisements, propaganda bulletins, sermons, and political speeches. These three uses of language—the practical, the literary, and the hortatory—are not sharply divided. They may be thought of as three points of a triangle; most actual specimens of written language fall somewhere within the triangle. Most poetry conveys some information, and some poetry has a design on the reader. But language becomes *literature* when the desire to communicate experience predominates.

the eggs are spotted and do not exceed three; and perhaps that the eagle's "great power of vision, the vast height to which it soars in the sky, the wild grandeur of its abode, have . . . commended it to the poets of all nations."*

But unless we are interested in this information only for practical purposes, we are likely to feel a little disappointed, as though we had grasped the feathers of the eagle but not its soul. True, we have learned many facts about the eagle, but we have missed somehow its lonely majesty, its power, and the "wild grandeur" of its surroundings that would make the eagle something living rather than a mere museum specimen. For the living eagle we must turn to literature.

THE EAGLE

He clasps the crag with crooked hands;
Close to the sun in lonely lands,
Ringed with the azure world, he stands.

The wrinkled sea beneath him crawls;
He watches from his mountain walls,
And like a thunderbolt he falls.

Alfred, Lord Tennyson (1809–1892)

QUESTIONS

1. What is peculiarly effective about the expressions "crooked hands," "close to the sun," "ringed with the azure world," "wrinkled," "crawls," and "like a thunderbolt"?

2. Notice the formal pattern of the poem, particularly the contrast of "he stands" in the first stanza and "he falls" in the second. Is there any other contrast between the two stanzas?

If the preceding poem has been read well, the reader will feel that he has enjoyed a significant experience and understands eagles better, though in a different way, than he did from the encyclopedia article alone. For if the article *analyzes* man's experience with eagles, the poem in some sense *synthesizes* such an experience. Indeed, the two approaches to experience—the scientific and the literary—may be said to complement each other. And it may be contended that the kind of

* *Encyclopedia Americana,* IX, 473–74.

understanding one gets from the second is at least as valuable as the kind he gets from the first.

Literature, then, exists to communicate significant experience—significant because concentrated and organized. Its function is not to tell us *about* experience but to allow us imaginatively to *participate* in it. It is a means of allowing us, through the imagination, to live more fully, more deeply, more richly, and with greater awareness. It can do this in two ways: by *broadening* our experience—that is, by making us acquainted with a range of experience with which, in the ordinary course of events, we might have no contact—or by *deepening* our experience—that is, by making us feel more poignantly and more understandingly the everyday experiences all of us have.

Two false approaches often taken to poetry can be avoided if we keep this conception of literature firmly in mind. The first approach always looks for a lesson or a bit of moral instruction. The second expects to find poetry always beautiful. Let us consider a song from Shakespeare:

WINTER

When icicles hang by the wall,
 And Dick the shepherd blows his nail,
And Tom bears logs into the hall,
 And milk comes frozen home in pail,
When blood is nipped and ways be foul,   5
Then nightly sings the staring owl,
   "Tu-whit, tu-who!"
A merry note,
While greasy Joan doth keel° the pot.   skim

When all aloud the wind doth blow,   10
 And coughing drowns the parson's saw,
And birds sit brooding in the snow,
 And Marian's nose looks red and raw,
When roasted crabs° hiss in the bowl,   crab apples
Then nightly sings the staring owl,   15
   "Tu-whit, tu-who!"
A merry note,
While greasy Joan doth keel the pot.

William Shakespeare (1564–1616)

1. What are the meanings of *nail* (2) and *saw* (11)?

2. Is the owl's cry really a *merry* note? How are this adjective and the verb *sings* employed?

3. In what way does the owl's cry contrast with the other details of the poem?

In the poem "Winter" Shakespeare is attempting to communicate the quality of winter life around a sixteenth-century English country house. But instead of telling us flatly that winter in such surroundings is cold and in many respects unpleasant, though with some pleasant features too (the adjectives *cold, unpleasant,* and *pleasant* are not even used in the poem), he gives us a series of concrete homely details that suggest these qualities and enable us, imaginatively, to experience this winter life ourselves. The shepherd lad blows on his fingernails to warm his hands; the milk freezes in the pail between the cowshed and the kitchen; the roads are muddy; the folk listening to the parson have colds; the birds "sit brooding in the snow"; and the servant girl's nose is raw from cold. But pleasant things are in prospect. Logs are being brought in for a fire, hot cider or ale is being prepared, and the kitchen maid is making a hot soup or stew. In contrast to all these homely, familiar details of country life comes in the mournful, haunting, and eerie note of the owl.

Obviously the poem contains no moral. Readers who always look in poetry for some lesson, message, or noble truth about life are bound to be disappointed. Moral-hunters see poetry as a kind of sugar-coated pill—a wholesome truth or lesson made palatable by being put into pretty words. What they are really after is a sermon—not a poem, but something inspirational. Yet "Winter," which has appealed to readers now for nearly four centuries, is not inspirational and contains no moral preachment.

Neither is the poem "Winter" beautiful. Though it is appealing in its way and contains elements of beauty, there is little that is really beautiful in red raw noses, coughing in chapel, nipped blood, foul roads, and greasy kitchen maids. Yet some readers think that poetry deals exclusively with beauty—with sunsets, flowers, butterflies, love, God—and that the one appropriate response to any poem is, after a moment of awed silence, "Isn't that beautiful!" For such readers poetry is a precious affair, the enjoyment only of delicate souls, removed from the heat and sweat of ordinary life. But theirs is too narrow an approach to poetry. The function of poetry is sometimes to be ugly rather than beautiful. And poetry may deal with common colds and greasy kitchen maids as legitimately as with sunsets and flowers. Consider another example:

DULCE ET DECORUM EST

Bent double, like old beggars under sacks,
Knock-kneed, coughing like hags, we cursed through sludge,
Till on the haunting flares we turned our backs,
And towards our distant rest began to trudge.
Men marched asleep. Many had lost their boots,   5
But limped on, blood-shod. All went lame, all blind;
Drunk with fatigue; deaf even to the hoots
Of gas-shells dropping softly behind.

Gas! GAS! Quick, boys!—An ecstasy of fumbling,
Fitting the clumsy helmets just in time,   10
But someone still was yelling out and stumbling
And flound'ring like a man in fire or lime.—
Dim through the misty panes and thick green light,
As under a green sea, I saw him drowning.

In all my dreams before my helpless sight   15
He plunges at me, guttering, choking, drowning.

If in some smothering dreams, you too could pace
Behind the wagon that we flung him in,
And watch the white eyes writhing in his face,
His hanging face, like a devil's sick of sin,   20
If you could hear, at every jolt, the blood
Come gargling from the froth-corrupted lungs
Bitter as the cud
Of vile, incurable sores on innocent tongues,—
My friend, you would not tell with such high zest   25
To children ardent for some desperate glory,
The old lie: *Dulce et decorum est*
Pro patria mori.

Wilfred Owen (1893–1918)

QUESTIONS

1. The Latin quotation, from the Roman poet Horace, means "It is sweet and becoming to die for one's country." (Wilfred Owen died fighting for England in World War I, a week before the armistice.) What is the poem's comment on this statement?

2. List the elements of the poem that to you seem not beautiful and therefore unpoetic. Are there any elements of beauty in the poem?

3. How do the comparisons in lines 1, 14, 20, and 23–24 contribute to the effectiveness of the poem?

Poetry takes all life as its province. Its primary concern is not with beauty, not with philosophical truth, not with persuasion, but with experience. Beauty and philosophical truth are aspects of experience, and the poet is often engaged with them. But poetry as a whole is concerned with all kinds of experience—beautiful or ugly, strange or common, noble or ignoble, actual or imaginary. One of the paradoxes of human existence is that all experience—even painful experience—when transmitted through the medium of art is, for the good reader, enjoyable. In real life, death and pain and suffering are not pleasurable, but in poetry they may be. In real life, getting soaked in a rainstorm is not pleasurable, but in poetry it can be. In actual life, if we cry, usually we are unhappy; but if we cry in a movie, we are manifestly enjoying it. We do not ordinarily like to be terrified in real life, but we sometimes seek movies or books that will terrify us. We find some value in all intense living. To be intensely alive is the opposite of being dead. To be dull, to be bored, to be imperceptive is in one sense to be dead. Poetry comes to us bringing life and therefore pleasure. Moreover, art focuses and so organizes experience as to give us a better understanding of it. And to understand life is partly to be master of it.

Between poetry and other forms of imaginative literature there is no sharp distinction. You may have been taught to believe that poetry can be recognized by the arrangement of its lines on the page or by its use of rime and meter. Such superficial tests are almost worthless. The Book of Job in the Bible and Melville's *Moby Dick* are highly poetical, but a versified theorem in physics is not.* The difference between poetry and other literature is one only of degree. Poetry is the most condensed and

*For instance, the following, found accidentally by Bliss Perry (*A Study of Poetry* [Boston: Houghton Mifflin, 1920], p. 155) in a textbook, *The Parallelo-*

9

concentrated form of literature, saying most in the fewest number of words. It is language whose individual lines, either because of their own brilliance or because they focus so powerfully what has gone before, have a higher voltage than most language has. It is language that grows frequently incandescent, giving off both light and heat.

Ultimately, therefore, poetry can be recognized only by the response made to it by a good reader. But there is a catch here. We are not all good readers. If we were, there would be no purpose for this book. And if you are a poor reader, much of what has been said about poetry so far must have seemed nonsensical. "How," you may ask, "can poetry be described as moving or exciting, when I have found it dull and boring? Poetry is just a fancy way of writing something that could be said more simply." So might a color-blind man deny that there is such a thing as color.

The act of communication involved in reading poetry is like the act of communication involved in receiving a message by radio. Two factors are involved: a transmitting station and a receiving set. The completeness of the communication depends on both the power and clarity of the transmitter and the sensitivity and tuning of the receiver. When a person reads a poem and no experience is transmitted, either the poem is not a good poem or the reader is a poor reader or not properly tuned. With new poetry, we cannot always be sure which is at fault. With older poetry, if it has acquired critical acceptance—has been enjoyed by generations of good readers—we may assume that the receiving set is at fault. Fortunately, the fault is not irremediable. Though we cannot all become expert readers, we can become good enough to find both pleasure and value in much good poetry, or we can increase the amount of pleasure we already find in poetry and the number of kinds of poetry we find it in. To help you increase your sensitivity and range as a receiving set is the purpose of this book.

---

gram of Forces, is not. Printed as verse, it has the same meter and rime scheme as Tennyson's *In Memoriam:*

> And hence no force, however great,
> Can draw a cord, however fine,
> Into a horizontal line
> Which shall be absolutely straight.

Poetry, finally, is a kind of multidimensional language. Ordinary language—the kind we use to communicate information—is one-dimensional. It is directed at only part of the listener, his understanding. Its one dimension is intellectual. Poetry, which is language used to communicate experience, has at least four dimensions. If it is to communicate experience, it must be directed at the *whole* man, not just at his understanding. It must involve not only his intelligence but also his senses, emotions, and imagination. Poetry, to the intellectual dimension, adds a sensuous dimension, an emotional dimension, and an imaginative dimension.

Poetry achieves its extra dimensions—its greater pressure per word and its greater tension per poem—by drawing more fully and more consistently than does ordinary language on a number of language resources, none of which is peculiar to poetry. These various resources form the subjects of a number of the following chapters. Among them are connotation, imagery, metaphor, symbol, paradox, irony, allusion, sound repetition, rhythm, and pattern. Using these resources and the materials of life, the poet shapes and makes his poem. Successful poetry is never effusive language. If it is to come alive it must be as cunningly put together and as efficiently organized as a tree. It must be an organism whose every part serves a useful purpose and cooperates with every other part to preserve and express the life that is within it.

SPRING

When daisies pied and violets blue,
   And lady-smocks all silver-white,
And cuckoo-buds of yellow hue
   Do paint the meadows with delight,
The cuckoo then, on every tree,   5
Mocks married men; for thus sings he,
              "Cuckoo!
Cuckoo, cuckoo!" O word of fear,
Unpleasing to a married ear!

When shepherds pipe on oaten straws, 10
   And merry larks are ploughmen's clocks,
When turtles tread, and rooks, and daws,
   And maidens bleach their summer smocks,
The cuckoo then, on every tree,
Mocks married men; for thus sings he, 15
                  "Cuckoo!
Cuckoo, cuckoo!" O word of fear,
Unpleasing to a married ear!

William Shakespeare (1564–1616)

QUESTIONS

1. Vocabulary: *pied* (1), *lady-smocks* (2), *oaten straws* (10), *turtles* (12), *tread* (12), *daws* (12).

2. This song is a companion piece to "Winter." In what respects are the two poems similar? How do they contrast? What details show that this poem, like "Winter," was written by a realist, not simply by a man carried away with the beauty of spring?

3. The word *cuckoo* is "unpleasing to a married ear" because it sounds like *cuckold*. Cuckolds were a frequent butt of humor in earlier English literature. If you do not know the meaning of the word, look it up.

4. Is the tone of this poem solemn or light and semihumorous?

WAS A MAN

Was a man, was a two-
faced man, pretended
he wasn't who he was,
who, in a men's room,
faced his hung-over 5
face in a mirror hung
over the towel rack.
The mirror was cracked.
Shaving close in that
looking glass, he nicked 10
his throat, bled blue
blood, grabbed a new
towel to patch the wrong
scratch, knocked off

the mirror and, facing   15
himself, almost intact,
in final terror hung
the wrong face back.

Philip Booth (b. 1925)

QUESTION

If we take this poem literally, it is absurd. Is any truth implied in the
absurdity?

THE TWA CORBIES

As I was walking all alane,°	alone
I heard twa corbies° making a mane;°	two ravens; moan
The tane° unto the tither did say,	one
"Where sall we gang° and dine the day?"	shall we go
"In behint yon auld fail dyke,°	old turf wall 5
I wot° there lies a new-slain knight;	know
And naebody kens° that he lies there,	knows
But his hawk, his hound, and his lady fair.	
"His hound is to the hunting gane,	
His hawk to fetch the wild-fowl hame,	10
His lady's ta'en anither mate,	
So we may mak our dinner sweet.	
"Ye'll sit on his white hause-bane,°	neck-bone
And I'll pike° out his bonny blue een;°	pick; eyes 14
Wi' ae° lock o' his gowden° hair	With one; golden
We'll theek° our nest when it grows bare.	thatch
"Mony a one for him maks mane,°	moan
But nane sall ken whar he is gane;	
O'er his white banes, when they are bare,	
The wind sall blaw for evermair."	20

Anonymous

QUESTIONS

1. Here is an implied story of false love, murder, and disloyalty. What
purpose is served by having the story told from the point of view of the "twa
corbies"? How do they emphasize the atmosphere of the poem?

13

2. Although we do not know exactly what happened to the knight, much is suggested. What is implied by the fact that "mony a one for him maks mane" but no one knows what has become of him except his hawk, his hound, and his lady? What is implied by the fact that he is "new-slain" but his lady has already taken another mate? Does the poem lose or gain in effect by not being entirely clear?

3. The language of the old English and Scottish folk ballads, of which this is one, presents a considerable initial obstacle, but if you accept it you will probably find that it contributes a unique flavor. An English critic has written of this poem: "Modernize the spelling [of the last stanza], and you have destroyed . . . the key of the poem: the thin high music of the lament, the endlessly subtle variations on the *a* sound, the strange feeling that all things have been unified with the shrillness of the wind through the heather."* Does this seem to you a valid comment?

4. How would you describe the experience created by the poem?

LOVE AND A QUESTION

A Stranger came to the door at eve,
    And he spoke the bridegroom fair.
He bore a green-white stick in his hand,
    And, for all burden, care.
He asked with the eyes more than the lips   5
    For a shelter for the night,
And he turned and looked at the road afar
    Without a window light.

The bridegroom came forth into the porch
    With "Let us look at the sky,   10
And question what of the night to be,
    Stranger, you and I."
The woodbine leaves littered the yard,
    The woodbine berries were blue,
Autumn, yes, winter was in the wind;   15
    "Stranger, I wish I knew."

Within, the bride in the dusk alone
    Bent over the open fire,

*T. R. Henn, *The Apple and the Spectroscope* (London: Methuen, 1951), p. 11.

Her face rose-red with the glowing coal
    And the thought of the heart's desire.   20
The bridegroom looked at the weary road,
    Yet saw but her within,
And wished her heart in a case of gold
    And pinned with a silver pin.

The bridegroom thought it little to give   25
    A dole of bread, a purse,
A heartfelt prayer for the poor of God,
    Or for the rich a curse;
But whether or not a man was asked
    To mar the love of two   30
By harboring woe in the bridal house,
    The bridegroom wished he knew.

Robert Frost (1874–1963)

QUESTIONS

1. The bridegroom in this poem is faced with a dilemma (a choice between two actions neither of which is satisfactory). How is the question he ponders in the last stanza to be answered?

2. What is the symbolic significance of the Stranger? Does this poem deal with a unique experience or does it have universal meaning?

3. Like "The Twa Corbies" this poem is a BALLAD (a narrative but songlike poem written in a stanzaic form repeated throughout the poem). Compare the two poems in intent and significance.

VIEW OF A PIG*

The pig lay on a barrow dead.
It weighed, they said, as much as three men.
Its eyes closed, pink white eyelashes.
Its trotters stuck straight out.

Such weight and thick pink bulk   5
Set in death seemed not just dead.
It was less than lifeless, further off.
It was like a sack of wheat.

*Mr. Hughes recorded "View of a Pig" (LP, Spoken Arts, SA 944).

I thumped it without feeling remorse.
One feels guilty insulting the dead,   10
Walking on graves. But this pig
Did not seem able to accuse.

It was too dead. Just so much
A poundage of lard and pork.
Its last dignity had entirely gone.   15
It was not a figure of fun.

Too dead now to pity.
To remember its life, din, stronghold
Of earthly pleasure as it had been,
Seemed a false effort, and off the point.   20

Too deadly factual. Its weight
Oppressed me—how could it be moved?
And the trouble of cutting it up!
The gash in its throat was shocking, but not pathetic.

Once I ran at a fair in the noise   25
To catch a greased piglet
That was faster and nimbler than a cat,
Its squeal was the rending of metal.

Pigs must have hot blood, they feel like ovens.
Their bite is worse than a horse's—   30
They chop a half-moon clean out.
They eat cinders, dead cats.

Distinctions and admirations such
As this one was long finished with.
I stared at it a long time. They were going to scald it,   35
Scald it and scour it like a doorstep.

Ted Hughes (b. 1930)

QUESTIONS

1. About what central contrast does the poem pivot?
2. With what other creatures is the pig, dead and alive, compared or contrasted? Is the poet finally interested in the difference or the similarity between it and other creatures?
3. What, essentially, is the poem about?

Terence is Housman himself.

place is in a tavern.

TERENCE, THIS IS STUPID STUFF

"Terence, this is stupid stuff: — *poetry – stupid 'cause he*
You eat your victuals fast enough; *talks about things dead.*
There can't be much amiss, 'tis clear,
To see the rate you drink your beer.
But oh, good Lord, the verse you make,   5
It gives a chap the belly-ache.
The cow, the old cow, she is dead;
It sleeps well, the horned head:
We poor lads, 'tis our turn now
To hear such tunes as killed the cow.   10
Pretty friendship 'tis to rhyme
Your friends to death before their time
Moping melancholy mad:
Come, pipe a tune to dance to, lad." *Suggests gay poetry instead of unhappy.*

    Why, if 'tis dancing you would be,
There's brisker pipes than poetry.
Say, for what were hop-yards meant,
Or why was Burton built on Trent?
Oh many a peer of England brews
Livelier liquor than the Muse,   20
And malt does more than Milton can
To justify God's ways to man.
Ale, man, ale's the stuff to drink
For fellows whom it hurts to think:
Look into the pewter pot   25
To see the world as the world's not.
And faith, 'tis pleasant till 'tis past:
The mischief is that 'twill not last.
Oh I have been to Ludlow fair
And left my necktie God knows where,   30
And carried half-way home, or near,
Pints and quarts of Ludlow beer:
Then the world seemed none so bad,
And I myself a sterling lad;
And down in lovely muck I've lain,   35
Happy till I woke again.
Then I saw the morning sky:
Heigho, the tale was all a lie;

people who are afraid to face the real world.

realistic of drunk

The world, it was the old world yet,
I was I, my things were wet,   40
And nothing now remained to do
But begin the game anew. — *get drunk again.*

Therefore, since the world has still
Much good, but much less good than ill,
And while the sun and moon endure   45
Luck's a chance, but trouble's sure,
I'd face it as a wise man would,
And train for ill and not for good.
'Tis true, the stuff I bring for sale — *'tis poetry*
Is not so brisk a brew as ale: 50
Out of a stem that scored the hand *wrung out of painful*
I wrung it in a weary land. *experience in Reality*
But take it: if the smack is sour,
The better for the embittered hour;
It should do good to heart and head   55
When your soul is in my soul's stead;
And I will friend you, if I may,
In the dark and cloudy day.

There was a king reigned in the East:
There, when kings will sit to feast,   60
They get their fill before they think
With poisoned meat and poisoned drink.
He gathered all that springs to birth
From the many-venomed earth;
First a little, thence to more,   65
He sampled all her killing store;
And easy, smiling, seasoned sound,
Sate the king when healths went round.
They put arsenic in his meat
And stared aghast to watch him eat;   70
They poured strychnine in his cup
And shook to see him drink it up:
They shook, they stared as white's their shirt:
Them it was their poison hurt.
—I tell the tale that I heard told.   75
Mithridates, he died old.

A. E. Housman (1859–1936)

The world has more bad than good. Hope for best & prepare for worst.

QUESTIONS

1. *Terence* (1) is Housman's poetic name for himself. Housman's poetry is largely pessimistic or sad; and this poem, placed near the end of his volume *A Shropshire Lad*, is his defense of the kind of poetry he wrote. Who is the speaker in the first fourteen lines? Who is the speaker in the rest of the poem? What is "the stuff I bring for sale" (49)?

2. *Hops* (17) and *malt* (21) are principal ingredients of beer and ale. *Burton-upon-Trent* (18) is an English city famous for its breweries. *Milton* (21), in the invocation of his epic poem *Paradise Lost*, declares that his purpose is to "justify the ways of God to men." What, in Housman's eyes, is the efficacy of liquor in helping one live a difficult life?

3. What six lines of the poem most explicitly sum up the poet's philosophy? Most people like reading material that is cheerful and optimistic (on the argument that "there's enough suffering and unhappiness in the world already"). What for Housman is the value of pessimistic and tragic literature?

4. *Mithridates* (76) was a king of Pontus and a contemporary of Julius Caesar; his "tale" is told in Pliny's *Natural History*. What is the connection of this last verse paragraph with the rest of the poem?

CONSTANTLY RISKING ABSURDITY*

Constantly risking absurdity
     and death
  whenever he performs
     above the heads
        of his audience   5
 the poet like an acrobat
   climbs on rime
     to a high wire of his own making
and balancing on eyebeams
     above a sea of faces   10
  paces his way
    to the other side of day
 performing entrechats
    and slight-of-foot tricks
and other high theatrics   15
    and all without mistaking
   any thing
     for what it may not be

*Mr. Ferlinghetti recorded "Constantly Risking Absurdity" (LP, Fantasy, 7004).

For he's the super realist

　　　　　　　　who must perforce perceive　　　　　　　20
　　　taut truth
　　　　　　　　before the taking of each stance or step
　in his supposed advance
　　　　　　　　toward that still higher perch
where Beauty stands and waits　　　　　　　25
　　　　　　　　with gravity
　　　　　　　　　　to start her death-defying leap
　　And he
　　　a little charleychaplin man
　　　　　　　　who may or may not catch　　　　　　　30
　　　her fair eternal form
　　　　　　　　spreadeagled in the empty air
　　　of existence

Lawrence Ferlinghetti (b. 1919)

QUESTIONS

1. Vocabulary: *entrechats* (13). What meanings have "above the heads" (4), "slight-of-foot tricks" (14), "high theatrics" (15), "with gravity" (26)?

2. The poet, it is said, "climbs on rime" (7). To what extent does this poem utilize rime and other sound correspondences? Point out examples.

3. What statement does the poem make about poetry, truth, and beauty?

4. What additional comments about poetry are implied by the figure of speech employed?

5. Does Ferlinghetti take poets and poetry seriously? Solemnly?

THROUGHOUT THE WORLD

Throughout the world, if it were sought,
Fair words enough a man shall find:
They be good cheap, they cost right nought,
Their substance is but only wind:
　　　But well to say and so to mean,
　　　That sweet accord is seldom seen.

Sir Thomas Wyatt (1503?–1542)

Reading
the Poem

The primary purpose of this book is to develop your ability to understand and appreciate poetry. Here are some preliminary suggestions:

1. Read a poem more than once. A good poem will no more yield its full meaning on a single reading than will a Beethoven symphony on a single hearing. Two readings may be necessary simply to let you get your bearings. And if the poem is a work of art, it will repay repeated and prolonged examination. One does not listen to a good piece of music once and forget it; one does not look at a good painting once and throw it away. A poem is not like a newspaper, to be hastily read and cast into the wastebasket. It is to be hung on the wall of one's mind.

2. Keep a dictionary by you and use it. It is futile to try to understand poetry without troubling to learn the meanings of the words of which it is composed. One might as well attempt to play tennis without a ball. One of your primary purposes while in college should be to build a good vocabulary, and the study of poetry gives you an excellent opportunity. A few other reference books will also be invaluable. Particularly desirable are a good book on mythology (your instructor can recommend one) and a Bible.

3. Read so as to hear the sounds of the words in your mind. Poetry is written to be heard: its meanings are conveyed through sound as well as through print. Every word is therefore important. The best way to read a poem is just the opposite of the best way to read a newspaper. One reads a newspaper as rapidly as he can; one should read a poem as slowly

as he car. When you cannot read a poem aloud, lip-read it: form the words with your tongue and mouth though you do not utter them. With ordinary reading material, lip reading is a bad habit; with poetry it is a good habit.

4. Always pay careful attention to what the poem is saying. Though one should be conscious of the sounds of the poem, he should never be so exclusively conscious of them that he pays no attention to what the poem means. For some readers reading a poem is like getting on board a rhythmical roller coaster. The car starts, and off they go, up and down, paying no attention to the landscape flashing past them, arriving at the end of the poem breathless, with no idea of what it has been about.* This is the wrong way to read a poem. One should make the utmost effort to follow the thought continuously and to grasp the full implications and suggestions. Because a poem says so much, several readings may be necessary, but on the very first reading one should determine which noun goes with which verb.

5. Practice reading poems aloud. When you find one you especially like, make your roommate or a friend listen to it. Try to read it to him in such a way that he will like it too. (a) Read it affectionately, but not affectedly. The two extremes oral readers often fall into are equally deadly. One is to read as if one were reading a tax report or a railroad timetable, unexpressively, in a monotone. The other is to elocute, with artificial flourishes and vocal histrionics. It is not necessary to put emotion into reading a poem. The emotion is already there. It only wants a fair chance to get out. It will express *itself* if the poem is read naturally and sensitively. (b) Of the two extremes, reading too fast offers greater danger than reading too slow. Read slowly enough that each word is clear and distinct and that the meaning has time to sink in. Remember that your roommate does not have the advantage, as you do, of having the text before him. Your ordinary rate of reading will probably be too fast. (c) Read the poem so that the rhythmical pattern is felt but not exaggerated. Remember that poetry is written in sentences, just as prose is, and that punctuation is a signal as to how it should be read. Give all grammatical pauses their full due. Do not distort the natural pronunciation of words or a normal accentuation of the sentence to fit into what

---

*Some poems encourage this type of reading. When this is so, usually the poet has not made the best use of his rhythm to support his sense.

you have decided is its metrical pattern. One of the worst ways to read a poem is to read it ta-*dum* ta-*dum* ta-*dum* with an exaggerated emphasis on every other syllable. On the other hand, it should not be read as if it were prose. An important test of your reading will be how you handle the end of a line when there is no punctuation there. A frequent mistake of the beginning reader is to treat each line as if it were a complete thought, whether grammatically complete or not, and to drop his voice at the end of it. A frequent mistake of the sophisticated reader is to take a running start upon approaching the end of a line and fly over it as if it were not there. The line is a rhythmical unit, and its end should be observed whether there is punctuation or not. If there is no punctuation, one observes it ordinarily by the slightest of pauses or by holding onto the last word in the line just a little longer than usual. One should not drop his voice. In line 12 of the following poem, one should hold onto the word *although* longer than if it occurred elsewhere in the line. But one should not lower his voice on it: it is part of the clause that follows in the next stanza.

THE MAN HE KILLED

Had he and I but met
By some old ancient inn,
We should have sat us down to wet
Right many a nipperkin!°   half-pint cup

But ranged as infantry,   5
And staring face to face,
I shot at him as he at me,
And killed him in his place.

I shot him dead because—
Because he was my foe,   10
Just so: my foe of course he was;
That's clear enough; although

He thought he'd 'list, perhaps,
Off-hand-like—just as I—
Was out of work—had sold his traps—   15
No other reason why.

Yes; quaint and curious war is!
You shoot a fellow down
You'd treat, if met where any bar is,
Or help to half-a-crown.   20

Thomas Hardy (1840–1928)

QUESTIONS

1. Vocabulary: *traps* (15).

2. In informational prose the repetition of a word like *because* (9–10) would be an error. What purpose does the repetition serve here? Why does the speaker repeat to himself his "clear" reason for killing a man (10–11)? The word *although* (12) gets more emphasis than it ordinarily would because it comes not only at the end of a line but at the end of a stanza. What purpose does this emphasis serve? Can the redundancy of "old ancient" (2) be poetically justified?

3. Someone has defined poetry as "the expression of elevated thought in elevated language." Comment on the adequacy of this definition in the light of Hardy's poem.

To aid us in the understanding of a poem, we may ask ourselves a number of questions about it. One of the most important is: *Who is the speaker and what is the occasion?* A cardinal error of beginning readers is to assume always that the speaker is the poet himself. A far safer course is to assume always that the speaker is someone other than the poet himself. For even when the poet does speak directly and express his own thoughts and emotions, he does so ordinarily as a representative human being rather than as an individual who lives at a particular address, dislikes dill pickles, and favors blue neckties. We must always be cautious about identifying anything in a poem with the biography of the poet. Like the novelist and the playwright, he is fully justified in changing actual details of his own experience to make the experience of the poem more universal. We may well think of every poem, therefore, as being to some degree *dramatic*, that is, the utterance of a fictional character rather than of the poet himself. Many poems are expressly dramatic.

In "The Man He Killed" the speaker is a soldier; the occasion is his having been in battle and killed a man—obviously for the first time in his life. We can tell a good deal about him. He is not a career soldier:

he enlisted only because he was out of work. He is a workingman: he speaks a simple and colloquial language (*nipperkin, 'list, off-hand-like, traps*), and he has sold the tools of his trade—he may have been a tinker or plumber. He is a friendly, kindly sort who enjoys a neighborly drink of ale in a bar and will gladly lend a friend a half crown when he has it. He has known what it is to be poor. In any other circumstances he would have been horrified at taking a human life. He has been given pause as it is. He is trying to figure it out. But he is not a deep thinker and thinks he has supplied a reason when he has only supplied a name: "I killed the man . . . because he was my foe." The critical question, of course, is *Why was the man his "foe"*? Even the speaker is left unsatisfied by his answer, though he is not analytical enough to know what is wrong with it. Obviously this poem is expressly dramatic. We need know nothing about Thomas Hardy's life (he was never a soldier and never killed a man) to realize that the poem is dramatic. The internal evidence of the poem tells us so.

A second important question that we should ask ourselves upon reading any poem is *What is the central purpose of the poem?** The purpose may be to tell a story, to reveal human character, to impart a vivid impression of a scene, to express a mood or an emotion, or to convey to us vividly some idea or attitude. Whatever the purpose is, we must determine it for ourselves and define it mentally as precisely as possible. Only then can we fully understand the function and meaning of the various details in the poem, by relating them to this central purpose. Only then can we begin to assess the value of the poem and determine whether it is a good one or a poor one. In "The Man He Killed" the central purpose is quite clear: it is to make us realize more keenly the irrationality of war. The puzzlement of the speaker may be our puzzlement. But even if we are able to give a more sophisticated answer than his as to why men kill each other, we ought still to have a greater awareness, after reading the poem, of the fundamental irrationality in war

---

*Our only reliable evidence of the poem's purpose, of course, is the poem itself. External evidence, when it exists, though often helpful, may also be misleading. Some critics have objected to the use of such terms as "purpose" and "intention" altogether; we cannot know, they maintain, what was *attempted* in the poem; we can know only what was *done*. Philosophically this position is impeccable. Yet it is possible to make *inferences* about what was attempted, and such inferences furnish a convenient and helpful way of talking about poetry.

that makes men kill who have no grudge against each other and who might under different circumstances show each other considerable kindness.

IS MY TEAM PLOUGHING

"Is my team ploughing,
    That I was used to drive
And hear the harness jingle
    When I was man alive?"

Aye, the horses trample,   5
    The harness jingles now;
No change though you lie under
    The land you used to plough.

"Is football playing
    Along the river shore,   10
With lads to chase the leather,
    Now I stand up no more?"

Aye, the ball is flying,
    The lads play heart and soul;
The goal stands up, the keeper   15
    Stands up to keep the goal.

"Is my girl happy,
    That I thought hard to leave,
And has she tired of weeping
    As she lies down at eve?"   20

Aye, she lies down lightly,
    She lies not down to weep:
Your girl is well contented.
    Be still, my lad, and sleep.

"Is my friend hearty,   25
    Now I am thin and pine;
And has he found to sleep in
    A better bed than mine?"

Yes, lad, I lie easy,
    I lie as lads would choose;   30

I cheer a dead man's sweetheart,
　　Never ask me whose.

A. E. Housman (1859–1936)

　1. What is meant by *whose* in line 32?
　2. Is Housman cynical in his observation of human nature and human life?
　3. The word *sleep* in the concluding stanzas suggests three different meanings. What are they? How many meanings are suggested by the word *bed?*

Once we have answered the question *What is the central purpose of the poem?* we can consider another question, equally important to full understanding: *By what means is that purpose achieved?* It is important to distinguish means from ends. A student on an examination once used the poem "Is My Team Ploughing" as evidence that A. E. Housman believed in immortality, because in it a man speaks from the grave. This is as naive as to say that Thomas Hardy in "The Man He Killed" joined the army because he was out of work. The purpose of Housman's poem is to communicate poignantly a certain truth about human life: life goes on after our deaths pretty much as it did before—our dying does not disturb the universe. This purpose is achieved by means of a fanciful dramatic framework in which a dead man converses with his still living friend. The framework tells us nothing about whether Housman believed in immortality (as a matter of fact, he did not). It is simply an effective means by which we *can* learn how Housman felt a man's death affected the life he left behind. The question *By what means is the purpose of the poem achieved?* is partially answered by describing the poem's dramatic framework, if it has any. The complete answer requires an accounting of various resources of communication that it will take us the rest of this book to discuss.

The most important preliminary advice we can give for reading poetry is to maintain always, while reading it, the utmost mental alertness. The most harmful idea one can get about poetry is that its purpose is to soothe and relax and that the best place to read it is lying in a

27

hammock with a cool drink beside one and low music in the background. One *can* read poetry lying in a hammock but only if he refuses to put his mind in the same attitude as his body. Its purpose is not to soothe and relax but to arouse and awake, to shock one into life, to make one more alive. Poetry is not a substitute for a sedative.

An analogy can be drawn between reading poetry and playing tennis. Both offer great enjoyment if the game is played hard. A good tennis player must be constantly on the tip of his toes, concentrating on his opponent's every move. He must be ready for a drive to the right or a drive to the left, a lob overhead or a drop shot barely over the net. He must be ready for top spin or underspin, a ball that bounces crazily to the left or crazily to the right. He must jump for the high ones and run for the far ones. He will enjoy the game almost exactly in proportion to the effort he puts into it. The same is true of poetry. Great enjoyment is there, but this enjoyment demands a mental effort equivalent to the physical effort one puts into tennis.

The reader of poetry has one advantage over the tennis player. The poet is not trying to win a match. He may expect the reader to stretch for his shots, but he *wants* the reader to return them.

EXERCISES

Most of the poems in this book are accompanied by study questions that are by no means exhaustive. Following is a list of questions that you may apply to any poem or that your instructor may wish to use, in whole or in part, to supplement the questions to any particular poem. You will not be able to answer many of them until you have read further into the book.

1. Who is the speaker? What kind of person is he?
2. To whom is he speaking? What kind of person is he?
3. What is the occasion?
4. What is the setting in time (time of day, season, century, etc.)?
5. What is the setting in place (indoors or out, city or country, nation, etc.)?
6. What is the central purpose of the poem?
7. State the central idea or theme of the poem in a sentence.
8. Discuss the tone of the poem. How is it achieved?
9. a. Outline the poem so as to show its structure and development, or
   b. Summarize the events of the poem.
10. Paraphrase the poem.

11. Discuss the diction of the poem. Point out words that are particularly well chosen and explain why.
12. Discuss the imagery of the poem. What kinds of imagery are used?
13. Point out examples of metaphor, simile, personification, and metonymy and explain their appropriateness.
14. Point out and explain any symbols. If the poem is allegorical, explain the allegory.
15. Point out and explain examples of paradox, overstatement, understatement, and irony. What is their function?
16. Point out and explain any allusions. What is their function?
17. Point out significant examples of sound repetition and explain their function.
18. a. What is the meter of the poem?
    b. Copy the poem and mark its scansion.
19. Discuss the adaptation of sound to sense.
20. Describe the form or pattern of the poem.
21. Criticize and evaluate the poem.

IT IS NOT GROWING LIKE A TREE

It is not growing like a tree
In bulk, doth make man better be;
Or standing long an oak, three hundred year,
To fall a log at last, dry, bald, and sere:
     A lily of a day   5
     Is fairer far in May,
Although it fall and die that night;
It was the plant and flower of light.
In small proportions we just beauties see;
And in short measures, life may perfect be.   10

Ben Jonson (1573?–1637)

QUESTIONS

1. Your instructor may occasionally ask you, as a test of your understanding of a poem at its lowest level, or as a means of clearing up misunderstanding, to paraphrase its content. To PARAPHRASE a poem means to restate it in different language, so as to make its prose sense as plain as possible. The paraphrase may be longer or shorter than the poem, but it should contain as far as possible all the ideas in the poem in such a way as to make them

clear to a puzzled reader. Figurative language should be reduced when possible to literal language; metaphors should be turned into similes. Though it is neither necessary nor possible to avoid using some words occurring in the original, you should in general use your own language.

The central idea of the above poem is approximately this: life is to be measured by its excellence, not by its length. The poem may be paraphrased as follows:

> A man does not become more excellent by simply growing in size, as a tree grows, nor by merely living for a very long time, as an oak does, only to die at length, old, bald, and wizened. A lily that lives only for one day in the spring is far more estimable than the long-lived tree, even though it dies at nightfall, for while it lives it is the essence and crown of beauty and excellence. Thus we may see perfect beauty in small things. Thus human life, too, may be most excellent though very brief.

2. A paraphrase is useful only if you understand that it is the barest, most inadequate approximation of what the poem really says and is no more equivalent to the poem than a corpse is equivalent to a man. Once having made a paraphrase, you should endeavor to see how far short of the poem it falls and why. In what respects does the above poem say more, and say it more memorably, than the paraphrase?

3. Does *bald* (4) apply only to the man or also to the log? May line 8 be interpreted in a way other than the way the paraphrase interprets it? What is the meaning of *just* (9)? Could *measures* (10) mean anything in addition to "amounts"? Comment on the effectiveness of the comparisons to tree and lily.

GENIUS IN BEAUTY

> Beauty like hers is genius. Not the call
>   Of Homer's or of Dante's heart sublime—
>   Not Michael's hand furrowing the zones of time—
> Is more with compassed mysteries musical;
> Nay, not in Spring's or Summer's sweet footfall   5
>   More gathered gifts exuberant Life bequeathes
>   Than doth his sovereign face, whose love-spell breathes
> Even from its shadowed contour on the wall.
>
> As many men are poets in their youth,
>   But for one sweet-strung soul the wires prolong   10
>   Even through all change the indomitable song;

So in likewise the envenomed years, whose tooth
Rends shallower grace with ruin void of ruth,
    Upon this beauty's power shall wreak no wrong.

Dante Gabriel Rossetti (1828–1882)

QUESTIONS

1. This sonnet might be paraphrased as follows:

> Beauty like hers is extraordinary—beyond nature. Neither the
> sublime poetry of Homer or Dante nor the immortal paintings of
> Michelangelo are more richly and inexplicably harmonious and
> beautiful. Life does not bestow a greater variety and richness of
> gifts even in the sweet seasons of spring and summer than does
> her queenly face, which casts a love-enchantment even from its
> shadow on the wall.
>
> Just as many men show poetical talent when they are young,
> while only a rare individual remains poetically gifted all his life, so
> in like manner many women are beautiful when they are young,
> but her beauty will survive the ravages of time.

Show how certain words in the poem (for example, *genius*) are more pregnant with meaning than their substitutes in the paraphrase. What effect do
such words as *call* (1), *heart* (2), *hand* (3), *footfall* (5), and *breathes* (7)
have on the poem that is missing from the paraphrase? What is lost through
the omission of such phrases as "compassed mysteries musical" (4), "ruin
void of ruth" (13), and "wreak no wrong" (14)? In what other respects is
the paraphrase notably less satisfactory than the poem?

2. Should the poem be read as saying that the lady's face, though it
changes as she grows older, will be beautiful through all its changes and
stay beautiful until her death? Or should it be read as saying that the lady's
beauty is unchanging and will last even beyond her death? May the poem be
read both ways?

BEDTIME STORY

Long long ago when the world was a wild place
Planted with bushes and peopled by apes, our
Mission Brigade was at work in the jungle.
    Hard by the Congo

Once, when a foraging detail was active   5
Scouting for green-fly, it came on a grey man, the

Last living man, in the branch of a baobab
  Stalking a monkey.

Earlier men had disposed of, for pleasure,
Creatures whose names we scarcely remember—   10
Zebra, rhinoceros, elephants, wart-hog,
  Lion, rats, deer. But

After the wars had extinguished the cities
Only the wild ones were left, half-naked
Near the Equator: and here was the last one,   15
  Starved for a monkey.

By then the Mission Brigade had encountered
Hundreds of such men: and their procedure,
History tells us, was only to feed them:
  Find them and feed them;   20

Those were the orders. And this was the last one.
Nobody knew that he was, but he was. Mud
Caked on his flat grey flanks. He was crouched, half-
  Armed with a shaved spear

Glinting beneath broad leaves. When their jaws cut   25
Swathes through the bark and he saw fine teeth shine,
Round eyes roll round and forked arms waver
  Huge as the rough trunks

Over his head, he was frightened. Our workers
Marched through the Congo before he was born, but   30
This was the first time perhaps that he'd seen one.
  Staring in hot still

Silence, he crouched there: then jumped. With a long swing
Down from his branch, he had angled his spear too
Quickly, before they could hold him, and hurled it   35
  Hard at the soldier

Leading the detail. How could he know Queen's
Orders were only to help him? The soldier
Winched when the tipped spear pricked him. Unsheathing his
  Sting was a reflex.   40

Later the Queen was informed. There were no more
Men. An impetuous soldier had killed off,

Purely by chance, the penultimate primate.
    When she was certain,

Squadrons of workers were fanned through the Congo   45
Detailed to bring back the man's picked bones to be
Sealed in the archives in amber. I'm quite sure
    Nobody found them

After the most industrious search, though.
Where had the bones gone? Over the earth, dear,   50
Ground by the teeth of the termites, blown by the
    Wind, like the dodo's.

George MacBeth (b. 1932)

QUESTIONS

1. Vocabulary: *penultimate* (43), *primate* (43).
2. Who is speaking? Describe him. To whom is he speaking? When?
3. What comments does the poem suggest about the nature, history, and destiny of the human species? Are contrasts implied between the human species and the speaker's species?
4. What is the force of the final comparison to the dodo (52)?
5. How would you read the first two stanzas aloud? The last three?

DEVIL, MAGGOT AND SON*

Three things seek my death,
    Hard at my heels they run—
Hang them, sweet Christ, all three,—
    Devil, maggot and son.

So much does each of them crave   5
    The morsel that falls to his share,
He cares not a thrauneen° what   straw
    Falls to the other pair.

If the devil, that crafty one,
    Can capture my soul in sin   10
He'll leave my flesh to the worm,
    My money to my kin.

*Translated from the Irish.

33

My sons think more of the money
 That will come to them when I die
Than a soul that they could not spend,   15
 A body that none would buy.

And how would the maggots fare
 On a soul too thin to eat
And money too tough to chew?
 The maggots must have meat.   20

Christ, speared by the blind man,
 Christ, nailed to a naked tree,
The three that are seeking my end
 Hang them, sweet Christ, all three!

Frank O'Connor (1903–1966)

QUESTIONS

 1. Who and what kind of person is the speaker?
 2. According to medieval Christian belief, the Roman soldier Longinus, who thrust a spear into Christ's side at the crucifixion, was blind (21). What element in this poem most underscores its horror?

THE MILL

The miller's wife had waited long,
 The tea was cold, the fire was dead;
And there might yet be nothing wrong
 In how he went and what he said:
"There are no millers any more,"   5
 Was all that she had heard him say;
And he had lingered at the door
 So long that it seemed yesterday.

Sick with a fear that had no form
 She knew that she was there at last;   10
And in the mill there was a warm
 And mealy fragrance of the past.
What else there was would only seem
 To say again what he had meant;
And what was hanging from a beam   15
 Would not have heeded where she went.

And if she thought it followed her,
  She may have reasoned in the dark
That one way of the few there were
  Would hide her and would leave no mark: 20
Black water, smooth above the weir
  Like starry velvet in the night,
Though ruffled once, would soon appear
  The same as ever to the sight.

Edwin Arlington Robinson (1869–1935)

QUESTIONS

1. What is the meaning of the miller's remark in line 5? Can we give an approximate date for the setting of the poem in time?

2. What does the miller's wife find in the mill in stanza 2? What does she do in stanza 3?

3. Poets, especially modern poets, are often accused of being perversely obscure. Certainly this poem tells its story in a roundabout way—by hints and implications rather than by direct statements. Is there any justification for this "obscurity" or has the poet indeed been needlessly unclear?

4. What details of the poem especially bring it to life as experience?

CUPID AND MY CAMPASPE

Cupid and my Campaspe played
At cards for kisses—Cupid paid:
He stakes his quiver, bow, and arrows,
His mother's doves and team of sparrows,
Loses them too; then down he throws   5
The coral of his lip, the rose
Growing on's cheek (but none knows how);
With these the crystal of his brow,
And then the dimple of his chin:
All these did my Campaspe win.   10
At last he set her both his eyes—
She won, and Cupid blind did rise.
  O Love! has she done this to thee?
  What shall, alas, become of me?

John Lyly (1554?–1606)

QUESTION

To convey a truth about his sweetheart, the speaker has invented a myth (the card game) using well-known mythical figures (Cupid and Venus). What does this myth enable him to say about Campaspe? Can you generalize from this instance anything about the nature and uses of myth in general? How does your answer relate to the discussion of means and ends on page 27?

HOW ROSES CAME RED

Roses at first were white,
    Till they could not agree
Whether my Sappho's breast
    Or they more white should be.

But being vanquished quite,
    A blush their cheeks bespread;
Since which, believe the rest,
    The roses first came red.

Robert Herrick (1591–1674)

QUESTION

Distinguish means from end in this poem. Was it written by a naturalist or a lover?

A STUDY OF READING HABITS

When getting my nose in a book
Cured most things short of school,
It was worth ruining my eyes
To know I could still keep cool,
And deal out the old right hook   5
To dirty dogs twice my size.

Later, with inch-thick specs,
Evil was just my lark:
Me and my cloak and fangs
Had ripping times in the dark.   10
The women I clubbed with sex!
I broke them up like meringues.

Don't read much now: the dude
Who lets the girl down before
The hero arrives, the chap   15
Who's yellow and keeps the store,
Seem far too familiar. Get stewed:
Books are a load of crap.

Philip Larkin (b. 1922)

QUESTIONS

1. The three stanzas delineate three stages in the speaker's life. Describe each.

2. What kind of person is the speaker? What kind of books does he read? May he be identified with the poet?

3. Contrast the advice given by the speaker in stanza 3 with the advice given by Terence in "Terence, This Is Stupid Stuff" (page 17). Are A. E. Housman and Philip Larkin at odds in their attitudes toward drinking and reading? Discuss.

WHEN ADAM DAY BY DAY

When Adam day by day
    Woke up in Paradise,
He always used to say
    "Oh, this is very nice."

But Eve from scenes of bliss
    Transported him for life.
The more I think of this
    The more I beat my wife.

A. E. Housman (1859–1936)

QUESTION

What conclusions may be legitimately drawn from this poem about its author?

Denotation and Connotation

A primary distinction between the practical use of language and the literary use is that in literature, especially in poetry, a *fuller* use is made of individual words. To understand this, we need to examine the composition of a word.

The average word has three component parts: sound, denotation, and connotation. It begins as a combination of tones and noises, uttered by the lips, tongue, and throat, for which the written word is a notation. But it differs from a musical tone or a noise in that it has a meaning attached to it. The basic part of this meaning is its DENOTATION or denotations: that is, the dictionary meaning or meanings of the word. Beyond its denotations, a word may also have connotations. The CONNOTATIONS are what it suggests beyond what it expresses: its overtones of meaning. It acquires these connotations by its past history and associations, by the way and the circumstances in which it has been used. The word *home*, for instance, by denotation means only a place where one lives, but by connotation it suggests security, love, comfort, and family. The words *childlike* and *childish* both mean "characteristic of a child," but *childlike* suggests meekness, innocence, and wide-eyed wonder, while *childish* suggests pettiness, willfulness, and temper tantrums. If we name over a series of coins: *nickel, peso, lira, shilling, sen, doubloon,* the word *doubloon,* to four out of five readers, will immediately suggest pirates, though one will find nothing about pirates in looking up its meaning in the dictionary. Pirates are part of its connotation.

Connotation is very important to the poet, for it is one of the means by which he can concentrate or enrich his meaning—say more in fewer words. Consider, for instance, the following short poem:

THERE IS NO FRIGATE LIKE A BOOK

There is no frigate like a book
To take us lands away,
Nor any coursers like a page
Of prancing poetry.
This traverse may the poorest take
Without oppress of toll;
How frugal is the chariot
That bears the human soul!

Emily Dickinson (1830–1886)

In this poem Emily Dickinson is considering the power of a book or of poetry to carry us away, to let us escape from our immediate surroundings into a world of the imagination. To do this she has compared literature to various means of transportation: a boat, a team of horses, a wheeled land vehicle. But she has been careful to choose kinds of transportation and names for them that have romantic connotations. *Frigate* suggests exploration and adventure; *coursers*, beauty, spirit, and speed; *chariot*, speed and the ability to go through the air as well as on land. (Compare "Swing Low, Sweet Chariot" and the myth of Phaethon, who tried to drive the chariot of Apollo, and the famous painting of Aurora with her horses, once hung in almost every school.) How much of the meaning of the poem comes from this selection of vehicles and words is apparent if we try to substitute for them, say, *steamship, horses,* and *streetcar*.

QUESTIONS

1. What is lost if *miles* is substituted for *lands* (2) or *cheap* for *frugal* (7)?

2. How is *prancing* (4) peculiarly appropriate to poetry as well as to coursers? Could the poet have without loss compared a book to coursers and poetry to a frigate?

39

3. Is this account appropriate to all kinds of poetry or just to certain kinds? That is, was the poet thinking of poems like Wilfred Owen's "Dulce et Decorum Est" (page 8) or of poems like Coleridge's "Kubla Khan" (page 304) and Walter de la Mare's "The Listeners" (page 306)?

Just as a word has a variety of connotations, so also it may have more than one denotation. If we look up the word *spring* in the dictionary, for instance, we will find that it has between twenty-five and thirty distinguishable meanings: It may mean (1) a pounce or leap, (2) a season of the year, (3) a natural source of water, (4) a coiled elastic wire, etc. This variety of denotation, complicated by additional tones of connotation, makes language confusing and difficult to use. Any person using words must be careful to define by context precisely the meanings that he wishes. But the difference between the writer using language to communicate information and the poet is this: the practical writer will always attempt to confine his words to one meaning at a time; the poet will often take advantage of the fact that the word has more than one meaning by using it to mean more than one thing at the same time. Thus when Edith Sitwell in one of her poems writes, "This is the time of the wild spring and the mating of tigers," she uses the word *spring* to denote both a season of the year and a sudden leap, and she uses *tigers* rather than *lambs* or *birds* because it has a connotation of fierceness and wildness that the other two lack.

ON A GIRDLE

That which her slender waist confined
Shall now my joyful temples bind;
No monarch but would give his crown
His arms might do what this has done.

It was my heaven's extremest sphere,   5
The pale which held that lovely deer.
My joy, my grief, my hope, my love,
Did all within this circle move!

A narrow compass, and yet there
Dwelt all that's good and all that's fair;   10

Give me but what this riband bound,
Take all the rest the sun goes round.

Edmund Waller (1606–1687)

QUESTIONS

1. Vocabulary: *girdle; pale* (6).
2. The poem is based on the notion of circles and what they contain. Point out six kinds of circles mentioned in the poem. What is the speaker willing to trade?
3. What word in the first stanza has two operative denotations? What word in the second is a pun?
4. Sensitive reading of poetry requires not only that we recognize all relevant meanings of its words but that we reject irrelevant meanings. What modern meanings of *girdle* and *fair* (10) must we reject if this poem is not to be ridiculous?
5. Try to explain why the poet chose his wording rather than one of the following alternatives: *thin* for *slender* (1), *forehead* for *temples* (2), *ruler* for *monarch* (3), *fence* for *pale* (6), *pretty* for *lovely* (6).

A frequent misconception of poetic language is that the poet seeks always the most beautiful or noble-sounding words. What he really seeks are the most *meaningful* words, and these vary from one context to another. Language has many levels and varieties, and the poet may choose from them all. His words may be grandiose or humble, fanciful or matter of fact, romantic or realistic, archaic or modern, technical or everyday, monosyllabic or polysyllabic. Usually his poem will be pitched pretty much in one key. The words in Emily Dickinson's "There Is No Frigate Like a Book" and those in Thomas Hardy's "The Man He Killed" (page 23) are chosen from quite different areas of language, but each poet has chosen the words most meaningful for his own poetic context. Sometimes a poet may import a word from one level or area of language into a poem composed mostly of words from a different level or area. If he does this clumsily, the result will be incongruous and sloppy. If he does it skillfully, the result will be a shock of surprise and an increment of meaning for the reader. In fact, the many varieties of language open to the poet provide his richest resource. His task is one of constant exploration and discovery. He searches always for the secret affinities of words that allow them to be brought together with soft explosions of meaning.

THE NAKED AND THE NUDE* ✓

For me, the naked and the nude
(By lexicographers construed
As synonyms that should express
The same deficiency of dress
Or shelter) stand as wide apart   5
As love from lies, or truth from art.

Lovers without reproach will gaze
On bodies naked and ablaze;
The hippocratic eye will see
In nakedness, anatomy;   10
And naked shines the Goddess when
She mounts her lion among men.

The nude are bold, the nude are sly
To hold each treasonable eye.
While draping by a showman's trick   15
Their dishabille in rhetoric,
They grin a mock-religious grin
Of scorn at those of naked skin.

The naked, therefore, who compete
Against the nude may know defeat;   20
Yet when they both together tread
The briary pastures of the dead,
By Gorgons with long whips pursued,
How naked go the sometime nude!

Greeks monsters [handwritten annotation]

Robert Graves (b. 1895)

QUESTIONS

1. Vocabulary: *lexicographers* (2), *construed* (2), *hippocratic* (9), *dishabille* (16), *Gorgons* (23).

2. What kind of language is used in lines 2–5? Why? (For example, why is *deficiency* used in preference to *lack*? Purely because of meter?)

3. What is meant by *rhetoric* (16)? Why is the word *dishabille* used in this line instead of some less fancy word?

4. Explain why the poet chose his wording instead of the following alter-

*Mr. Graves recorded "The Naked and the Nude" (LP, Library of Congress, PL 20).

natives: *brave* for *bold* (13), *clever* for *sly* (13), *clothing* for *draping* (15), *smile* for *grin* (17).

5. What, for the poet, is the difference in connotation between *naked* and *nude*? Try to explain reasons for the difference. If your own sense of the two words differs from that of Graves, state the difference and give reasons to support your sense of them.

6. Explain the reversal in the last line.

The person using language to convey information is largely indifferent to the sound of his words and is hampered by their connotations and multiple denotations. He tries to confine each word to a single exact meaning. He uses, one might say, a fraction of the word and throws the rest away. The poet, on the other hand, tries to use as much of the word as he can. He is interested in sound and uses it to reinforce meaning (see chapter 13). He is interested in connotation and uses it to enrich and convey meaning. And he may use more than one denotation.

The purest form of practical language is scientific language. The scientist needs a precise language for conveying information precisely. The fact that words have multiple denotations and various overtones of meaning is a hindrance to him in accomplishing his purpose. His ideal language would be a language with a one-to-one correspondence between word and meaning; that is, every word would have one meaning only, and for every meaning there would be only one word. Since ordinary language does not fulfill these conditions, he has invented one that does. A statement in his language looks something like this:

$$SO_2 + H_2O = H_2SO_3$$

In such a statement the symbols are entirely unambiguous; they have been stripped of all connotation and of all denotations but one. The word *sulfurous*, if it occurred in poetry, might have all kinds of connotations: fire, smoke, brimstone, hell, damnation. But H_2SO_3 means one thing and one thing only: sulfurous acid.

The ambiguity and multiplicity of meanings that words have, then, are an obstacle to the scientist but a resource to the poet. Where the scientist wants singleness of meaning, the poet wants richness of meaning. Where the scientist needs and has invented a strictly one-dimensional language, in which every word is confined to one denotation, the poet needs a multidimensional language, and he creates it partly by using a multidimensional vocabulary, in which, to the dimension of denotation he adds the dimensions of connotation and sound.

The poet, we may say, plays on a many-stringed instrument. And he sounds more than one note at a time.

The first problem in reading poetry, therefore, or in reading any kind of literature, is to develop a sense of language, a feeling for words. One needs to become acquainted with their shape, their color, and their flavor. There are two ways of doing this: extensive use of the dictionary and extensive reading.

EXERCISES

1. Robert Frost has said that "Poetry is what evaporates from all translations." On the basis of this chapter, can you explain why this statement is true? How much of a word can be translated?

2. Which of the following words have the most "romantic" connotations?
   a. horse ( ) steed ( ) equine quadruped ( )
   b. China ( ) Cathay ( )
   Which of the following is the most emotionally connotative?
   c. mother ( ) female parent ( ) dam ( )
   Which of the following have the more favorable connotations?
   d. average ( ) mediocre ( )
   e. secret agent ( ) spy ( )
   f. adventurer ( ) adventuress ( )

3. Fill each blank with the word richest in meaning in the given context. Explain.
   a. I still had hopes, my latest hours to crown,
      Amidst these humble bowers to lay me down;
      To husband out life's _____ at the close,   *candle, taper*
      And keep the flame from wasting by repose.
               Goldsmith

   b. She was a _____ of delight   *ghost, phantom,*
      When first she gleamed upon my sight.   *spectre, spook*
               Wordsworth

   c. His sumptuous watch-case, though concealed it lies,
      Like a good conscience, _____ joy sup-   *perfect, solid,*
      plies.   *Edward Young*   *thorough*

d. Charmed magic _____ opening on the foam — *casements, windows*

Of _____ seas, in faery lands forlorn. — *dangerous, perilous*
                                      Keats

e. Thou _____ unravished bride of quiet- — *still, yet*
   ness.   *Keats*

f. I'll _____ the guts into the neighbor — *bear, carry, convey,*
   room.   *Shakespeare* — *lug*

g. The iron tongue of midnight hath _____ — *said, struck, told*
   twelve.   *Shakespeare*

h. In poetry each word reverberates like the note of a well-tuned _____ and always leaves — *banjo, guitar, lyre* behind it a multitude of vibrations.   *Joubert*

i. I think that with this _____ new alli- — *holy, sacred*
   ance
     I may ensure the public, and defy
  All other magazines of art or science.   *Byron*

j. Care on thy maiden brow shall put
  A wreath of wrinkles, and thy foot
  Be shod with pain: not silken dress
  But toil shall _____ thy loveliness. — *clothe, tire, weary*
                               C. Day Lewis

4. Ezra Pound has defined great literature as being "simply language charged with meaning to the utmost possible degree." Would this be a good defini- tion of poetry? The word *charged* is roughly equivalent to *filled*. Why is *charged* a better word in Pound's definition? What do its associations with storage batteries, guns, and dynamite suggest about poetry?

———————————————

RICHARD CORY

Whenever Richard Cory went down town,
We people on the pavement looked at him:
He was a gentleman from sole to crown,
Clean favored, and imperially slim.

And he was always quietly arrayed,
And he was always human when he talked;   5

But still he fluttered pulses when he said,
"Good-morning," and he glittered when he walked.

And he was rich—yes, richer than a king— 10
And admirably schooled in every grace:
In fine, we thought that he was everything
To make us wish that we were in his place.

So on we worked, and waited for the light, — *the hope for future*
And went without the meat, and cursed the bread;
And Richard Cory, one calm summer night, 15
Went home and put a bullet through his head.

Edwin Arlington Robinson (1869–1935)

QUESTIONS *Suggest atmosphere & being happy*

1. In how many senses is Richard Cory a gentleman?

2. The word *crown* (3), meaning the top of the head, is familiar to you from "Jack and Jill," but why does Robinson use the unusual phrase "from sole to crown" instead of the common "from head to foot" or "from top to toe"?

3. List the words in the poem that express or suggest the idea of aristocracy or royalty.

4. Try to explain why the poet chose his wording rather than the following alternatives: *sidewalk* for *pavement* (2), *good-looking* for *clean favored* (4), *thin* for *slim* (4), *dressed* for *arrayed* (5), *courteous* for *human* (6), *wonderfully* for *admirably* (10), *trained* for *schooled* (10), *manners* for *every grace* (10), *in short* for *in fine* (11). What other examples of effective diction do you find in the poem?

5. Why is "Richard Cory" a good name for the character in this poem?

6. This poem is a good example of how ironic contrast (see chapter 7) generates meaning. The poem makes no direct statement about life; it simply relates an incident. What larger meanings about life does it suggest?

7. A leading American critic has said of this poem: "In 'Richard Cory' . . . we have a superficially neat portrait of the elegant man of mystery; the poem builds up deliberately to a very cheap surprise ending; but all surprise endings are cheap in poetry, if not, indeed, elsewhere, for poetry is written to be read not once but many times."* Do you agree with this evaluation of the poem? Discuss.

*Yvor Winters, *Edwin Arlington Robinson* (Norfolk, Conn., New Directions, 1946), p. 52.

THE RICH MAN ✓

The rich man has his motor-car,
   His country and his town estate.
He smokes a fifty-cent cigar
   And jeers at Fate.

He frivols through the livelong day,   5
   He knows not Poverty her pinch.
His lot seems light, his heart seems gay,
   He has a cinch.

Yet though my lamp burns low and dim,
   Though I must slave for livelihood—   10
Think you that I would change with him?
   You bet I would!

                 Franklin P. Adams (1881–1960)

QUESTIONS

  1. What meanings has *lot* (7)?
  2. Bearing in mind the criticism cited of Robinson's "Richard Cory," state whether you think that poem or this has more poetic value. Which poem is merely clever? Which is something more?

[handwritten: Scene is outside or place where can see outside & gardens]
[handwritten: Scene is training camp in army]

NAMING OF PARTS* *[handwritten: rifle represents]*

[handwritten: 2 personae — instructor describing rifle & another man thinking about something else, because half-listening to lecture]

To-day we have naming of parts. Yesterday,
We had daily cleaning. And to-morrow morning,
We shall have what to do after firing. But to-day,
To-day we have naming of parts. Japonica
Glistens like coral in all of the neighboring gardens,   5
   And to-day we have naming of parts."
This is the lower sling swivel. And this *[handwritten: or rifle — brace for carrying rifles.]*
Is the upper sling swivel, whose use you will see, *[handwritten: rest gun on or stack like tripod]*
When you are given your slings. And this is the piling swivel,
Which in your case you have not got. The branches   10
Hold in the gardens their silent, eloquent gestures, *[handwritten: clear, expressive — trees respond to gestures]*
   Which in our case we have not got." —

*Mr. Reed recorded "Naming of Parts" (LP, Library of Congress, PL 26).

This is the safety-catch, which is always released
With an easy flick of the thumb. And please do not let me
See anyone using his finger. You can do it quite easy   15
If you have any strength in your thumb. The blossoms
Are fragile and motionless, never letting anyone see
      Any of them using their finger. *— artificial means of sex which*
flowers don't have to have.
And this you can see is the bolt. The purpose of this
Is to open the breech, as you see. We can slide it   20
Rapidly backwards and forwards: we call this
Easing the spring. And rapidly backwards and forwards
The early bees are assaulting and fumbling the flowers: *— bees pollinate*
releasing —They call it easing the Spring. *flowers. Bees symbolize*
tensions into season. *the male & flowers, the*
They call it easing the Spring: it is perfectly easy *female,*   25
If you have any strength in your thumb: like the bolt,
And the breech, and the cocking-piece, and the point of balance, *women balance men, one*
Which in our case we have not got; and the almond-blossom *must have*
Silent in all of the gardens and the bees going backwards and forwards, *sex for balanced*
      For to-day we have naming of parts.   30

Recruit is thinking of sex.
Life cycle shown.   Henry Reed (b. 1914)
Contrast between nature & natural, and artificial.

QUESTIONS

    1. What basic contrasts are represented by the trainees and the gardens?
    2. What is it that the trainees "have not got"?
    3. How many senses have the phrases "easing the Spring" (stanza 4) and "point of balance" (27)?
    4. What differences of language and rhythm do you find between the lines concerning "naming of parts" and those describing the gardens?
    5. Does the repetition of certain phrases throughout the poem have any special function, or is it only a kind of refrain?

There is a sergent is lecturing **JUDGING DISTANCES***

Not only how far away, but the way that you say it
Is very important. Perhaps you may never get
The knack of judging a distance, but at least you know
How to report on a landscape: the central sector,

*Mr. Reed recorded "Judging Distances" (LP, Library of Congress, PL 20).

The right of arc and that, which we had last Tuesday,　　　　　5
　　And at least you know

place to Clock.

That maps are of time, not place, so far as the army
Happens to be concerned—the reason being,
Is one which need not delay us. Again, you know
There are three kinds of tree, three only, the fir and the poplar,　　10
And those which have bushy tops to; and lastly
　　That things only seem to be things.

A barn is not called a barn, to put it more plainly,
Or a field in the distance, where sheep may be safely grazing.
You must never be over-sure. You must say, when reporting:　　15
At five o'clock in the central sector is a dozen *- Comparing to place in Clock*
Of what appear to be animals; whatever you do,
　　Don't call the bleeders *sheep*. *- sheep bleat*

I am sure that's quite clear; and suppose, for the sake of example,
The one at the end, asleep, endeavors to tell us　　20
What he sees over there to the west, and how far away,
After first having come to attention. There to the west,
On the fields of summer the sun and the shadows bestow
　　Vestments of purple and gold.

The still white dwellings are like a mirage in the heat,　　25
And under the swaying elms a man and a woman
Lie gently together. Which is, perhaps, only to say
That there is a row of houses to the left of arc,- *military terms*
And that under some poplars a pair of what appear to be humans
　　Appear to be loving.　　　　　30

Well that, for an answer, is what we might rightly call
Moderately satisfactory only, the reason being,
Is that two things have been omitted, and those are important.
The human beings, now: in what direction are they,
And how far away, would you say? And do not forget　　35
　　There may be dead ground in between. *- Gullys, etc that are important*
　　　wasted time　　　　*in military planning.*
There may be dead ground in between; and I may not have got
The knack of judging a distance; I will only venture
A guess that perhaps between me and the apparent lovers,
(Who, incidentally, appear by now to have finished,)　　40

At seven o'clock from the houses, is roughly a distance
   Of about one year and a half.

Henry Reed (b. 1914)

QUESTIONS

  1. In what respect are maps "of time, not place" (7) in the army?

  2. Though they may be construed as belonging to the same speaker, there are two speaking voices in this poem. Identify each and put quotation marks around the lines spoken by the second voice.

  3. Two kinds of language are used in this poem—army "officialese" and the language of human experience. What are the characteristics of each? What is the purpose of each? Which is more precise?

  4. The word *bleeders* (18)—i.e., "bloody creatures"—is British profanity. To which of the two kinds of language does it belong? Or is it perhaps a third kind of language?

  5. As in "Naming of Parts" (these two poems are part of a series of three with the general title "Lessons of War") the two kinds of language used might possibly be called "unpoetic" and "poetic." Is the "unpoetic" language *really* unpoetic? In other words, is its use inappropriate in these two poems? Explain.

  6. The phrase "dead ground" (36) takes on symbolic meaning in the last stanza. What is its literal meaning? What is its symbolic meaning? What does the second speaker mean by saying that the distance between himself and the lovers is "about one year and a half" (42)? In what respect is the contrast between the recruits and the lovers similar to that between the recruits and the gardens in "Naming of Parts"? What meanings are generated by the former contrast?

BASE DETAILS

If I were fierce, and bald, and short of breath,
  I'd live with scarlet Majors at the Base,
And speed glum heroes up the line to death.
  You'd see me with my puffy petulant face,
Guzzling and gulping in the best hotel,   5
  Reading the Roll of Honor. "Poor young chap,"
I'd say—"I used to know his father well;
  Yes, we've lost heavily in this last scrap."
And when the war is done and youth stone dead,
I'd toddle safely home and die—in bed.   10

Siegfried Sassoon (1886–1967)

1. Vocabulary: *petulant* (4).

2. In what two ways may the title be interpreted? (Both words have two pertinent meanings.) What applications has *scarlet* (2)? What is the force of *fierce* (1)? Try to explain why the poet chose his wording rather than the following alternatives: *fleshy* for *puffy* (4), "eating and drinking" for "guzzling and gulping" (5), *battle* for *scrap* (8), *totter* for *toddle* (10).

3. Who evidently is the speaker? (The poet, a British captain in World War I, was decorated for bravery on the battlefield.) Does he mean what he says? What is the purpose of the poem?

SACRAMENTAL MEDITATION VI

Am I thy gold? Or purse, Lord, for thy wealth;
    Whether in mine or mint refined for thee?
I'm counted so, but count me o'er thyself,
    Lest gold-washed face, and brass in heart I be.
I fear my touchstone touches when I try°   °test 5
    Me, and my counted gold too overly.

Am I new-minted by thy stamp indeed?
    Mine eyes are dim; I cannot clearly see.
Be thou my spectacles that I may read
    Thine image and inscription stamped on me.   10
If thy bright image do upon me stand,
    I am a golden angel in thy hand.

Lord, make my soul thy plate: thine image bright
    Within the circle of the same enfoil.
And on its brims in golden letters write   15
    Thy superscription in an holy style.
Then I shall be thy money, thou my hoard:
    Let me thy angel be, be thou my Lord.

                     Edward Taylor (1642?–1729)

1. Vocabulary: *touchstone* (5), *superscription* (16).

2. In lines 13–14 the word *plate* means a gold disc and *enfoil* means to place on a bright background (as one mounts a jewel on a foil). What steps in the process of turning gold ore into gold coin are referred to in the poem?

3. In line 5 the phrase "my touchstone touches" is probably to be in-

terpreted as "the touches of my touchstone." What fear does the speaker express in stanza 1? What hope in stanza 2? What prayer in stanza 3?

4. What meanings have *refined* (2) and *count* and *counted* (3, 6)? On what meanings of *angel* (12, 18) does the poem pivot? For what reasons is *golden* rather than *silver* or *bronze* used for the coinage in the poem?

PORTRAIT D'UNE FEMME

Your mind and you are our Sargasso Sea,
London has swept about you this score years
And bright ships left you this or that in fee:
Ideas, old gossip, oddments of all things,
Strange spars of knowledge and dimmed wares of price.   5
Great minds have sought you—lacking someone else.
You have been second always. Tragical?
No. You preferred it to the usual thing:
One dull man, dulling and uxorious,
One average mind—with one thought less, each year.   10
Oh, you are patient. I have seen you sit
Hours, where something might have floated up.
And now you pay one. Yes, you richly pay.
You are a person of some interest, one comes to you
And takes strange gain away: 15
Trophies fished up; some curious suggestion;
Fact that leads nowhere; and a tale for two,
Pregnant with mandrakes, or with something else
That might prove useful and yet never proves,
That never fits a corner or shows use,   20
Or finds its hour upon the loom of days:
The tarnished, gaudy, wonderful old work;
Idols, and ambergris and rare inlays.
These are your riches, your great store; and yet
For all this sea-hoard of deciduous things,   25
Strange woods half sodden, and new brighter stuff:
In the slow float of differing light and deep,
No! there is nothing! In the whole and all,
Nothing that's quite your own.

                               Yet this is you.   30

                              Ezra Pound (b. 1885)

1. Vocabulary: *in fee* (3), *uxorious* (9), *mandrakes* (18), *ambergris* (23), *deciduous* (25). *[falling off]*

2. The Sargasso Sea, an area of still water in the North Atlantic, is legendarily a place where ships have become entangled in seaweed and where the ocean floor is littered with sunken vessels and their scattered cargoes. What kind of woman is Pound describing? In what ways is her mind like the Sargasso Sea?

3. Pound seeks to create an impression of the rich and strange, as opposed to the dull and average. How does he do it?

4. Comment on the phrases "in fee" (3), "of price" (5), "richly pay" (13), "of some interest" (14), "strange gain" (15), "your riches" (24), "your great store" (24), "this sea-hoard" (25). What do they have in common? What is their effect?

5. Comment on the phrase "pregnant with mandrakes" (18). Why do these two words go well together?

6. Pound might have called his poem "Portrait of a Woman" or "Portrait of a Lady." Which would have been more accurate? What advantages does the French title have over either?

THE WRITTEN WORD

A	B
The spoken or written word	The written word
Should be as clean as a bone,	Should be clean as bone,
As clear as is the light,	Clear as light,
As firm as is a stone.	Firm as stone.
Two words will never serve	Two words are not
As well as one alone.	As good as one.

QUESTION

Which of the above versions of a poem, by an anonymous writer, is the better? Why?

Imagery

Experience comes to us largely through the senses. My experience of a spring day, for instance, may consist partly of certain emotions I feel and partly of certain thoughts I think, but most of it will be a cluster of sense impressions. It will consist of seeing blue sky and white clouds, budding leaves and daffodils; of hearing robins and bluebirds singing in the early morning; of smelling damp earth and blossoming hyacinths; and of feeling a fresh wind against my cheek. The poet seeking to express his experience of a spring day must therefore provide a selection of the sense impressions he has. Like Shakespeare (page 55), he must give the reader "daisies pied" and "lady-smocks all silver-white" and "merry larks" and the song of the cuckoo and maidens bleaching their summer smocks. Without doing so he will probably fail to evoke the emotions that accompanied his sensations. His language, therefore, must be more sensuous than ordinary language. It must be more full of imagery.

IMAGERY may be defined as the representation through language of sense experience. Poetry appeals directly to our senses, of course, through its music and rhythm, which we actually hear when it is read aloud. But indirectly it appeals to our senses through imagery, the representation to the imagination of sense experience. The word *image* perhaps most often suggests a mental picture, something seen in the mind's eye—and *visual* imagery is the most frequently occurring kind of imagery in poetry. But an image may also represent a sound; a smell; a taste; a tactile experience, such as hardness, wetness, or cold; an internal sensation, such as hunger, thirst, or nausea; or movement or tension in the muscles or joints. If we wished to be scientific, we could extend this list further, for psychologists no longer confine themselves to five or even six senses, but for purposes of discussing poetry the above classification should ordinarily be sufficient.

MEETING AT NIGHT ✓

The gray sea and the long black land;
And the yellow half-moon large and low;
And the startled little waves that leap
In fiery ringlets from their sleep,
As I gain the cove with pushing prow,   5
And quench its speed i' the slushy sand.

Then a mile of warm sea-scented beach;
Three fields to cross till a farm appears;
A tap at the pane, the quick sharp scratch
And blue spurt of a lighted match,   10
And a voice less loud, through its joys and fears,
Than the two hearts beating each to each!

Robert Browning (1812–1889)

"Meeting at Night" is a poem about love. It makes, one might say, a number of statements about love: being in love is a sweet and exciting experience; when one is in love everything seems beautiful to him, and the most trivial things become significant; when one is in love his sweetheart seems the most important object in the world. But the poet actually *tells* us none of these things directly. He does not even use the word *love* in his poem. His business is to communicate experience, not information. He does this largely in two ways. First, he presents us with a specific situation, in which a lover goes to meet his sweetheart. Second, he describes the lover's journey so vividly in terms of sense impressions that the reader not only sees and hears what the lover saw and heard but also shares his anticipation and excitement.

Every line in the poem contains some image, some appeal to the senses: the gray sea, the long black land, the yellow half-moon, the startled little waves with their fiery ringlets, the blue spurt of the lighted match—all appeal to our sense of sight and convey not only shape but also color and motion. The warm sea-scented beach appeals to the senses of both smell and touch. The pushing prow of the boat on the slushy sand, the tap at the pane, the quick sharp scratch of the match, the low speech of the lovers, and the sound of their two hearts beating— all appeal to the sense of hearing.

PARTING AT MORNING ✓

Round the cape of a sudden came the sea,
And the sun looked over the mountain's rim:
And straight was a path of gold for him,
And the need of a world of men for me.

Robert Browning (1812–1889)

QUESTIONS

1. This poem is a sequel to "Meeting at Night." *Him* (3) refers to the sun. Does the last line mean that the lover needs the world of men or that the world of men needs the lover? Or both?

2. Does the sea *actually* come suddenly around the cape or *appear* to? Why does Browning mention the *effect* before its *cause* (the sun looking over the mountain's rim)?

3. Do these two poems, taken together, suggest any larger truths above love? Browning, in answer to a question, said that the second part is the man's confession of "how fleeting is the belief (implied in the first part) that such raptures are self-sufficient and enduring—as for the time they appear."

The sharpness and vividness of any image will ordinarily depend on how specific it is and on the poet's use of effective detail. The word *hummingbird*, for instance, conveys a more definite image than does *bird*, and *ruby-throated hummingbird* is sharper and more specific still. It is not necessary, however, that for a vivid representation something be completely described. One or two especially sharp and representative details will ordinarily serve the alert reader, allowing his imagination to fill in the rest. Tennyson in "The Eagle" (page 5) gives only one detail about the eagle itself—that he clasps the crag with "crooked hands"— but this detail is an effective and memorable one. Robinson tells us that Richard Cory (page 45) was "clean favored," "slim," and "quietly arrayed," but the detail that really brings Cory before us is that he "glittered when he walked." Browning, in "Meeting at Night," calls up a whole scene with "A tap at the pane, the quick sharp scratch/And blue spurt of a lighted match."

Since imagery is a peculiarly effective way of evoking vivid experience, and since it may be used by the poet to convey emotion and suggest ideas as well as to cause a mental reproduction of sensations, it is an invaluable resource of the poet. In general, he will seek concrete or image-bearing words in preference to abstract or non-image-bearing words. We cannot evaluate a poem, however, by the amount or quality of its imagery alone. Sense impression is only one of the elements of experience. A poet may attain his ends by other means. We must never judge any single element of a poem except in reference to the total intention of that poem.

Late in Day's winter

THE DARKLING THRUSH — *pessimistic poem*

I leant upon a coppice gate   *thicket*
    When Frost was specter-gray,
And Winter's dregs made desolate
    The weakening eye of day.
The tangled bine-stems scored the sky   5
    Like strings of broken lyres, *represent poet.*
And all mankind that haunted nigh
    Had sought their household fires.

Comparison of The land's sharp features seemed to be
    The Century's corpse outleant,   *reminds him of*
His crypt the cloudy canopy,   *funeral.*
    The wind his death-lament.
The ancient pulse of germ and birth
    Was shrunken hard and dry,
And every spirit upon earth   15
    Seemed fervorless as I.   *lost faith*   *pessimistic*

At once a voice arose among
    The bleak twigs overhead   *a bird starts singing*
In a full-hearted evensong
    Of joy illimited;   20

An aged thrush, frail, gaunt, and small,
   In blast-beruffled plume,
Had chosen thus to fling his soul—
   Upon the growing gloom.

So little cause for carolings   25
   Of such ecstatic sound
Was written on terrestrial things   *earthly*
   Afar or nigh around,
That I could think there trembled through
   His happy good-night air   30
Some blessed Hope, whereof he knew
   And I was unaware.

December 1900.

Thomas Hardy (*1840–1928*)

QUESTIONS

  1. Vocabulary: *coppice* (1). *thicket of small trees or bushes*

  2. What three periods of time simultaneously end in the poem? What is the emotional effect of these terminations?

  3. Two emotional states are contrasted in the poem. Pick out the words that contribute to each. How many belong to images?

  4. The image in lines 5–6 is visual. What additional values does it have?

  5. Define as precisely as possible the change, if any, produced by the thrush's song in the outlook of the speaker. Does the bird know of a hope unknown to the speaker? Does the speaker think it does? Why does the bird sing? Is this an optimistic poem?

ON MOONLIT HEATH AND LONESOME BANK

On moonlit heath and lonesome bank
   The sheep beside me graze;
And yon the gallows used to clank
   Fast by the four cross ways.

A careless shepherd once would keep   5
   The flocks by moonlight there,
And high amongst the glimmering sheep
   The dead man stood on air.

They hang us now in Shrewsbury jail:
    The whistles blow forlorn,   10
And trains all night groan on the rail
    To men that die at morn.

There sleeps in Shrewsbury jail to-night,
    Or wakes, as may betide,
A better lad, if things went right,   15
    Than most that sleep outside.

And naked to the hangman's noose
    The morning clocks will ring
A neck God made for other use
    Than strangling in a string.   20

And sharp the link of life will snap,
    And dead on air will stand
Heels that held up as straight a chap
    As treads upon the land.

So here I'll watch the night and wait   25
    To see the morning shine,
When he will hear the stroke of eight
    And not the stroke of nine;

And wish my friend as sound a sleep
    As lads' I did not know,   30
That shepherded the moonlit sheep
    A hundred years ago.

A. E. Housman (1859–1936)

QUESTIONS

1. Housman explains in a note to lines 5–6 that "Hanging in chains was called keeping sheep by moonlight." Where is this idea repeated?

2. What is the speaker's attitude toward his friend? Toward other young men who have died by hanging? What is the purpose of the reference to the young men hanged "a hundred years ago"?

3. Discuss the kinds of imagery present in the poem and their role in the development of the dramatic situation.

4. Discuss the use of language in stanza 5.

SPRING ✓ — traditional poem of spring

Nothing is so beautiful as spring—
 When weeds, in wheels, shoot long and lovely and lush;
 Thrush's eggs look little low heavens, and thrush
Through the echoing timber does so rinse and wring
The ear, it strikes like lightnings to hear him sing;   5
 The glassy peartree leaves and blooms, they brush
 The descending blue; that blue is all in a rush
With richness; the racing lambs too have fair their fling.

What is all this juice and all this joy?
 A strain of the earth's sweet being in the beginning 10
In Eden garden.—Have, get, before it cloy,
 Before it cloud, Christ, lord, and sour with sinning,
Innocent mind and Mayday in girl and boy,
 Most, O maid's child, thy choice and worthy the winning.

Gerard Manley Hopkins (1844–1889)

beginning of
man compares to spring, which is beginning of life.

Compares spring to Garden of Eden
and Mayday.
Mayday is picking of flowers and pagant.
girl & boy are innocent like
Adam & Eve will be

QUESTIONS

1. The first line makes an abstract statement. How is this statement brought to carry conviction? it

2. The sky is described as being "all in a rush/With richness" (7–8). In what other respects is the poem "rich"?

3. The author was a Catholic priest as well as a poet. To what two things does he compare the spring in lines 9–14? In what ways are the comparisons appropriate?

A DESCRIPTION OF THE MORNING ✓

Now hardly here and there a hackney-coach
Appearing, showed the ruddy morn's approach.
Now Betty from her master's bed had flown,
And softly stole to discompose her own.
The slip-shod 'prentice from his master's door   5
Had pared the dirt, and sprinkled round the floor.
Now Moll had whirled her mop with dextrous airs,
Prepared to scrub the entry and the stairs.
The youth with broomy stumps began to trace

The kennel's edge, where wheels had worn the place.   10
The small-coal man was heard with cadence deep,
Till drowned in shriller notes of chimney-sweep.
Duns at his lordship's gate began to meet;
And Brickdust Moll had screamed through half the street.
The turnkey now his flock returning sees,   15
Duly let out a-nights to steal for fees.
The watchful bailiffs take their silent stands;
And schoolboys lag with satchels in their hands.

Jonathan Swift (1667–1745)

QUESTIONS

    hired coach

1. Vocabulary: *hardly* (1), *hackney-coach* (1), *kennel* (10), *duns* (13), *turnkey* (15), *bailiffs* (17).

2. The images in this poem differ sharply from those in the previous poem. Do they differ also from the expectations set up by the title? What is the poem's purpose?

3. The poem gives a good brief picture of London street life in the eighteenth century. List the various types of people mentioned and explain what each is doing. (The "youth with broomy stumps" in line 9 is apparently searching for salvage.)

STOP

In grimy winter dusk
We slowed for a concrete platform;
The pillars passed more slowly;
A paper bag leapt up.

The train banged to a standstill.   5
Brake-steam rose and parted.
Three chipped-at blocks of ice
Sprawled on a baggage-truck.

Out in that glum, cold air
The broken ice lay glintless,   10
But the truck was painted blue
On side, wheels, and tongue,

A purple, glowering blue
Like the phosphorus of Lethe

Or Queen Persephone's gaze   15
In the numb fields of the dark.

Richard Wilbur (b. 1921)

QUESTIONS

1. What senses are the images of the poem addressed to? What is their combined effect?

2. *Lethe* (14), in Greek mythology, was the river of oblivion flowing out of Hades. *Persephone* (15) was queen of death and the underworld. Literally this poem simply describes the stopping of a train at a small way-station. What do the title, the action, the images, and the comparisons make it suggest?

TO AUTUMN

Season of mists and mellow fruitfulness,
    Close bosom-friend of the maturing sun;
Conspiring with him how to load and bless
    With fruit the vines that round the thatch-eaves run;
To bend with apples the mossed cottage-trees,   5
    And fill all fruit with ripeness to the core;
        To swell the gourd, and plump the hazel shells
With a sweet kernel; to set budding more,
    And still more, later flowers for the bees,
    Until they think warm days will never cease,   10
        For Summer has o'er-brimmed their clammy cells.

Who hath not seen thee oft amid thy store?
    Sometimes whoever seeks abroad may find
Thee sitting careless on a granary floor,
    Thy hair soft-lifted by the winnowing wind;   15
Or on a half-reaped furrow sound asleep,
    Drowsed with the fume of poppies, while thy hook
        Spares the next swath and all its twined flowers:
And sometimes like a gleaner thou dost keep
    Steady thy laden head across a brook;   20
    Or by a cider-press, with patient look,
        Thou watchest the last oozings hours by hours.

Where are the songs of Spring? Ay, where are they?
    Think not of them, thou hast thy music too,—
While barred clouds bloom the soft-dying day,   25
    And touch the stubble-plains with rosy hue;
Then in a wailful choir the small gnats mourn
    Among the river sallows, borne aloft
        Or sinking as the light wind lives or dies;
And full-grown lambs loud bleat from hilly bourn;   30
    Hedge-crickets sing; and now with treble soft
    The red-breast whistles from a garden-croft;
        And gathering swallows twitter in the skies.

John Keats (1795–1821)

QUESTIONS

1. Vocabulary: *hook* (17), *sallows* (28), *bourn* (30), *croft* (32).
2. How many kinds of imagery do you find in the poem? Give examples of each.
3. Are the images arranged haphazardly or are they carefully organized? In answering this question, consider: (a) With what aspect of autumn is each stanza particularly concerned? (b) What kind of imagery is dominant in each stanza? (c) What time of the season is presented in each stanza? (d) Is there any progression in time of day?
4. What is Autumn personified as in stanza 2? Is there any suggestion of personification in the other two stanzas?
5. Although the poem is primarily descriptive, what attitude toward transience and passing beauty is implicit in it?

DRIVING TO TOWN LATE TO MAIL A LETTER

It is a cold and snowy night. The main street is deserted.
The only things moving are swirls of snow.
As I lift the mailbox door, I feel its cold iron.
There is a privacy I love in this snowy night.
Driving around, I will waste more time.

Robert Bly (b. 1926)

Figurative Language 1

Metaphor, Personification, Metonymy

> *Poetry provides the one permissible*
> *way of saying one thing and meaning*
> *another.* **ROBERT FROST**

Let us assume that your roommate has just come in out of a rainstorm and you say to him, "Well, you're a pretty sight! Got slightly wet, didn't you?" And he replies, "Wet? I'm drowned! It's raining cats and dogs outside, and my raincoat's just like a sieve!"

It is likely that you and your roommate understand each other well enough, and yet if you examine this conversation literally, that is to say unimaginatively, you will find that you have been speaking nonsense. Actually you have been speaking figuratively. You have been saying less than what you mean, or more than what you mean, or the opposite of what you mean, or something else than what you mean. You did not mean that your roommate was a pretty sight but that he was a wretched sight. You did not mean that he got slightly wet but that he got very wet. Your roommate did not mean that he got drowned but that he got drenched. It was not raining cats and dogs; it was raining water. And your roommate's raincoat is so unlike a sieve that not even a baby would confuse them.

If you are familiar with Molière's play *Le Bourgeois Gentilhomme*,

64

you will remember how delighted M. Jourdain was to discover that he had been speaking prose all his life. You may be equally surprised to discover that you have been speaking a kind of subpoetry all your life. The difference between your figures of speech and the poet's is that yours are worn and trite, his fresh and original.

On first examination, it might seem absurd to say one thing and mean another. But we all do it and with good reason. We do it because we can say what we want to say more vividly and forcefully by figures than we can by saying it directly. And we can say more by figurative statement than we can by literal statement. Figures of speech are another way of adding extra dimensions to language. We shall examine their usefulness more particularly later in this chapter.

Broadly defined, a FIGURE OF SPEECH is any way of saying something other than the ordinary way, and some rhetoricians have classified as many as 250 separate figures. For our purposes, however, a figure of speech is more narrowly definable as a way of saying one thing and meaning another, and we need be concerned with no more than a dozen. FIGURATIVE LANGUAGE—language using figures of speech—is language that cannot be taken literally.

METAPHOR and SIMILE are both comparisons between things essentially unlike. The only distinction is that in simile the comparison is *expressed*, by the use of some word or phrase such as *like, as, than, similar to,* or *resembles*. In metaphor the comparison is *implied*—that is, the figurative term is *substituted for* or *identified with* the literal term. When Shakespeare writes in "Spring" (page 11) that "merry larks are plough-men's clocks," he is using a metaphor, for he identifies larks with clocks. When Tennyson writes that the eagle "clasps the crag with crooked hands" (page 5), he is using a metaphor, for he substitutes crooked hands for claws. Later, when he says that the eagle falls "like a thunderbolt," he uses a simile.

A HILLSIDE THAW ✓

To think to know the country and not know
The hillside on the day the sun lets go
Ten million silver lizards out of snow!
As often as I've seen it done before
I can't pretend to tell the way it's done.   5

65

It looks as if some magic of the sun
Lifted the rug that bred them on the floor
And the light breaking on them made them run.
But if I thought to stop the wet stampede,
And caught one silver lizard by the tail,   10
And put my foot on one without avail,
And threw myself wet-elbowed and wet-kneed
In front of twenty others' wriggling speed,—
In the confusion of them all aglitter,
And birds that joined in the excited fun   15
By doubling and redoubling song and twitter,
I have no doubt I'd end by holding none.

It takes the moon for this. The sun's a wizard
By all I tell; but so's the moon a witch.
From the high west she makes a gentle cast   20
And suddenly, without a jerk or twitch,
She has her spell on every single lizard.
I fancied when I looked at six o'clock
The swarm still ran and scuttled just as fast.
The moon was waiting for her chill effect.   25
I looked at nine: the swarm was turned to rock
In every lifelike posture of the swarm,
Transfixed on mountain slopes almost erect.
Across each other and side by side they lay.
The spell that so could hold them as they were   30
Was wrought through trees without a breath of storm
To make a leaf, if there had been one, stir.
It was the moon's: she held them until day,
One lizard at the end of every ray.
The thought of my attempting such a stay!   35

Robert Frost (1874–1963)

QUESTIONS

1. The literal equivalents of the silver lizards and the lizards turned to rock are never named in the poem. What are they?

2. A poet may use a variety of metaphors or similes in developing a subject, or may, as Frost does here, develop a single metaphor at length (this poem is an excellent example of an EXTENDED OR SUSTAINED METAPHOR). What are the advantages of each type of development?

3. Though primarily descriptive of nature, this poem also reveals a good deal about the nature of the speaker and of the poet. What is his relationship to nature? Is he serious in ascribing to the moon the transformation effected in the second half of the poem? If not, what quality of mind is here displayed, and how is it seen elsewhere in the poem?

PERSONIFICATION consists in giving the attributes of a human being to an animal, an object, or an idea. It is really a subtype of metaphor, an implied comparison in which the figurative term of the comparison is always a human being. When Frost calls the sun a wizard and the moon a witch, he is personifying objects. When Keats describes autumn as a harvester "sitting careless on a granary floor" or "on a half-reaped furrow sound asleep"(page 62), he is personifying a concept. Personifications differ in the degree to which they ask the reader actually to visualize the literal term in human form. In Keats's comparison we are asked to make a complete identification of autumn with a human being. In Frost's, we are asked to think of the sun and moon as having only human (or superhuman) powers. In "The Twa Corbies" (page 13), we are asked to think of the two ravens as speaking, thinking, and feeling like human beings, but not as having human form. In Browning's reference to "the startled little waves" (page 55), a personification is barely suggested; we would make a mistake if we tried to visualize the waves in human form or even, really, to think of them as having human emotions.*

Closely related to personification is APOSTROPHE, which consists in addressing someone absent or something nonhuman as if it were alive and present and could reply to what is being said. When the speaker in James Joyce's poem (page 188) cries out, "My love, my love, my love, why have you left me alone?" he is apostrophizing his departed sweet-

---

*The various figures of speech blend into each other, and it is sometimes difficult to classify a specific example as definitely metaphor or symbol, symbolism or allegory, understatement or irony, irony or paradox. Often a given example may exemplify two or more figures at once. When Hardy writes of the "weakening eye of day" (page 57), the metaphorical substitution of *eye* for *sun* has the secondary effect of personifying *day*. In the poem "A White Rose" (page 84), beginning "The red rose whispers of passion," the red rose is personified by the verb *whispers* but is at the same time a symbol. The important consideration in reading poetry is not that we classify figures definitively but that we construe them correctly.

heart. The speaker in Shakespeare's "Fear No More the Heat o' the Sun" (page 342) is apostrophizing the body of a dead boy. William Blake apostrophizes the tiger throughout his famous poem (page 302) but does not otherwise personify it. Keats apostrophizes as well as personifies autumn (page 62). Personification and apostrophe are both ways of giving life and immediacy to one's language, but since neither requires great imaginative power on the part of the poet—apostrophe especially does not—they may degenerate into mere mannerisms and are to be found as often in bad and mediocre poetry as in good. We need to distinguish between their effective use and their merely conventional use.

DR. SIGMUND FREUD DISCOVERS THE SEA SHELL

Science, that simple saint, cannot be bothered
Figuring what anything is for:
Enough for her devotions that things are
And can be contemplated soon as gathered.

She knows how every living thing was fathered,   5
She calculates the climate of each star,
She counts the fish at sea, but cannot care
Why any one of them exists, fish, fire or feathered.

Why should she? Her religion is to tell
By rote her rosary of perfect answers.   10
Metaphysics she can leave to man:
She never wakes at night in heaven or hell

Staring at darkness. In her holy cell
There is no darkness ever: the pure candle
Burns, the beads drop briskly from her hand.   15

Who dares to offer Her the curled sea shell!
She will not touch it!—knows the world she sees
Is all the world there is! Her faith is perfect!

And still he offers the sea shell. . . .
                    What surf
Of what far sea upon what unknown ground   20
Troubles forever with that asking sound?
What surge is this whose question never ceases?

Archibald MacLeish (b. 1892)

1. Vocabulary: *metaphysics* (11).

2. This poem employs an extended personification. List the ways in which science is appropriately compared to a saint. In what way is its faith *perfect* (18)?

3. Who is *he* in line 19?

4. Who was Sigmund Freud, and what discoveries did he make about human nature?

5. What does the sea shell represent?

THE SEA-GULL

Hark to the whimper of the sea-gull;
He weeps because he's not an ea-gull.
Suppose you were, you silly sea-gull,
Could you explain it to your she-gull?

Ogden Nash (b. 1902)

QUESTION

What is lost in effectiveness, and why, if the last two lines are rewritten thus:

But if it were, how could the sea-gull
Explain the matter to its she-gull?

SYNECDOCHE (the use of the part for the whole) and METONYMY (the use of something closely related for the thing actually meant) are alike in that both substitute some significant detail or aspect of an experience for the experience itself. Thus, Shakespeare uses synecdoche when he says that the cuckoo's song is unpleasing to a "married ear" (page 11), for he means a married *man*. Robert Graves uses synecdoche in "The Naked and the Nude" (page 42) when he refers to a doctor as a "hippocratic eye," and T. S. Eliot uses it in "The Love Song of J. Alfred Prufrock" when he refers to a crab or lobster as "a pair of ragged claws" (page 284). Shakespeare uses metonymy when he says that the yellow cuckoo-buds "paint the meadows with delight" (page 11), for he means with bright color, which produces delight. Robert Frost uses metonymy in "Out, Out—" (page 135) when he describes an injured boy holding up his cut hand "as if to keep/The life from spilling," for literally he means to keep the blood from spilling. In each case, however, there is a gain in vividness and meaning. Eliot, by substituting for the crab that part which seizes its prey, tells us something important about the crab and makes us see it more vividly. Shakespeare, by referring to bright color as "delight" evokes not only the visual effect but the emotional response it arouses. Frost tells us both that the boy's hand is bleeding and that his life is in danger.

Many synecdoches and metonymies, of course, like many metaphors, have become so much a part of the language that they no longer strike us as figurative; such is the case with *redskin* for Indian, *paleface* for white man, and *salt* and *tar* for sailor. Such figures are referred to as dead metaphors or dead figures. Synecdoche and metonymy are so much alike that it is hardly worth while to distinguish between them, and the latter term is increasingly coming to be used for both. In this book metonymy will be used for both figures—that is, for any figure in which a part or something closely related is substituted for the thing literally meant.

LINES ON A PAID MILITIA*

The country rings around with loud alarms,
And raw in fields the rude militia swarms;
Mouths without hands; maintained at vast expense,
In peace a charge, in war a weak defense:
Stout once a month they march, a blustering band,   5
And ever, but in times of need, at hand.
This was the morn when, issuing on the guard,
Drawn up in rank and file they stood prepared
Of seeming arms to make a short essay,
Then hasten to be drunk, the business of the day.   10

John Dryden (1631–1700)

QUESTIONS

1. Vocabulary: *essay* (9).
2. Comment on the meanings or force of *charge* (4), *business* (10).
3. The art of this passage depends on effective juxtapositions. Point out and comment on the most effective.

*From *Cymon and Iphigenia*.

4. Explain the meaning of "mouths without hands" (3). Although this book proposes that the single term *metonymy* be used for the figures once distinguished as metonymy and synecdoche, it may be instructive to make the distinction here. Which is *mouths*? Which is *hands*? Why?

We said at the beginning of this chapter that figurative language often provides a more effective means of saying what we mean than does direct statement. What are some of the reasons for that effectiveness?

First, figurative language affords us imaginative pleasure. Imagination might be described in one sense as that faculty or ability of the mind that proceeds by sudden leaps from one point to another, that goes up a stair by leaping in one jump from the bottom to the top rather than by climbing up one step at a time.* The mind takes delight in these sudden leaps, in seeing likenesses between unlike things. We have probably all taken pleasure in staring into a fire and seeing castles and cities and armies in it, or in looking into the clouds and shaping them into animals or faces, or in seeing a man in the moon. We name our plants and flowers after fancied resemblances: jack-in-the-pulpit, babies'-breath, Queen Anne's lace. Figures of speech are therefore satisfying in themselves, providing us with a source of pleasure in the exercise of the imagination.

Second, figures of speech are a way of bringing additional imagery into verse, of making the abstract concrete, of making poetry more sensuous. When MacLeish personifies science (page 68), he gives body and form to what had previously been only a concept. When Robert Frost's bridegroom thinks of his bride (page 15) and wishes "her heart in a case of gold/And pinned with a silver pin," he objectifies an inner feeling in precise visual terms. When Robert Browning compares the crisping waves to "fiery ringlets" (page 55), he starts with one image and transforms it into three. Figurative language is a way of multiplying the sense appeal of poetry.

Third, figures of speech are a way of adding emotional intensity to otherwise merely informative statements and of conveying attitudes along

*It is also the faculty of mind that is able to "picture" or "image" absent objects as if they were present. It was with imagination in this sense that we were concerned in the chapter on imagery.

with information. If we say, "So-and-so is a rat" or "My feet are killing me," our meaning is as much emotional as informative. When Thomas Hardy compares "tangled bine-stems" to "strings of broken lyres" (page 57), he not only draws an exact visual comparison but also conjures up a feeling of despondency through the suggestion of discarded instruments no longer capable of making music. When Wilfred Owen compares a soldier caught in a gas attack to a man drowning under a green sea (page 8), he conveys a feeling of despair and suffocation as well as a visual image.

Fourth, figures of speech are a means of concentration, a way of saying much in brief compass. Like words, they may be multidimensional. Consider, for instance, the merits of comparing life to a candle, as Shakespeare does in a passage from *Macbeth* (page 137). Life is like a candle in that it begins and ends in darkness; in that while it burns, it gives off light and energy, is active and colorful; in that it gradually consumes itself, get shorter and shorter; in that it can be snuffed out at any moment; in that it is brief at best, burns only for a short duration. Possibly your imagination can suggest other similarities. But at any rate, Macbeth's compact metaphorical description of life as a "brief candle" suggests certain truths about life that would require dozens of words to state in literal language. At the same time it makes the abstract concrete, provides imaginative pleasure, and adds a degree of emotional intensity.

Obviously one of the necessary abilities for reading poetry is the ability to interpret figurative language. Every use of figurative language involves a risk of misinterpretation, though the risk is well worth taking. For the person who can translate the figure, the dividends are immense. Fortunately all people have imagination to some degree, and imagination can be cultivated. By practice one's ability to interpret figures of speech can be increased.

EXERCISES

1. Identify each of the following quotations as literal or figurative. If figurative, explain what is being compared to what and explain the appropriateness of the comparison. EXAMPLE: "Talent is a cistern; genius is a fountain." ANSWER: A metaphor. Talent = cistern; genius = fountain. Talent exists in finite supply; it can be used up. Genius is inexhaustible, ever renewing.

a. O tenderly the haughty day
   Fills his blue urn with fire.   *Emerson*

b. It is with words as with sunbeams—the more they are condensed, the
   deeper they burn.   *Robert Southey*

c. Joy and Temperance and Repose
   Slam the door on the doctor's nose.   *Anonymous*

d. The pen is mightier than the sword.   *Edward Bulwer-Lytton*

e. The strongest oaths are straw
   To the fire i' the blood.   *Shakespeare*

f. The Cambridge ladies . . . live in furnished souls.   *E. E. Cummings*

g. The green lizard and the golden snake,
   Like unimprisoned flames, out of their trance awake.   *Shelley*

h. Dorothy's eyes, with their long brown lashes, looked very much like
   her mother's.   *Laetitia Johnson*

i. Is this the face that launched a thousand ships?   *Marlowe*

j. What should such fellows as I do crawling between earth and heaven?
                                                    Shakespeare

k. Love's feeling is more soft and sensible
   Than are the tender horns of cockled snails.   *Shakespeare*

l. The tawny-hided desert crouches watching her.   *Francis Thompson*

m. . . . Let us sit upon the ground
   And tell sad stories of the death of kings.   *Shakespeare*

n. See, from his [Christ's, on the cross] head, his hands, his side
   Sorrow and love flow mingled down.   *Isaac Watts*

o. Now half [of the departing guests] to the setting moon are gone,
   And half to the rising day.   *Tennyson*

p. I do not know whether my present poems are better than the earlier
   ones. But this is certain: they are much sadder and sweeter, like pain
   dipped in honey.   *Heinrich Heine*

q. . . . clouds. . . . Shepherded by the slow, unwilling wind.   *Shelley*

r. Let us eat and drink, for tomorrow we shall die.   *Isaiah 22:13*

s. Let us eat and drink, for tomorrow we may die.
                              Common misquotation of the above

2. What is the most important difference between the following two poems?
   Explain.

THE DESERTED HOUSE

There's no smoke in the chimney,
  And the rain beats on the floor;
There's no glass in the window,
  There's no wood in the door;
And heather grows behind the house,   5
  And the sand lies before.

No hand hath trained the ivy,
  The walls are gray and bare;
The boats upon the sea sail by,
  Nor ever tarry there.   10
No beast of the field comes nigh,
  Nor any bird of the air.

Mary Coleridge (1861–1907)

THE OLD HOUSE

A very, very old house I know—
And ever so many people go,
Past the small lodge, forlorn and still,
Under the heavy branches, till
Comes the blank wall, and there's the door.   5
Go in they do; come out no more.
No voice says aught; no spark of light
Across that threshold cheers the sight;
Only the evening star on high
Less lonely makes a lonely sky,   10
As, one by one, the people go
Into that very old house I know.

Walter de la Mare (1873–1956)

LOVE *metonymy for God.*

Love bade me welcome; yet my soul drew back,
  Guilty of dust and sin.
But quick-eyed Love, observing me grow slack
  From my first entrance in,

Drew nearer to me, sweetly questioning 5
    If I lacked anything.

"A guest," I answered, "worthy to be here."
    Love said, "You shall be he."
"I, the unkind, ungrateful? Ah my dear,
    I cannot look on Thee." 10
Love took my hand, and smiling, did reply,
    "Who made the eyes but I?"

"Truth, Lord, but I have marred them; let my shame
    Go where it doth deserve."
"And know you not," says Love, "who bore the blame?" 15
    "My dear, then I will serve."
"You must sit down," says Love, "and taste my meat."
    So I did sit and eat.

Directly relates to Christianity

                    George Herbert (1593–1633)

QUESTIONS

1. This little drama has two characters. Characterize the guest. Characterize the host. What is the relationship between them?

2. Should *Love* be considered a personification or a metonymy? Explain.

3. To what kind of feast is the guest being invited? Is the *meat* (17) any meat or something special?

THE GUITARIST TUNES UP

With what attentive courtesy he bent
Over his instrument;
Not as a lordly conquerer who could
Command both wire and wood,
But as a man with a loved woman might,
Inquiring with delight
What slight essential things she had to say
Before they started, he and she, to play.

                    Frances Cornford (1886–1960)

QUESTION

Explore the comparison. Does it principally illuminate the guitarist or the lovers or both? What one word brings its two terms together?

2 lovers – He is leaving but only parting physical, not spiritually

A VALEDICTION: FORBIDDING MOURNING

As virtuous men pass mildly away,
  And whisper to their souls to go,
While some of their sad friends do say,
  {The breath goes now, and some say, no:

reference to deathbed, but only comparison

So let us melt, and make no noise,   5
  No tear-floods, nor sigh-tempests move, – *don't cry in public*
'Twere profanation of our joys
  To tell the laity our love.

Moving of th' earth brings harms and fears,
  Men reckon what it did and meant,   10
But trepidation of the spheres, – *belief that spheres together move others*
  Though greater far, is innocent.

Destroy harmony of universe

Dull sublunary lovers' love
  (Whose soul is sense) cannot admit
Absence, because it doth remove   15
  Those things which elemented it.

But we by a love so much refined,
  That ourselves know not what it is,   *Our love is so refined that we don't need sex.*
Inter-assured of the mind,
  Care less, eyes, lips, and hands to miss.   20

Our two souls therefore, which are one,
  Though I must go, endure not yet
A breach, but an expansion, – *When they part, they really expanding.*
  Like gold to airy thinness beat.

If they be two, they are two so   25
  As stiff twin compasses are two,
Thy soul the fixed foot, makes no show
  To move, but doth, if th' other do.

And though it in the center sit,
  Yet when the other far doth roam,   30
It leans, and hearkens after it, – *Compass spreads*
  And grows erect, as that comes home.

Such wilt thou be to me, who must
  Like th' other foot, obliquely run;

Simile
Parting of lovers
Death of virtuous man

Thy firmness makes my circle just,
And makes me end, where I begun. —*Come back to lover*

John Donne (1572–1631)

QUESTIONS

1. Vocabulary: *valediction* (title), *profanation* (7), *laity* (8), *trepidation* (11), *innocent* (12), *sublunary* (13), *elemented* (16). Line 11 is a reference to the spheres of the Ptolemaic cosmology, whose movement caused no such disturbance as does a movement of the earth—that is, an earthquake.

2. Is the speaker in the poem about to die? Or about to leave on a journey?

3. The poem is organized around a contrast of two kinds of lovers: the *laity* (8) and, as their opposite, the priesthood. What two major contrasts are drawn between these two kinds of lovers?

4. Find and explain three similes and one metaphor used to describe the parting of true lovers. The figure in the last three stanzas is one of the most famous in English literature. Demonstrate its appropriateness by obtaining a drawing compass or by using two pencils to imitate the two legs.

5. What kind of language is used in the poem? Is the language consonant with the figures of speech?

TO HIS COY MISTRESS

Had we but world enough, and time,
This coyness, lady, were no crime.
We would sit down, and think which way
To walk, and pass our long love's day.
Thou by the Indian Ganges' side   5
Shouldst rubies find; I by the tide
Of Humber would complain. I would
Love you ten years before the Flood,
And you should, if you please, refuse
Till the conversion of the Jews.   10
My vegetable love should grow
Vaster than empires, and more slow;
An hundred years should go to praise
Thine eyes, and on thy forehead gaze;
Two hundred to adore each breast,   15
But thirty thousand to the rest;

77

An age at least to every part,
And the last age should show your heart.
For, lady, you deserve this state,
Nor would I love at lower rate.   20
  But at my back I always hear
Time's wingèd chariot hurrying near;
And yonder all before us lie
Deserts of vast eternity.
Thy beauty shall no more be found,   25
Nor, in thy marble vault, shall sound
My echoing song; then worms shall try
That long-preserved virginity,
And your quaint honor turn to dust,
And into ashes all my lust: 30
The grave's a fine and private place,
But none, I think, do there embrace.
  Now therefore, while the youthful hue
Sits on thy skin like morning dew,
And while thy willing soul transpires   35
At every pore with instant fires,
Now let us sport us while we may,
And now, like amorous birds of prey,
Rather at once our time devour
Than languish in his slow-chapped power.   40
Let us roll all our strength and all
Our sweetness up into one ball,
And tear our pleasures with rough strife
Thorough° the iron gates of life.   through
Thus, though we cannot make our sun   45
Stand still, yet we will make him run.

Andrew Marvell (1621–1678)

QUESTIONS

  1. Vocabulary: *mistress* (title), *Humber* (7), *transpires* (35), *chapped*
(40).

  2. Outline the speaker's argument in three sentences, beginning with
If, But, and *Therefore.* Is the speaker urging his mistress to marry him?

  3. Explain the appropriateness of "vegetable love" (11). What simile in
the third section contrasts with it and how? What image in the third section

contrasts with the distance between the Ganges and the Humber in section one?

4. Explain the figures in lines 22, 24, and 40 and their implications.

5. Explain the last two lines. For what is *sun* a metonymy?

6. Is this poem principally about love or about time? If the latter, what might making love represent? What philosophy is the poet advancing here?

THE FOLLY OF BEING COMFORTED

One that is ever kind said yesterday:
"Your well-belovèd's hair has threads of grey,
And little shadows come about her eyes;
Time can but make it easier to be wise
Though now it seems impossible, and so   5
All that you need is patience."

                                 Heart cries, "No,
I have not a crumb of comfort, not a grain.
Time can but make her beauty over again:
Because of that great nobleness of hers
The fire that stirs about her, when she stirs,   10
Burns but more clearly. O she had not these ways
When all the wild summer was in her gaze."

O heart! O heart! if she'd but turn her head,
You'd know the folly of being comforted.

William Butler Yeats (1865–1939)

QUESTIONS

1. For some thirty years Yeats suffered an unrequited love for a famous Irish beauty who was working in the cause of Irish freedom. What comfort is here held out to him? On what grounds does he reject it? What is the meaning of the last two lines?

2. Find two personifications, one apostrophe, and five metaphors in the poem, and comment on their effectiveness.

DREAM DEFERRED

What happens to a dream deferred?

    Does it dry up
    like a raisin in the sun?

Or fester like a sore—
And then run?
Does it stink like rotten meat?   5
Or crust and sugar over—
like a syrupy sweet?

Maybe it just sags
like a heavy load.

Or does it explode?   10

Langston Hughes (1902–1967)

QUESTIONS

1. Of the six images, five are similes. Which is a metaphor? Comment on its position and its effectiveness.

2. Since the dream could be any dream, the poem is general in its implication. What happens to your understanding of it on learning that its author was an American Negro?

THE HAND THAT SIGNED THE PAPER FELLED A CITY

The hand that signed the paper felled a city;
Five sovereign fingers taxed the breath,
Doubled the globe of dead and halved a country;
These five kings did a king to death.

The mighty hand leads to a sloping shoulder,   5
The finger joints are cramped with chalk;
A goose's quill has put an end to murder
That put an end to talk.

The hand that signed the treaty bred a fever,
And famine grew, and locusts came;   10
Great is the hand that holds dominion over
Man by a scribbled name.

The five kings count the dead but do not soften
The crusted wound nor stroke the brow;
A hand rules pity as a hand rules heaven;   15
Hands have no tears to flow.

Dylan Thomas (1914–1953)

QUESTIONS

1. This poem is developed around one main metonymy and one main metaphor. Identify each and discuss its effectiveness. What other parts or faculties of human beings, besides the one Thomas chose, are often used for the whole human being? Justify Thomas's choice.

2. Identify a second metonymy in the second stanza. Distinguish metaphorical from literal language in the last line of the first stanza.

3. What are the significance of the "sloping shoulder" (5) and the "finger joints . . . cramped with chalk" (6)?

4. Discuss the meaning of line 15.

UPON MISTRESS SUSANNA SOUTHWELL, HER FEET

Her pretty feet
Like snails did creep
A little out, and then,
As if they playèd at bo-peep,
Did soon draw in again.

Robert Herrick (1591–1674)

ENTICER

A married man who begs his friend,
A bachelor, to wed and end
His lonesome, sorry state,
Is like a bather in the sea,
Goose-pimpled, blue from neck to knee,
Who cries, "The water's great!"

Richard Armour (b. 1906)

Figurative Language 2

Symbol, Allegory

THE ROAD NOT TAKEN* ✓

Two roads diverged in a yellow wood, — *choices in life*
And sorry I could not travel both
And be one traveler, long I stood
And looked down one as far as I could
To where it bent in the undergrowth;   5

Then took the other, as just as fair,
And having perhaps the better claim,
Because it was grassy and wanted wear;
Though as for that the passing there
Had worn them really about the same,   10

And both that morning equally lay
In leaves no step had trodden black.
Oh, I kept the first for another day!
Yet knowing how way leads on to way,
I doubted if I should ever come back.   15

I shall be telling this with a sigh
Somewhere ages and ages hence:
Two roads diverged in a wood, and I—

---

*Mr. Frost recorded "The Road Not Taken" (LP, National Council of Teachers of English, RL 20-1; or LP, Library of Congress, PL 20; or LP, Caedmon, TC 1060.)

I took the one less traveled by,
And that has made all the difference.   20

                                        Robert Frost (1874–1963)

QUESTIONS

1. Does the speaker feel that he made the wrong choice in taking the road "less traveled by"? If not, why does he sigh? What does he regret?

2. Why does the choice between two roads that seem very much alike make such a big difference many years later?

A SYMBOL may be roughly defined as something that means *more* than what it is. "The Road Not Taken," for instance, concerns a choice made between two roads by a person out walking in the woods. He would like to explore both roads. He tells himself that he will explore one and then come back and explore the other, but he knows that he shall probably be unable to do so. By the last stanza, however, we realize that the poet is talking about something more than the choice of paths in a wood, for such a choice would be relatively unimportant, while this choice is one that will make a great difference in the speaker's life and that he will remember with a sigh "ages and ages hence." We must interpret his choice of a road as a symbol for any choice in life between alternatives that appear almost equally attractive but will result through the years in a large difference in the kind of experience one knows.

Image, metaphor, and symbol shade into each other and are sometimes difficult to distinguish. In general, however, an image means only what it is; a metaphor means something other than what it is; and a symbol means what it is and something more too.* If I say that a shaggy brown dog was rubbing its back against a white picket fence, I am talking about nothing but a dog (and a picket fence) and am therefore presenting an image. If I say, "Some dirty dog stole my wallet at the party," I am not talking about a dog at all and am therefore using a metaphor. But if I say, "You can't teach an old dog new tricks," I am talking not only about dogs but about living creatures of any species and

---

*This account does not hold for nonliterary symbols such as the letters of the alphabet and algebraic signs (the symbol ∞ for infinity or = for equals). Here, the symbol is meaningless except as it stands for something else, and the connection between the sign and what it stands for is purely arbitrary.

am therefore speaking symbolically. Images, of course, do not cease to be images when they become incorporated in metaphors or symbols. If we are discussing the sensuous qualities of "The Road Not Taken" we should refer to the two leaf-strewn roads in the yellow wood as an image; if we are discussing the significance of the poem, we talk about them as symbols.

Symbols vary in the degree of identification and definition that their authors give them. Frost in this poem forces us to interpret the choice of roads symbolically by the degree of importance he gives it in the last stanza. Sometimes poets are much more specific in identifying their symbols. Sometimes they do not identify them at all. Consider, for instance, the following two poems.

A WHITE ROSE

The red rose whispers of passion,
    And the white rose breathes of love;
Oh, the red rose is a falcon,
    And the white rose is a dove.

But I send you a cream-white rosebud,
    With a flush on its petal tips;
For the love that is purest and sweetest
    Has a kiss of desire on the lips.

John Boyle O'Reilly (1844–1890)

QUESTIONS

1. Could the poet have made the white rose a symbol of passion and the red rose a symbol of love? Why not?

2. In the second stanza, why does the speaker send a rosebud rather than a rose?

MY STAR

All that I know
    Of a certain star
Is, it can throw
    (Like the angled spar)

Now a dart of red,   5
    Now a dart of blue;
Till my friends have said
    They would fain see, too,
My star that dartles the red and the blue!
Then it stops like a bird; like a flower, hangs furled: 10
    They must solace themselves with the Saturn above it.
What matter to me if their star is a world?
    Mine has opened its soul to me; therefore I love it.

Robert Browning (1812–1889)

In his first two lines O'Reilly indicates so clearly that his red rose is a symbol of physical desire and his white rose a symbol of spiritual attachment that when we get to the metaphor in the third line we unconsciously substitute passion for the red rose in our minds, knowing without thinking that what O'Reilly is really likening is falcons and passion, not falcons and roses. Similarly in the second stanza, the symbolism of the white rosebud with pink tips is specifically indicated in the last two lines, although, as a matter of fact, it would have been clear from the first stanza. In Browning's poem, on the other hand, there is nothing specific to tell us that Browning is talking about anything other than just a star, and it is only the star's importance to him that makes us suspect that he is talking about something more.

The symbol is the richest and at the same time the most difficult of the poetical figures. Both its richness and its difficulty result from its imprecision. Although the poet may pin down the meaning of his symbol to something fairly definite and precise, as O'Reilly does in "A White Rose," more often the symbol is so general in its meaning that it is able to suggest a great variety of more specific meanings. It is like an opal that flashes out different colors when slowly turned in the light. The choice in "The Road Not Taken," for instance, concerns some choice in life, but what choice? Was it a choice of profession? (Frost took the road "less traveled by" in deciding to become a poet.) A choice of hobby? A choice of wife? It might be any or all or none of these. We cannot determine what particular choice the poet had in mind, if any, and it is not important that we do so. The general meaning of the poem is clear enough. It is an expression of regret that the possibilities of life-experience are so sharply limited. One must live with one wife, have one native country, follow one profession. The speaker in the poem would have liked to explore both roads, but he could explore only one. The person with a craving for life, however satisfied with his own choice, will always long for the realms of experience that had to be passed by. Because the symbol is a rich one, the poem suggests other meanings too. It affirms a belief in the possibility of choice and says something of the nature of choice—how each choice limits the range of possible future choices, so that we make our lives as we go, both freely choosing and being determined by past choices. Though not primarily a philosophical poem, it obliquely comments on the issue of free will versus determinism and indicates the poet's own position. It is able to do all these things, concretely and compactly, by its use of an effective symbol.

"My Star," if we interpret it symbolically, likewise suggests a variety of meanings. It has been most often interpreted as a tribute to Browning's wife, Elizabeth Barrett Browning. As one critic writes, "She shone upon his life like a star of various colors; but the moment the world attempted to pry into the secret of her genius, she shut off the light altogether."* The poem has also been taken to refer to Browning's own peculiar genius, "his gift for seeing in events and things a significance hidden from other men."† A third suggestion is that Browning was thinking of his own peculiar poetic style. He loved harsh, jagged sounds and rhythms and grotesque images; most people of his time found beauty only in the smoother-flowing, melodic rhythms and more conventionally poetic images of his contemporary Tennyson's style, which could be symbolized by Saturn in the poem. The point is not that any one of these interpretations is right or necessarily wrong. We cannot say what the poet had specifically in mind. Literally, the poem is an expression of affection for a particular star in the sky that has a unique beauty and fascination for the poet but in which no one else can see the qualities that the poet sees. If we interpret the poem symbolically, the star is a symbol for anything in life that has unique meanings and value for an

*William Lyon Phelps, *Robert Browning: How to Know Him* (Indianapolis: Bobbs-Merrill, 1932), p. 165.

†Quoted from William Clyde DeVane, *A Browning Handbook* (New York: Crofts, 1935), p. 202.

individual, which other people cannot see. Beyond this, the meaning is "open." And because the meaning is open, the reader is justified in bringing his own experience to its interpretation. Browning's cherished star might remind him of, for instance, an old rag doll he particularly loved as a child, though its button eyes were off and its stuffing coming out and it had none of the crisp bright beauty of waxen dolls with real hair admired by other children.

Between the extremes represented by "The White Rose" and "My Star" a poem may exercise all degrees of control over the range and meaning of its symbolism. Consider another example.

YOU, ANDREW MARVELL*

And here face down beneath the sun
And here upon earth's noonward height
To feel the always coming on
The always rising of the night:

To feel creep up the curving east   5
The earthly chill of dusk and slow
Upon those under lands the vast
And ever-climbing shadow grow

And strange at Ecbatan the trees
Take leaf by leaf the evening strange   10
The flooding dark about their knees
The mountains over Persia change

And now at Kermanshah the gate
Dark empty and the withered grass
And through the twilight now the late   15
Few travelers in the westward pass

And Baghdad darken and the bridge
Across the silent river gone
And through Arabia the edge
Of evening widen and steal on   20

And deepen on Palmyra's street
The wheel rut in the ruined stone

*Mr. MacLeish recorded "You, Andrew Marvell" (78 rpm, Harvard Vocarium, P–1220; or LP, Library of Congress, PL 29).

And Lebanon fade out and Crete
High through the clouds and overblown

And over Sicily the air   25
Still flashing with the landward gulls
And loom and slowly disappear
The sails above the shadowy hulls

And Spain go under and the shore
Of Africa the gilded sand   30
And evening vanish and no more
The low pale light across that land

Nor now the long light on the sea:
And here face downward in the sun
To feel how swift how secretly   35
The shadow of the night comes on . . .

Archibald MacLeish (b. 1892)

QUESTIONS

1. We ordinarily speak of *nightfall;* why does MacLeish speak of the
rising of the night? What implicit metaphorical comparison is suggested by
phrases like "rising of the night" (4), "the flooding dark" (11), "the
bridge/Across the silent river gone" (17–18), "deepen on Palmyra's street"
(21), "Spain go under" (29), and so on?

2. Does the comparative lack of punctuation serve any function in the
poem?

3. Ecbatan was founded in 700 B.C. and is associated in history with
Cyrus the Great, founder of the Persian Empire, and with Alexander the
Great. It and Kermanshah were ancient cities of Persia. Where are Baghdad,
Palmyra, Lebanon, Crete?

On the literal level, "You, Andrew Marvell" is about the coming
on of night. The poet, lying at noon full length in the sun somewhere
in the United States,* pictures in his mind the earth's shadow, halfway
around the world, moving silently westward over Persia, Syria, Crete,
Sicily, Spain, Africa, and finally the Atlantic—approaching swiftly, in
fact, the place where he himself lies. But the title of the poem tells us

*MacLeish has identified the fixed location of the poem as Illinois on the shore
of Lake Michigan.

that, though particularly concerned with the passage of a day, it is more generally concerned with the swift passage of time; for the title is an allusion to a famous poem on this subject by Andrew Marvell ("To His Coy Mistress," page 77) and especially to two lines of that poem:

But at my back I always hear
Time's wingèd chariot hurrying near.

Once we are aware of this larger concern of the poem, two symbolical levels of interpretation open to us. Marvell's poem is primarily concerned with the swift passing of man's life; and the word *night*, we know, if we have had any experience with other literature, is a natural and traditional metaphor or symbol for death. The poet, then, is thinking not only about the passing of a day but about the passing of his life. He is at present "upon earth's noonward height"—in the full flush of manhood—but he is acutely conscious of the declining years ahead and of "how swift how secretly" his death comes on.

If we are to account fully for all the data of the poem, however, a third level of interpretation is necessary. What has dictated the poet's choice of geographical references? The places named, of course, progress from east to west; but they have a further linking characteristic. Ecbatan, Kermanshah, Baghdad, and Palmyra are all ancient or ruined cities, the relics of past empires and crumbled civilizations. Lebanon, Crete, Sicily, Spain, and North Africa are places where civilization once flourished more vigorously than it does at present. On a third level, then, the poet is concerned, not with the passage of a day nor with the passage of a lifetime, but with the passage of historical epochs. The poet's own country—the United States—now shines "upon earth's noonward height" as a favored nation in the sun of history, but its civilization, too, will pass.

Meanings ray out from a symbol, like the corona around the sun or like connotations around a richly suggestive word. But the very fact that a symbol may be so rich in its meanings makes it necessary that we use the greatest tact in its interpretation. Though Browning's "My Star" might, if memory and reason be stretched, make us think of a rag doll, still we should not go around telling people that in this poem Browning uses the star to symbolize a rag doll, for this interpretation is private, idiosyncratic, and narrow. The poem allows it but does not itself suggest it. Moreover, we should never assume that because the meaning of a symbol is more or less open, we may make it mean anything we choose.

We would be wrong, for instance, in interpreting the choice in "The Road Not Taken" as some choice between good and evil, for the poem tells us that the two roads are much alike and that both lie "in leaves no step had trodden black." Whatever the choice is, it is a choice between two goods. Whatever our interpretation of a symbolical poem, it must be tied firmly to the facts of the poem. We must not let loose of the string and let our imaginations go ballooning up among the clouds. Because the symbol is capable of adding so many dimensions to a poem, it is a peculiarly effective resource of the poet, but it is also peculiarly susceptible of misinterpretation by the untrained or incautious reader.

Accurate interpretation of the symbol requires delicacy, tact, and good sense. The reader must keep his balance while walking a tightrope between too little and too much—between underinterpretation and overinterpretation. If he falls off, however, it is much more desirable that he fall off on the side of too little. The reader who reads "The Road Not Taken" as being only about a choice between two roads in a wood has at least gotten part of the experience that the poem communicates, but the reader who reads into it anything he chooses might as well discard the poem and simply daydream.

Above all, we should avoid the disease of seeing symbols everywhere, like a man with hallucinations, whether there are symbols there or not. It is better to miss a symbol now and then than to walk constantly among shadows and mirages.

TO THE VIRGINS, TO MAKE MUCH OF TIME

Gather ye rosebuds while ye may,
　　Old Time is still a-flying;
And this same flower that smiles today
　　Tomorrow will be dying.

The glorious lamp of heaven, the Sun,   5
　　The higher he's a-getting,
The sooner will his race be run,
　　And nearer he's to setting.

That age is best which is the first,
　　When youth and blood are warmer;   10
But being spent, the worse, and worst
　　Times still succeed the former.

Then be not coy, but use your time;
And while ye may, go marry;
For having lost but once your prime,   15
You may forever tarry.

Robert Herrick (1591–1674)

QUESTIONS

1. The first two stanzas might be interpreted literally if the third and fourth stanzas did not force us to interpret them symbolically. What do the rosebuds symbolize (stanza 1)? What does the course of a day symbolize (stanza 2)? Does the poet fix the meaning of the rosebud symbol in the last stanza or merely name *one* of its specific meanings?

2. How does the title help us interpret the meaning of the symbol? Why did Herrick use *virgins* instead of *maidens*?

3. Why is such haste necessary in gathering the rosebuds? True, the blossoms die quickly, but they are replaced by others. Who *really* is dying?

4. What are the "worse, and worst" times (11)? Why?

5. Why did the poet use his wording rather than the following alternative: *blooms* for *smiles* (3), *course* for *race* (7), *used* for *spent* (11), *spend* for *use* (13)?

ALLEGORY is a narrative or description that has a second meaning beneath the surface one. Although the surface story or description may have its own interest, the author's major interest is in the ulterior meaning. When Pharaoh in the Bible, for instance, has a dream in which seven fat kine are devoured by seven lean kine, the story does not really become significant until Joseph interprets its allegorical meaning: that Egypt is to enjoy seven years of fruitfulness and prosperity followed by seven years of famine. Allegory has been defined sometimes as an extended metaphor and sometimes as a series of related symbols. But it is usually distinguishable from both of these. It is unlike extended metaphor in that it involves a *system* of related comparisons rather than one comparison drawn out. It differs from symbolism in that it puts less emphasis on the images for their own sake and more on their ulterior meanings. Also, these meanings are more fixed. In allegory usually there is a one-to-one correspondence between the details and a single set of ulterior meanings. In complex allegories the details may have more than

91

one meaning, but these meanings tend to be definite. Meanings do not ray out from allegory as they do from a symbol.

Allegory is less popular in modern literature than it was in medieval and Renaissance writing, and it is much less often found in short poems than in long works such as *The Faerie Queene, Everyman,* and *Pilgrim's Progress.* It has sometimes, especially with political allegory, been used to conceal meaning rather than reveal it (or, rather, to conceal it from some people while revealing it to others). Though less rich than the symbol, allegory is an effective way of making the abstract concrete and has occasionally been used effectively even in fairly short poems.

PEACE

> Sweet Peace, where dost thou dwell? I humbly crave,
> Let me once know.
> I sought thee in a secret cave,
> And asked, if Peace were there.
> A hollow wind did seem to answer, No,   5
> Go seek elsewhere.
>
> I did; and going did a rainbow note.
> Surely, thought I,
> This is the lace of Peace's coat:
> I will search out the matter.   10
> But while I looked the clouds immediately
> Did break and scatter.
>
> Then went I to a garden and did spy
> A gallant flower,
> The crown imperial. Sure, said I,   15
> Peace at the root must dwell.
> But when I digged, I saw a worm devour
> What showed so well.
>
> At length I met a rev'rend good old man,
> Whom when for Peace   20
> I did demand, he thus began:
> There was a Prince of old
> At Salem° dwelt, who lived with good increase   Jerusalem
> Of flock and fold.

He sweetly lived; yet sweetness did not save 25
    His life from foes.
  But after death out of his grave
    There sprang twelve stalks of wheat;
Which many wond'ring at, got some of those
    To plant and set. 30

It prospered strangely, and did soon disperse
    Through all the earth:
  For they that taste it do rehearse,
    That virtue lies therein,
A secret virtue, bringing peace and mirth 35
    By flight of sin.

Take of this grain, which in my garden grows,
    And grows for you;
  Make bread of it: and that repose
    And peace which ev'rywhere 40
With so much earnestness you do pursue,
    Is only there.

George Herbert (1593–1633)

QUESTIONS

1. Who was the Prince (22)? What were the twelve stalks of wheat (28)? What is the grain (37)?

2. Should the secret cave (stanza 1), the rainbow (stanza 2), and the garden (stanza 3) be taken merely in the sense of "I searched everywhere" or should they be assigned more precise meanings?

EXERCISE

Determine whether *sleep*, in the following poems, is literal, metaphorical, symbolical, or other. In each case explain and justify your answer.

1. "On Moonlit Heath and Lonesome Bank," page 58, line 13.
2. Same poem, line 29.
3. "Stopping by Woods on a Snowy Evening," page 150.
4. "The Chimney Sweeper," page 116.
5. "Is My Team Ploughing," page 26.
6. "The Second Coming," page 103.
7. "Ulysses," page 96, line 5.

STARS, I HAVE SEEN THEM FALL

Stars, I have seen them fall,
   But when they drop and die
No star is lost at all
   From all the star-sown sky.
The toil of all that be
   Helps not the primal fault;
It rains into the sea,
   And still the sea is salt.

A. E. Housman (1859–1936)

QUESTION

Relate the symbols employed to the meaning of the poem.

THE SICK ROSE

O Rose, thou art sick!
The invisible worm
That flies in the night,
In the howling storm,

Has found out thy bed
Of crimson joy,
And his dark secret love
Does thy life destroy.

William Blake (1757–1827)

QUESTIONS

1. As in Browning's "My Star" the meaning of the symbolism here is left
open. The poem might be interpreted as being only about a rose that has
been attacked on a stormy night by a cankerworm. But the connotations of
certain words and details are so powerful as to suggest that something more

is meant: "sick" (applied to a flower), "invisible," "night," "howling storm," "joy," "dark secret love." May we say that the worm symbolizes any corrupting agent that destroys something beautiful by feeding upon it or making love to it?

2. Some specific interpretations of the poem are that it refers to the destruction of love by selfishness, possessiveness, or jealousy; of innocence by experience; of humanity by Satan; of imagination by reason. Do these suggestions seem plausible? Do you think of others?

3. Besides being a symbol, the rose is to some degree personified. What words in the poem contribute to this personification?

ALL THAT TIME

I saw two trees embracing.
One leaned on the other
as if to throw her down.
But she was the upright one.
Since their twin youth, maybe she   5
had been pulling him toward her
all that time,

and finally almost uprooted him.
He was the thin, dry, insecure one,
the most wind-warped, you could see.   10
And where their tops tangled
it looked like he was crying
on her shoulder.
On the other hand, maybe he

had been trying to weaken her,   15
break her, or at least
make her bend
over backwards for him
just a little bit.
And all that time   20
she was standing up to him

the best she could.
She was the most stubborn,
the straightest one, that's a fact.
But he had been willing   25
to change himself—

even if it was for the worse—
all that time.

At the top they looked like one
tree, where they were embracing.   30
It was plain they'd be
always together.
Too late now to part.
When the wind blew, you could hear
them rubbing on each other.   35

May Swenson (b. 1919)

QUESTIONS

1. What features of this poem demand that it be given a symbolical interpretation? What do the trees symbolize? Explain the last stanza.

2. Why is the poet so tentative in explaining the relationship of the two trees?

ULYSSES

It little profits that an idle king,
By this still hearth, among these barren crags,
Matched with an agèd wife, I mete and dole
Unequal laws unto a savage race,
That hoard, and sleep, and feed, and know not me.   5
I cannot rest from travel; I will drink
Life to the lees. All times I have enjoyed
Greatly, have suffered greatly, both with those
That loved me, and alone; on shore, and when
Through scudding drifts the rainy Hyades   10
Vext the dim sea. I am become a name;
For always roaming with a hungry heart
Much have I seen and known,—cities of men
And manners, climates, councils, governments,
Myself not least, but honored of them all;   15
And drunk delight of battle with my peers,
Far on the ringing plains of windy Troy.
I am a part of all that I have met;
Yet all experience is an arch wherethrough

Gleams that untraveled world, whose margin fades 20
For ever and for ever when I move.
How dull it is to pause, to make an end,
To rust unburnished, not to shine in use!
As though to breathe were life! Life piled on life
Were all too little, and of one to me 25
Little remains; but every hour is saved
From that eternal silence, something more,
A bringer of new things; and vile it were
For some three suns to store and hoard myself,
And this grey spirit yearning in desire 30
To follow knowledge like a sinking star,
Beyond the utmost bound of human thought.

This is my son, mine own Telemachus,
To whom I leave the scepter and the isle—
Well-loved of me, discerning to fulfil 35
This labor, by slow prudence to make mild
A rugged people, and through soft degrees
Subdue them to the useful and the good.
Most blameless is he, centered in the sphere
Of common duties, decent not to fail 40
In offices of tenderness, and pay
Meet adoration to my household gods,
When I am gone. He works his work, I mine.

There lies the port; the vessel puffs her sail:
There gloom the dark, broad seas. My mariners, 45
Souls that have toiled, and wrought, and thought with me—
That ever with a frolic welcome took
The thunder and the sunshine, and opposed
Free hearts, free foreheads—you and I are old;
Old age hath yet his honor and his toil. 50
Death closes all; but something ere the end,
Some work of noble note, may yet be done,
Not unbecoming men that strove with Gods.
The lights begin to twinkle from the rocks;
The long day wanes; the slow moon climbs; the deep 55
Moans round with many voices. Come, my friends,
'Tis not too late to seek a newer world.
Push off, and sitting well in order smite

The sounding furrows; for my purpose holds
To sail beyond the sunset, and the baths   60
Of all the western stars, until I die.
It may be that the gulfs will wash us down;
It may be we shall touch the Happy Isles,
And see the great Achilles, whom we knew.
Though much is taken, much abides; and though   65
We are not now that strength which in old days
Moved earth and heaven, that which we are, we are:
One equal temper of heroic hearts,
Made weak by time and fate, but strong in will
To strive, to seek, to find, and not to yield.   70

Alfred, Lord Tennyson (1809–1892)

QUESTIONS

1. Vocabulary: *Hyades* (10), *meet* (42).
2. Ulysses, king of Ithaca, is a legendary Greek hero, a major figure in Homer's *Iliad*, the hero of Homer's *Odyssey*, and a minor figure in Dante's *Divine Comedy*. After ten years at the siege of Troy, Ulysses set sail for home but, having incurred the wrath of the god of the sea, he was subjected to storms and vicissitudes and was forced to wander for another ten years, having many adventures and seeing most of the Mediterranean world before again reaching Ithaca, his wife, and his son. Once back home, according to Dante, he still wished to travel and "to follow virtue and knowledge." In Tennyson's poem, Ulysses is represented as about to set sail on a final voyage from which he will not return. Where is Ulysses standing during his speech? Whom is he addressing? Locate Ithaca on a map. Where exactly, in geographical terms, does Ulysses intend to sail (59–64)? (The Happy Isles were the Elysian fields, or Greek paradise; Achilles was another Greek prince, the hero of the *Iliad*, who was killed at the siege of Troy.)
3. Characterize Ulysses. What kind of person is he as Tennyson represents him?
4. What does Ulysses symbolize? What way of life is being recommended?
5. Find as many evidences as you can that Ulysses' desire for travel represents something more than mere wanderlust and wish for adventure.
6. Give two reasons why Tennyson might have Ulysses travel westward.
7. Interpret lines 18–21 and 26–29. What is symbolized by "the thunder and the sunshine" (48)? What do the two metonymies in line 49 stand for? What metaphor is implied in line 23?

may have killed the cat; more likely
the cat was just unlucky, or else curious
to see what death was like, having no cause
to go on licking paws, or fathering
litter on litter of kittens, predictably.   5

    Nevertheless, to be curious
is dangerous enough. To distrust
what is always said, what seems,
to ask odd questions, interfere in dreams,
leave home, smell rats, have hunches   10
does not endear him to those doggy circles
where well-smelt baskets, suitable wives, good lunches
are the order of things, and where prevails
much wagging of incurious heads and tails.

    Face it. Curiosity   15
will not cause him to die—
only lack of it will.
Never to want to see
the other side of the hill,
or that improbable country   20
where living is an idyll
(although a probable hell)
would kill us all.
Only the curious
have, if they live, a tale   25
worth telling at all.

    Dogs say he loves too much, is irresponsible,
is changeable, marries too many wives,
deserts his children, chills all dinner tables
with tales of his nine lives.   30
Well, he is lucky. Let him be
nine-lived and contradictory,
curious enough to change, prepared to pay
the cat price, which is to die
and die again and again,   35
each time with no less pain.
A cat minority of one

is all that can be counted on
to tell the truth. And what he has to tell
on each return from hell   40
is this: that dying is what the living do,
that dying is what the loving do,
and that dead dogs are those who do not know
that hell is where, to live, they have to go.

                                                Alastair Reid (b. 1926)

QUESTIONS

1. On the surface this poem is a dissertation on cats. What deeper comments does it make? Of what are cats and dogs, in this poem, symbols?
2. In what different senses are the words *death, die,* and *dying* here used?
3. Compare and contrast this poem in meaning and manner with "Ulysses."

HYMN TO GOD MY GOD, IN MY SICKNESS

Since I am coming to that holy room
   Where, with thy choir of saints for evermore,
I shall be made thy music, as I come
   I tune the instrument here at the door,
   And what I must do then, think here before.   5

Whilst my physicians by their love are grown
   Cosmographers, and I their map, who lie
Flat on this bed, that by them may be shown
   That this is my southwest discovery,   9
   Per fretum febris,° by these straits to die,   through the
                                                              raging of fever

I joy that in these straits I see my west;
   For though their currents yield return to none,
What shall my west hurt me? As west and east
   In all flat maps (and I am one) are one,
   So death doth touch the resurrection.   15

Is the Pacific Sea my home? Or are
   The eastern riches? Is Jerusalem?
Anyan,° and Magellan, and Gibralter,   Bering Strait
   All straits, and none but straits, are ways to them,
   Whether where Japhet dwelt, or Cham, or Sem.   20

We think that Paradise and Calvary,
  Christ's cross and Adam's tree, stood in one place;
Look Lord, and find both Adams met in me;
  As the first Adam's sweat surrounds my face,
  May the last Adam's blood my soul embrace.   25

So, in his purple wrapped receive me Lord,
  By these his thorns give me his other crown;
And as to others' souls I preached thy word,
  Be this my text, my sermon to mine own:
  Therefore, that he may raise, the Lord throws down.

John Donne (1572–1631)

QUESTIONS

1. Vocabulary: *cosmographers* (7).

2. For the last ten years of his life John Donne was Dean of St. Paul's Cathedral in London, and he is famous for his sermons (see lines 28–30) as well as his poems. According to his earliest biographer, this poem was written eight days before his death. What are "that holy room" (1) and "the instrument" (4)? What is Donne engaged in doing in stanza 1?

3. During Donne's lifetime such explorers as Henry Hudson and Martin Frobisher sought for a northwest passage to the East Indies. Why does Donne speak instead of a "southwest discovery" (9)? In what ways is his raging fever like a strait? What different meanings of the word *straits* (10) are operative here? What do the straits symbolize?

4. In what ways does Donne's body resemble a map?

5. Though the map is metaphorical, its parts are symbolical. What does the west symbolize? the east? the fact that west and east are one?

6. What meanings has the word *return* (12)? (Compare line 17.)

7. Japhet, Cham, and Sem (20), the sons of Noah, are in Christian legend the ancestors of three races of man, roughly identifiable with the populations of Europe, Africa, and Asia. What must one go through, according to Donne, to reach any place important? In what ways are the Pacific Ocean, the East Indies, and Jerusalem (16–17) each a fitting symbol for Donne's own destination?

8. The locations of Eden and Calvary (21) were identical according to early Christian scholars. How does this tie in with Donne's geographical symbolism? What connection is there between Adam's "sweat" (24) and Christ's "blood" (25)? Because Adam is said in the Bible to prefigure Christ (Romans 5:12–21), Christ is sometimes called the second Adam. How do the two Adams meet in Donne? What do sweat and blood (together and separately) symbolize?

9. For what are "eastern riches" (17), "his purple" (26), and "his thorns" (27) respectively metonymies? What do "purple" and "thorns" symbolize? What is Christ's "other crown" (27)?

10. With what earlier paradoxes in the poem does the paradox in the final line tie in? What, according to Donne, is the explanation and meaning of human suffering?

THE MARGRAVE'S BIRTHNIGHT

Up from many a sheeted valley,
From white woods as well,
Down too from each fleecy upland
Jingles many a bell

Jovial on the work-sad horses   5
Hitched to runners old
Of the toil-worn peasants sledging
Under sheepskins in the cold;

Till from every quarter gathered
Meet they on one ledge,   10
There from hoods they brush the snow off
Lighting from each sledge

Full before the Margrave's castle,
Summoned there to cheer
On his birth-night, in mid-winter,   15
Kept year after year.

O the hall, and O the holly!
Tables line each wall;
Guests as holly-berries plenty,
But—no host withal!   20

May his people feast contented
While at head of board
Empty throne and vacant cover
Speak the absent lord?

Minstrels enter. And the stewards   25
Serve the guests; and when,
Passing there the vacant cover,
Functionally then

Old observance grave they offer;
But no Margrave fair,   30
In his living aspect gracious,
Sits responsive there;

No, and never guest once marvels,
None the good lord name,
Scarce they mark void throne and cover—   35
Dust upon the same.

Mindless as to what importeth
Absence such in hall;
Tacit as the plough-horse feeding
In the palfrey's stall.   40

Ah, enough for toil and travail,
If but for a night
Into wine is turned the water,
Black bread into white.

Herman Melville (1819–1891)

QUESTIONS

1. Who is the Margrave? When is his birthnight? What is the significance of his absence and of the guests' failure to wonder at his absence?

2. Why did Melville choose the German title Margrave for the absent host rather than its English equivalent Marquis or some other title such as Prince, Baron, Earl, or Count?

3. Comment on the significance of the last stanza.

THE SECOND COMING

Turning and turning in the widening gyre
The falcon cannot hear the falconer;
Things fall apart; the centre cannot hold;
Mere anarchy is loosed upon the world,
The blood-dimmed tide is loosed, and everywhere
The ceremony of innocence is drowned;
The best lack all conviction, while the worst
Are full of passionate intensity.

Surely some revelation is at hand;
Surely the Second Coming is at hand.   10

103

[handwritten top margin: Things could continue to go around & round in cycles.]

The Second Coming! Hardly are those words out
When a vast image out of *Spiritus Mundi*
Troubles my sight: somewhere in sands of the desert
A shape with lion body and the head of a man,
A gaze blank and pitiless as the sun,   15
Is moving its slow thighs, while all about it
Reel shadows of the indignant desert birds.
The darkness drops again; but now I know
That twenty centuries of stony sleep
Were vexed to nightmare by a rocking cradle,   20
And what rough beast, its hour come round at last,
Slouches towards Bethlehem to be born? — *[handwritten: Anti-Christ or return to pagan]*

[handwritten left margin: Desert imagery; phynx represents pagan image. Civilization ruled by paganism.]

[handwritten left margin: Some kind of revolution must be at hand cause world in bad state.]

William Butler Yeats (1865–1939)

[handwritten: represents dragon or satan when he comes to get his.] *[handwritten: Where Christ was born, Ironic place to start.]*

QUESTIONS

1. Vocabulary: *gyre* (1).

2. In Christian legend the prophesied Second Coming may refer either to Christ or to Antichrist. *Spiritus Mundi* (12), literally world spirit, means the racial memory or collective unconscious mind of mankind. Yeats believed in a cyclical theory of history in which one historical era would be replaced by an opposite kind of era every two thousand years. Here, the anarchy in the world following World War I (the poem was written in 1919) heralds the end of the Christian era. What is symbolized by the falcon and the falconer (1–2)? What is the "shape with lion body and the head of a man" (14), and what does it symbolize? What are the "rocking cradle" (20) and the "rough beast" (21)? Discuss the effectiveness of these symbols.

LOVE SONG: I AND THOU*

Nothing is plumb, level or square:
    the studs are bowed, the joists
are shaky by nature, no piece fits
    any other piece without a gap
or pinch, and bent nails   5
    dance all over the surfacing
like maggots. By Christ
    I am no carpenter. I built

*Mr. Dugan recorded "Love Song: I and Thou" (LP, Library of Congress, PL 29).

the roof for myself, the walls
    for myself, the floors   10
for myself, and got
    hung up in it myself. I
danced with a purple thumb
    at this house-warming, drunk
with my prime whiskey: rage.   15
    Oh I spat rage's nails
into the frame-up of my work:
    it held. It settled plumb,
level, solid, square and true
    for that one moment. Then   20
it screamed and went on through
    skewing as wrong the other way.
God damned it. This is hell,
    but I planned it, I sawed it,
I nailed it, and I   25
    will live in it until it kills me.
I can nail my left palm
    to the left-hand cross-piece but
I can't do everything myself.
    I need a hand to nail the right,   30
a help, a love, a you, a wife.

Alan Dugan (b. 1923)

QUESTIONS

1. What clues are there that this house is not literal? What does it stand
for?

2. Why does the speaker swear "By Christ" rather than "By God" (7)?
Where else in the poem is Christ alluded to? What parallels and differences
does the speaker see between himself and Christ?

3. "God damned it" (23) at first sounds like another curse, but the past
tense makes its meaning more precise. What are the implications of lines
24–26? What implications are added in the phrase "by nature" (3)? What
meanings has "prime" (15)?

4. What is the meaning of the last three lines?

5. Allegory, symbol, and extended metaphor are often difficult to tell
apart, and perhaps have no fixed boundaries. (Some writers have defined
allegory as extended metaphor.) Classification is unimportant so long as

meanings are perceived. Nevertheless, how would you classify this? Do you see any differences between it and, say, Frost's "A Hillside Thaw" (page 65)?

EXERCISE

What are the essential differences between the following poems?

THE HOUSE ON THE HILL

They are all gone away,
 The House is shut and still,
There is nothing more to say.

Through broken walls and gray
 The winds blow bleak and shrill: 5
They are all gone away.

Nor is there one to-day
 To speak them good or ill:
There is nothing more to say.

Why is it then we stray   10
 Around the sunken sill?
They are all gone away,

And our poor fancy-play
 For them is wasted skill:
There is nothing more to say.   15

There is ruin and decay
 In the House on the Hill:
They are all gone away,
There is nothing more to say.

Edwin Arlington Robinson (1869–1935)

THE DESERTED HOUSE

Life and Thought have gone away
 Side by side,
Leaving door and windows wide:
 Careless tenants they!

All within is dark as night: 5
In the windows is no light;
And no murmur at the door,
So frequent on its hinge before.

Close the door, the shutters close,
Or through the windows we shall see   10
The nakedness and vacancy
Of the dark deserted house.

Come away: no more of mirth
Is here or merry-making sound.
The house was builded of the earth,   15
And shall fall again to ground.

Come away: for Life and Thought
Here no longer dwell;
But in a city glorious—
A great and distant city—have bought   20
A mansion incorruptible.
Would they could have stayed with us!

Alfred, Lord Tennyson (1809–1892)

EXERCISE

Which of the following poems are symbolical? Which are not?

ON A DEAD HOSTESS

Of this bad world the loveliest and best
Has smiled and said "Good Night," and gone to rest.

Hilaire Belloc (1870–1953)

WIND AND SILVER

Greatly shining,
The Autumn moon floats in the thin sky;
And the fish-ponds shake their backs and flash their dragon scales
As she passes over them.

Amy Lowell (1874–1925)

I MAY, I MIGHT, I MUST

If you will tell me why the fen
appears impassable, I then
Will tell you why I think that I
can get across it if I try.

Marianne Moore (b. 1887)

THE AMBER BEAD

I saw a fly within a bead
Of amber cleanly buried;
The urn was little, but the room
More rich than Cleopatra's tomb.

Robert Herrick (1591–1674)

SAFE UPON THE SOLID ROCK

Safe upon the solid rock the ugly houses stand:
Come and see my shining palace built upon the sand!

Edna St. Vincent Millay (1892–1950)

WESTERN WIND

O Western wind, when wilt thou blow
That the small rain down can rain?
Christ, that my love were in my arms,
And I in my bed again!

Anonymous

QUESTION
What is the connection between the first two lines and the last two?

Figurative
Language 3

Paradox, Overstatement, Understatement, Irony

Aesop tells the tale of a traveler who sought refuge with a Satyr on a bitter winter night. On entering the Satyr's lodging, he blew on his fingers, and was asked by the Satyr what he did it for. "To warm them up," he explained. Later, on being served with a piping hot bowl of porridge, he blew also on it, and again was asked what he did it for. "To cool it off," he explained. The Satyr thereupon thrust him out of doors, for he would have nothing to do with a man who could blow hot and cold with the same breath.

A PARADOX is an apparent contradiction that is nevertheless somehow true. It may be either a situation or a statement. Aesop's tale of the traveler illustrates a paradoxical situation. As a figure of speech, paradox is a statement. When Alexander Pope wrote that a literary critic of his time would "damn with faint praise," he was using a verbal paradox, for how can a man damn by praising?

When we understand all the conditions and circumstances involved in a paradox, we find that what at first seemed impossible is actually entirely plausible and not strange at all. The paradox of the cold hands and hot porridge is not strange to a man who knows that a stream of air directed upon an object of different temperature will tend to bring that object closer to its own temperature. And Pope's paradox is not strange when we realize that *damn* is being used figuratively, and that Pope means only that a too reserved praise may damage an author with the

109

public almost as much as adverse criticism. In a paradoxical statement the contradiction usually stems from one of the words being used figuratively or in more than one sense.

The value of paradox is its shock value. Its seeming impossibility startles the reader into attention and, thus, by the fact of its apparent absurdity, it underscores the truth of what is being said.

MY LIFE CLOSED TWICE

My life closed twice before its close;
    It yet remains to see
If Immortality unveil
    A third event to me,

So huge, so hopeless to conceive,
    As these that twice befell.
Parting is all we know of heaven,
    And all we need of hell.

Emily Dickinson (1830–1886)

QUESTIONS

1. Do lines 2–6 mean: (a) I do not know yet whether there is a life after death—a continued existence in heaven and hell or (b) I do not know yet whether my entry into heaven or hell—whichever place I go—will be as "huge" an event as two events that have already happened to me during my life? Or both?

2. The poem sets forth two or possibly three paradoxes: (a) that the speaker's life closed twice before its close; (b) (if we accept the second alternative above) that death and entry into immortality may possibly be "lesser" events than two not extraordinary occurrences that happened during the speaker's lifetime; (c) that parting from a loved one is *both* heaven and hell. Resolve (that is, explain) each of these paradoxes.

Overstatement, understatement, and verbal irony form a continuous series, for they consist, respectively, of saying more, saying less, and saying the opposite of what one really means.

OVERSTATEMENT, or *hyperbole*, is simply exaggeration but exaggeration in the service of truth. It is not the same as a fish story. If you say, "I'm starved!" or "You could have knocked me over with a feather!" or "I'll die if I don't pass this course!" you do not expect to be believed; you are merely adding emphasis to what you really mean. (And if you say, "There were literally millions of people at the dance!" you are merely piling one overstatement on top of another, for you really mean that "There were figuratively millions of people at the dance," or, literally, "The dance hall was very crowded.") Like all figures of speech, overstatement may be used with a variety of effects. It may be humorous or grave, fanciful or restrained, convincing or unconvincing. When Tennyson says of his eagle (page 5) that it is *Close* to the sun in lonely lands," he says what appears to be literally true, though we know from our study of astronomy that it is not. When Wordsworth reports of his daffodils in "I wandered lonely as a cloud" that they "stretched *in never-ending line*" along the margin of a bay, he too reports faithfully a visual appearance. When Frost says, at the conclusion of "The Road Not Taken" (page 82),

> I shall be saying this with a sigh
> Somewhere *ages and ages hence,*

we are scarcely aware of the overstatement, so quietly is the assertion made. Unskillfully used, however, overstatement may seem strained and ridiculous, leading us to react as Gertrude does to the player-queen's speeches in *Hamlet:* "The lady doth protest too much."

It is paradoxical that one can emphasize a truth either by overstating it or by understating it. UNDERSTATEMENT, or saying less than one means, may exist in what one says or merely in how one says it. If, for instance, upon sitting down to a loaded dinner plate, you say, "This looks like a good bite," you are actually stating less than the truth; but if you say, with Artemus Ward, that a man who holds his hand for half an hour in a lighted fire will experience "a sensation of excessive and disagreeable warmth," you are stating what is literally true but with a good deal less force than the situation might seem to warrant.

A RED, RED ROSE

O my luve is like a red, red rose,
  That's newly sprung in June.
O my luve is like the melodie
  That's sweetly played in tune.

As fair art thou, my bonnie lass,   5
  So deep in luve am I,

And I will luve thee still, my dear,
    Till a'° the seas gang° dry.   all; go

Till a' the seas gang dry, my dear,
    And the rocks melt wi' the sun!   10
And I will luve thee still, my dear,
    While the sands o' life shall run.

And fare thee weel, my only luve,
    And fare thee weel awhile!
And I will come again, my luve,   15
    Though it were ten thousand mile!

Robert Burns (1759–1796)

THE ROSE FAMILY

The rose is a rose,
And was always a rose.
But the theory now goes
That the apple's a rose,
And the pear is, and so's   5
The plum, I suppose.
The dear only knows
What will next prove a rose.
You, of course, are a rose—
But were always a rose.   10

Robert Frost (1874–1963)

QUESTION

Burns and Frost use the same metaphor in paying tribute to their loved ones;
otherwise their methods are opposed. Burns begins with a couple of conventionally poetic similes and proceeds to a series of overstatements. Frost begins with literal and scientific fact (the apple, pear, plum, and rose all belong
to the same botanical family, the Rosaceae), and then slips in his metaphor
so casually and quietly that the assertion has the effect of understatement.
What is the function of *of course* and *but* in the last two lines?

Like paradox, *irony* has meanings that extend beyond its use merely
as a figure of speech.

VERBAL IRONY, saying the opposite of what one means, is often confused with sarcasm and with satire, and for that reason it may be well to look at the meanings of all three terms. SARCASM and SATIRE both imply ridicule, one on the colloquial level, the other on the literary level. Sarcasm is simply bitter or cutting speech, intended to wound the feelings (it comes from a Greek word meaning to tear flesh). Satire is a more formal term, usually applied to written literature rather than to speech and ordinarily implying a higher motive: it is ridicule (either bitter or gentle) of human folly or vice, with the purpose of bringing about reform or at least of keeping other people from falling into similar folly or vice. Irony, on the other hand, is a literary device or figure that may be used in the service of sarcasm or ridicule or may not. It is popularly confused with sarcasm and satire because it is so often used as their tool: but irony may be used without either sarcastic or satirical intent, and sarcasm and satire may exist (though they do not usually) without irony. If, for instance, one of the members of your class raises his hand on the discussion of this point and says, "I don't understand," and your instructor replies, with a tone of heavy disgust in his voice, "Well, I wouldn't expect *you* to," he is being sarcastic but not ironical; he means exactly what he says. But if, after you have done particularly well on an examination, your instructor brings your test papers into the classroom saying, "Here's some *bad* news for you: you all got A's and B's!" he is being ironical but not sarcastic. Sarcasm, we may say, is cruel, as a bully is cruel: it intends to give hurt. Satire is both cruel and kind, as a surgeon is cruel and kind: it gives hurt in the interest of the patient or of society. Irony is neither cruel nor kind: it is simply a device, like a surgeon's scalpel, for performing any operation more skillfully.

Though verbal irony always implies the opposite of what is said, it has many gradations, and only in its simplest forms does it mean *only* the opposite of what is said. In more complex forms it means both what is said and the opposite of what is said, at once, though in different ways and with different degrees of emphasis. When Terence's critic, in "Terence, This Is Stupid Stuff" (page 17) says, "*Pretty* friendship 'tis to rhyme / Your friends to death before their time" (11–12), we may substitute the literal "sorry" for "pretty" with little or no loss of meaning. However, when Dryden writes of the paid militia (page 70) that they "hasten to be drunk, the *business* of the day," we cannot substitute "pleasure" for "business" without considerable loss of meaning, for while "business" here means pleasure—the opposite of what they are paid to be doing—it also means their chief activity of the day, what they are most in earnest about, what keeps them "busy" or occupied, and what, in fact, they do get paid for. On the other hand, when Dylan Thomas writes (page 80) "*Great* is the hand that holds dominion over / Man by a scribbled name," the meaning is mainly literal, with undertones of irony, for Thomas is emphasizing the great political power of the hand, but at the same time he is denying its moral greatness (it "doubled the globe of dead and halved a country") and its physical power (it "leads to a sloping shoulder" and its "finger joints are cramped with chalk").*

Like all figures of speech, verbal irony runs the danger of being misunderstood. With irony the risks are perhaps greater than with other figures, for if metaphor is misunderstood, the result may be simply bewilderment; but if irony is misunderstood, the reader goes away with exactly the opposite idea from what the user meant to convey. The results of misunderstanding if, for instance, you ironically called someone a villain, might be calamitous. For this reason the user of irony must be very skillful in its use, conveying by an altered tone or by a wink of the eye or pen, that he is speaking ironically; and the reader of literature must be always alert to recognize the subtle signs that irony is intended.

No matter how broad or obvious the irony, there will always be, in any large audience, a number who will misunderstand. The humorist Artemus Ward used to protect himself against these people by writing at the bottom of his newspaper column, "This is writ ironical." But irony is most delightful and most effective, for the good reader, when it is subtlest. It sets up a special understanding between writer and reader that may add either grace or force. If irony is too obvious, it sometimes seems merely crude. But if effectively used, it, like all figurative language, is capable of adding extra dimensions to meaning.

ON A CERTAIN LADY AT COURT

I know the thing that's most uncommon;—
Envy, be silent, and attend!—

*He is also drawing an ironical contrast between the terrifying consequences of its action and triviality of the means by which it accomplishes these consequences: "a scribbled name." This is irony of situation (see page 117).

I know a reasonable woman,
Handsome and witty, yet a friend.

Not warped by passion, awed by rumor,   5
Not grave through pride, or gay through folly,
An equal mixture of good humor,
And sensible soft melancholy.

"Has she no faults then," Envy says, "Sir?"
Yes, she has one, I must aver;   10
When all the world conspires to praise her,
The woman's deaf, and does not hear.

Alexander Pope (1688–1744)

QUESTIONS

1. Vocabulary: *attend* (2), *melancholy* (8), *conspires* (11).
2. Which line of the poem is ironical? To what purpose is irony put?
3. What other lines in the poem are figurative? Explain.

The term *irony* always implies some sort of discrepancy or incongruity. In verbal irony the discrepancy is between what is said and what is meant. In other forms the discrepancy may be between appearance and reality or between expectation and fulfillment. These other forms of irony are, on the whole, more important resources for the poet than is verbal irony. Two types, especially, are important for the beginning student to know.

In DRAMATIC IRONY* the discrepancy is not between what the speaker

---

*The term *dramatic irony*, which stems from Greek tragedy, often connotes something more specific and perhaps a little different from what I am developing here. It is used of a speech or an action in a story which has much greater significance to the audience than to the character who speaks or performs it, because of possession by the audience of knowledge the character does not have, as when the enemies of Ulysses, in the *Odyssey*, wish good luck and success to a man who the reader knows is Ulysses himself in disguise, or as when Oedipus, in the play by Sophocles, bends every effort to discover the murderer of Laius so that he may avenge the death, not knowing, as the audience does, that Laius is the man whom he himself once slew. I have appropriated the term for a perhaps slightly different situation, because no other suitable term exists. Both uses have the common characteristic—that the author conveys to the reader something different, or at least something more, than the character himself intends.

says and what he means but between what the speaker says and what the author means. The speaker's words may be perfectly straightforward, but the author, by putting these words in a particular speaker's mouth, may be indicating to the reader ideas or attitudes quite opposed to those the speaker is voicing. This form of irony is more complex than verbal irony and demands a more complex response from the reader. It may be used not only to convey attitudes but also to illuminate character, for the author who uses it is indirectly commenting not only upon the value of the ideas uttered but also upon the nature of the person who utters them. Such comment may be harsh, gently mocking, or sympathetic.

THE CHIMNEY SWEEPER

Common practice to all small children. They were good size to craw in chimneys.

When my mother died I was very young,
And my father sold me while yet my tongue
Could scarcely cry " 'weep! 'weep! 'weep! 'weep!"
So your chimneys I sweep, and in soot I sleep.

There's little Tom Dacre, who cried when his head,   5
That curled *curly hair* like a lamb's back, was shaved; so I said,
"Hush, Tom! never mind it, for, when your head's bare,
You know that the soot cannot spoil your white hair."

And so he was quiet, and that very night,
As Tom was asleeping, he had such a sight!   10
That thousands of sweepers, Dick, Joe, Ned, and Jack,
Were all of them locked up in coffins of black.

slavery — a death in life.
And by came an Angel who had a bright key,
he wishes this (gets to go out in air.)
And he opened the coffins and set them all free;
Then down a green plain leaping, laughing, they run,   15
And wash in a river, and shine in the sun.

Then naked and white, all their bags left behind,
They rise upon clouds and sport in the wind;
And the Angel told Tom, if he'd be a good boy,
Do good & will be rewarded later. Use religious faith. & will rise above this & will be happy in afterlife.
He'd have God for his father, and never want joy.   20

And so Tom awoke, and we rose in the dark,
And got with our bags and our brushes to work.

116   FIGURATIVE LANGUAGE 3

Though the morning was cold, Tom was happy and warm;
So if all do their duty they need not fear harm.

William Blake (1757–1827)

QUESTIONS

1. In the eighteenth century small boys, sometimes no more than four or five years old, were employed to climb up the narrow chimney flues and clean them, collecting the soot in bags. Such boys, sometimes sold to the master sweepers by their parents, were miserably treated by their masters and often suffered disease and physical deformity. Characterize the boy who speaks in this poem. How do his and the poet's attitudes toward his lot in life differ? How, especially, are the meanings of the poet and the speaker different in lines 3, 7–8, and 24?

2. The dream in lines 11–20, besides being a happy dream, is capable of symbolic interpretations. Point out possible significances of the sweepers' being "locked up in coffins of black" and the Angel's releasing them with a bright key to play upon green plains.

A third type of irony is IRONY OF SITUATION. This occurs when there is a discrepancy between the actual circumstances and those that would seem appropriate or between what one anticipates and what actually comes to pass. If a man and his second wife, on the first night of their honeymoon, are accidentally seated at the theater next to the man's first wife, we should call the situation ironical. When, in O. Henry's famous short story "The Gift of the Magi" a poor young husband pawns his most prized possession, a gold watch, in order to buy his wife a set of combs for her hair for Christmas, and his wife sells her most prized possession, her long brown hair, in order to buy a fob for her husband's watch, we call the situation ironical. When King Midas, in the famous fable, is granted his fondest wish, that anything he touch turn to gold, and then finds that he cannot eat because even his food turns to gold, we call the situation ironical. When Coleridge's Ancient Mariner finds himself in the middle of the ocean with "Water, water, everywhere" but not a "drop to drink," we call the situation ironical. In each case the circumstances are not what would seem appropriate or what we would expect.

Dramatic irony and irony of situation are powerful devices for the poet, for, like symbol, they enable him to suggest meanings without stating them—to communicate a great deal more than he says. We have seen one effective use of irony of situation in "Richard Cory" (page 45). Another is in "Ozymandias," which follows.

Irony and paradox may be trivial or powerful devices, depending on their use. At their worst they may degenerate into mere mannerism and mental habit. At their best they may greatly extend the dimensions of meaning in a work of literature. Because irony and paradox are devices that demand an exercise of critical intelligence, they are particularly valuable as safeguards against sentimentality.

OZYMANDIAS ✓

A statue of an Egyptian king who is supposed to be strong & powerful; yet, it is in ruins.

I met a traveller from an antique land
Who said: Two vast and trunkless legs of stone
Stand in the desert . . . Near them, on the sand,
Half sunk, a shattered visage lies, whose frown,
And wrinkled lip, and sneer of cold command,   5
Tell that its sculptor well those passions read   *the sculptor made him*
Which yet survive, stamped on these lifeless things,   *appear as he*
The hand that mocked them, and the heart that fed: *is.*
And on the pedestal these words appear:
"My name is Ozymandias, king of kings: 10
Look on my works, ye Mighty, and despair!"   *power*
Nothing beside remains. Round the decay   *Ironic reversal. Nothing of his mighty works remains.*
Of that colossal wreck, boundless and bare
The lone and level sands stretch far away.

Percy Bysshe Shelley (1792–1822)

Physical monuments don't last.

QUESTIONS

1. *Survive* (7) is a transitive verb with *hand* and *heart* as direct objects. Whose hand? Whose heart? What figure of speech is exemplified in *hand* and *heart*?

2. Characterize Ozymandias.

3. Ozymandias was an ancient Egyptian tyrant. This poem was first published in 1817. Of what is Ozymandias a *symbol*? What contemporary reference might the poem have had in Shelley's time?

4. What is the theme of the poem and how is it "stated"?

Identify each of the following quotations as literal or figurative. If figurative, identify the figure as paradox, overstatement, understatement, or irony and explain the use to which it is put (emotional emphasis, humor, satire, etc.).

1. Poetry is a language that tells us, through a more or less emotional reaction, something that cannot be said.   *Edwin Arlington Robinson*

2. Have not the Indians been kindly and justly treated? Have not the temporal things, the vain baubles and filthy lucre of this world, which were too apt to engage their worldly and selfish thoughts, been benevolently taken from them? And have they not instead thereof, been taught to set their affections on things above?   *Washington Irving*

3. A man who could make so vile a pun would not scruple to pick a pocket.   *John Dennis*

4. Last week I saw a woman flayed, and you will hardly believe how much it altered her person for the worse.   *Swift*

5. . . . Where ignorance is bliss,
   'Tis folly to be wise.   *Thomas Gray*

6. All night I made my bed to swim; with my tears I dissolved my couch.
   Psalms 6:6

7. Believe him, he has known the world too long,
   And seen the death of much immortal song.   *Pope*

8. Give me my Romeo: and, when he shall die,
   Take him and cut him out in little stars,
   And he will make the face of heaven so fine
   That all the world will be in love with night,
   And pay no worship to the garish sun.   *Juliet, in Shakespeare*

9. Immortality will come to such as are fit for it; and he who would be a great soul in the future must be a great soul now.   *Emerson*

10. Whoe'er their crimes for interest only quit,
    Sin on in virtue, and good deeds *commit*.   *Edward Young*

TO LUCASTA, GOING TO THE WARS

Tell me not, Sweet, I am unkind,
   That from the nunnery
Of thy chaste breast and quiet mind
   To war and arms I fly.

True, a new mistress now I chase,   5
    The first foe in the field;
And with a stronger faith embrace
    A sword, a horse, a shield.

Yet this inconstancy is such
    As you too shall adore;   10
I could not love thee, Dear, so much,
    Loved I not honor more.

Richard Lovelace (1618–1658)

QUESTIONS

    1. State the basic paradox of the poem in a sentence. How is the paradox
to be resolved?

    2. Do you find any words in the poem used in more than one meaning?

THE HABIT OF PERFECTION

Elected Silence, sing to me
And beat upon my whorlèd ear,
Pipe me to pastures still and be
The music that I care to hear.

Shape nothing, lips; be lovely-dumb: 5
It is the shut, the curfew sent
From there where all surrenders come
Which only makes you eloquent.

Be shellèd, eyes, with double dark
And find the uncreated light: 10
This ruck and reel which you remark
Coils, keeps, and teases simple sight.

Palate, the hutch of tasty lust,
Desire not to be rinsed with wine:
The can must be so sweet, the crust   15
So fresh that come in fasts divine!

Nostrils, your careless breath that spend
Upon the stir and keep of pride,

What relish shall the censers send
Along the sanctuary side!   20

O feel-of-primrose hands, O feet
That want the yield of plushy sward,
But you shall walk the golden street
And you unhouse and house the Lord.

And, Poverty, be thou the bride   25
And now the marriage feast begun,
And lily-colored clothes provide
Your spouse not labored-at nor spun.

Gerard Manley Hopkins (1844–1889)

QUESTIONS

1. Vocabulary: *ruck* (11), *remark* (11), *coils* (12), *hutch* (13), *stir* (18), *keep* (18), *censers* (19).

2. Gerard Manley Hopkins, in the year he wrote this poem, was converted to Roman Catholicism; he later became a Jesuit priest. In this poem he writes about the monastic, ascetic life of the priest, who traditionally takes vows of poverty (25). Line 24 refers to taking the Host from the tabernacle of the altar in a Catholic mass. What central paradox underlies the poem? How is this paradox developed in each of the separate stanzas?

3. Lines 27–28 are an allusion to Matthew 6:28–29. How does it contribute to the meaning of the poem?

4. What meanings have *Habit* (title)? *simple* (12)? *want* (22)?

LINES FOR A CHRISTMAS CARD

May all my enemies go to hell,
Noel, Noel, Noel, Noel.

Hilaire Belloc (1870–1953)

NO LONGER MOURN FOR ME

No longer mourn for me when I am dead
Than you shall hear the surly sullen bell
Give warning to the world that I am fled
From this vile world, with vilest worms to dwell.
Nay, if you read this line, remember not   5

The hand that writ it, for I love you so,
That I in your sweet thoughts would be forgot,
If thinking on me then should make you woe.
O, if, I say, you look upon this verse
When I perhaps compounded am with clay,   10
Do not so much as my poor name rehearse,
But let your love even with my life decay,
    Lest the wise world should look into your moan
    And mock you with me after I am gone.

William Shakespeare (1564–1616)

QUESTIONS

1. What paradoxical idea informs the first twelve lines of the poem, and how is it resolved?
2. What word in the concluding couplet is ironical?

SONG

The lark now leaves his watery nest,
    And climbing shakes his dewy wings;
He takes this window for the east,
    And to implore your light he sings:
Awake, awake! the morn will never rise   5
Till she can dress her beauty at your eyes.

The merchant bows unto the seaman's star,
    The plowman from the sun his season takes;
But still the lover wonders what they are
    Who look for day before his mistress wakes.   10
Awake, awake, break through your veils of lawn!
Then draw your curtains, and begin the dawn.

Sir William Davenant (1606–1668)

QUESTIONS

1. Vocabulary: *dress* (6), *lawn* (11).
2. To what does the speaker compare his sweetheart?
3. In developing his central figure, the speaker combines metonymy, personification, and metaphor with overstatement. Find examples of each.

THE LANGUID LADY

From *A Satire on Women*

The languid lady next appears in state,
Who was not born to carry her own weight;
She lolls, reels, staggers, till some foreign aid
To her own stature lifts the feeble maid.
Then, if ordained to so severe a doom,   5
She, by just stages, journeys round the room:
But, knowing her own weakness, she despairs
To scale the Alps—that is, ascend the stairs.
My fan! let others say, who laugh at toil;
Fan! hood! glove! scarf! is her laconic style;   10
And that is spoke with such a dying fall,
That Betty° rather sees, than hears the call;   the serving
The motion of her lips, and meaning eye,   maid
Piece out the idea her faint words deny.
O listen with attention most profound!   15
Her voice is but the shadow of a sound.
And help! oh help! her spirits are so dead,
One hand scarce lifts the other to her head.
If, there, a stubborn pin it triumphs o'er,
She pants! she sinks away! and is no more.   20
Let the robust and the gigantic carve,
Life is not worth so much, she'd rather starve;
But chew she must herself, ah cruel fate!
That Rosalinda can't by proxy eat.

Edward Young (1683–1765)

QUESTIONS

1. What figure of speech chiefly sustains this satirical excerpt?

2. Why did the poet choose his wording rather than the following alternatives: "other's aid" for "foreign aid" (3), "degrees" for "just stages" (6), "walks around" for "journeys round" (6), "spoken in a voice so small" for "spoke with such a dying fall" (11), "whisper" for "shadow" (16), "misplaced" for "stubborn" (19)?

3. Contrast the use of overstatement in this poem and the preceding one.

GIVE ME FOR LIFE

Give me for life the honest name,
Then take my due arrears of fame.
I am grown deaf, and shall become
A trifle deafer in the tomb.

Walter Savage Landor (1775–1864)

QUESTIONS

1. Vocabulary: *arrears* (2).
2. How young or old is the speaker? What does he consider important in life? What is his attitude toward fame? Why?
3. What figure of speech is used in the last line and a half?

AFTERWARDS

When the Present has latched its postern behind my tremulous stay,
  And the May month flaps its glad green leaves like wings,
Delicate-filmed as new-spun silk, will the neighbors say,
  "He was a man who used to notice such things"?

If it be in the dusk when, like an eyelid's soundless blink,   5
  The dewfall-hawk comes crossing the shades to alight
Upon the wind-warped upland thorn, a gazer may think,
  "To him this must have been a familiar sight."

If I pass during some nocturnal blackness, mothy and warm,
  When the hedgehog travels furtively over the lawn,   10
One may say, "He strove that such innocent creatures should
    come to no harm,
  But he could do little for them; and now he is gone."

If, when hearing that I have been stilled at last, they stand at
    the door,
  Watching the full-starred heavens that winter sees,
Will this thought rise on those who will meet my face no more,   15
  "He was one who had an eye for such mysteries"?

And will any say when my bell of quittance is heard in the gloom,
  And a crossing breeze cuts a pause in its outrollings,

Till they rise again, as they were a new bell's boom,
"He hears it not now, but used to notice such things"?   20

Thomas Hardy (1840–1928)

QUESTIONS

  1. Vocabulary: *postern* (1), *thorn* (7).

  2. Who is really making the comments that the speaker imagines his neighbors will make about him after his death? What is the manner of these comments?

1887

From Clee to heaven the beacon burns,
    The shires have seen it plain,
From north and south the sign returns
    And beacons burn again.

Look left, look right, the hills are bright,   5
    The dales are light between,
Because 'tis fifty years tonight
    That God has saved the Queen.

Now, when the flame they watch not towers
    About the soil they trod,   10
Lads, we'll remember friends of ours
    Who shared the work with God.

To skies that knit their heartstrings right,
    To fields that bred them brave,
The saviors come not home tonight: 15
    Themselves they could not save.

It dawns in Asia, tombstones show
    And Shropshire names are read;
And the Nile spills his overflow
    Beside the Severn's dead.   20

We pledge in peace by farm and town
    The Queen they served in war,
And fire the beacons up and down
    The land they perished for.

"God save the Queen" we living sing,   25
    From height to height 'tis heard;
And with the rest your voices ring,
    Lads of the Fifty-third.

Oh, God will save her, fear you not:
    Be you the men you've been,   30
Get you the sons your fathers got,
    And God will save the Queen.

                              A. E. Housman (1859–1936)

QUESTIONS

1. Vocabulary: *get* and *got* (31).

2. In 1887 England celebrated the fiftieth year of Queen Victoria's reign with beacon fires built on hilltops across the land. This poem, written in 1887, was published in a volume entitled *The Shropshire Lad*. *Clee* (1), in the Clee Hills, is a village, the *Severn* (20) a river; both are in Shropshire. Whom is the poet addressing? What is "the Fifty-third" (28)?

3. To what are lines 15–16 an allusion? If you do not know, check Mark 15:29–31. What is the poet's attitude toward the dead soldiers?

4. What is referred to in lines 8, 25, 29, and 32? Who, in the poet's view, will really "save the Queen"? What kind of irony is this?

◊ FORMAL APPLICATION

"The poets apparently want to rejoin the human race." Time

I shall begin by learning to throw
the knife, first at trees, until it sticks
in the trunk and quivers every time;

next from a chair, using only wrist
and fingers, at a thing on the ground,   5
a fresh ant hill or a fallen leaf,

then at a moving object, perhaps
a pieplate swinging on twine, until
I pot it at least twice in three tries.

Meanwhile, I shall be teaching the birds   10
that the skinny fellow in sneakers
is a source of suet and bread crumbs,

first putting them on a shingle nailed
to a pine tree, next scattering them
on the needles, closer and closer   15

to my seat, until the proper bird,
a towhee, I think, in black and rust
and gray, takes tossed crumbs six feet away.

Finally, I shall coordinate
conditioned reflex and functional   20
form and qualify as Modern Man.

You see the splash of blood and feathers
and the blade pinning it to the tree?
It's called an "Audubon Crucifix."

The phrase has pleasing (even pious)   25
connotations, like *Arbeit Macht Frei*,
"Molotov Cocktail," and *Enola Gay.*

Donald W. Baker (b. 1923)

QUESTIONS

1. *Arbeit Macht Frei* (26) ("Labor liberates") was the slogan of the
German Nazi Party. "Molotov Cocktail" (27), a homemade hand grenade
named after Stalin's foreign minister, was widely used during the Spanish
Civil War and World War II. *Enola Gay* (27) was the American plane
that dropped the first atom bomb on Hiroshima. In what ways are the connotations of these phrases—and of "Audubon Crucifix" (24)—"pleasing"?

2. What different kinds of irony operate in this poem? Discuss.

[handwritten: John Smith]

THE UNKNOWN CITIZEN*

[handwritten: speaker of poem is an official of state who's dedicating a monument to an unknown citizen.]

(To JS/07/M/378 This Marble Monument Is Erected by the State)

He was found by the Bureau of Statistics to be
One against whom there was no official complaint,
And all the reports on his conduct agree *[handwritten: like Tomb of Unknown Soldier so]*
That, in the modern sense of an old-fashioned word, he was a saint, *[handwritten: the state he]*
For in everything he did he served the Greater Community. *[handwritten: was just a number]*

[handwritten: Ideal citizen cause don't do anything - do nothing.]

*Mr. Auden recorded "The Unknown Citizen" (LP, Library of Congress,
PL 21).

[handwritten: highest thing a person could do is conform to govt. & society.]

[handwritten: Great Society!]

Except for the War till the day he retired
He worked in a factory and never got fired,
But satisfied his employers, Fudge Motors Inc. — *about Ford or Dodge*
Yet he wasn't a scab or odd in his views,
For his Union reports that he paid his dues,   10
(Our report on his Union shows it was sound)
And our Social Psychology workers found
That he was popular with his mates and liked a drink.
The Press are convinced that he bought a paper every day
And that his reactions to advertisements were normal in every way.   15
Policies taken out in his name prove that he was fully insured,
And his Health-card shows he was once in hospital but left it cured.
Both Producers Research and High-Grade Living declare
He was fully sensible to the advantages of the Installment Plan
And had everything necessary to the Modern Man,   20
A phonograph, a radio, a car and a frigidaire.
Our researchers into Public Opinion are content
That he held the proper opinions for the time of year;
When there was peace, he was for peace; when there was war, he went.
He was married and added five children to the population,   25
Which our Eugenist says was the right number for a parent of his
     generation, *person who deals w/ science of genetics*
And our teachers report that he never interfered with their education.
Was he free? Was he happy? The question is absurd:
Had anything been wrong, we should certainly have heard.

Don't care about his views
Bought the stuff
Like Gallup polls
Typical mr. Citizen
He couldn't be too happy because he hadn't done anything
Was the human existence worthwhile , Satirical
He really didn't feel anything. No feelings just cold, statistical statements

W. H. Auden (b. 1907)
in agreement with "Brave New World" & "1980"

QUESTIONS

1. Vocabulary: *scab* (9), *Eugenist* (26).

2. Explain the allusion and the irony in the title. Why was the citizen *unknown*?

3. This obituary of an unknown state "hero" was apparently prepared by a functionary of the state. Give an account of the citizen's life and character from Auden's own point of view.

4. What trends in modern life and social organization does the poem satirize?

DEPARTMENTAL*

An ant on the tablecloth
Ran into a dormant moth
Of many times his size.
He showed not the least surprise.
His business wasn't with such.   5
He gave it scarcely a touch,
And was off on his duty run.
Yet if he encountered one
Of the hive's enquiry squad
Whose work is to find out God   10
And the nature of time and space,
He would put him onto the case.
Ants are a curious race;
One crossing with hurried tread
The body of one of their dead   15
Isn't given a moment's arrest—
Seems not even impressed.
But he no doubt reports to any
With whom he crosses antennae,
And they no doubt report   20
To the higher up at court.
Then word goes forth in Formic:
"Death's come to Jerry McCormic,
Our selfless forager Jerry.
Will the special Janizary   25
Whose office it is to bury
The dead of the commissary
Go bring him home to his people.
Lay him in state on a sepal.
Wrap him for shroud in a petal.   30
Embalm him with ichor of nettle.
This is the word of your Queen."
And presently on the scene
Appears a solemn mortician;
And taking formal position   35
With feelers calmly atwiddle,

*Mr. Frost recorded "Departmental" (LP, Caedmon, TC 1060).

Seizes the dead by the middle,
And heaving him high in air,
Carries him out of there.
No one stands round to stare.   40
It is nobody else's affair.

It couldn't be called ungentle.
But how thoroughly departmental.

                                    Robert Frost (1874–1963)

QUESTIONS

1. Vocabulary: *dormant* (2), *Formic* (22), *Janizary* (25), *commissary* (27), *sepal* (29), *ichor* (31).

2. The poem is ostensibly about ants. Is it ultimately about ants? Give reasons to support your view that it is or is not.

3. What is the author's attitude toward the "departmental" organization of ant society? How is it indicated? Could this poem be described as "gently satiric"? If so, in what sense?

4. Compare and contrast this poem with "The Unknown Citizen" in content and manner.

THE CONSTANT LOVER

Out upon it! I have loved
    Three whole days together;
And am like to love three more,
    If it prove fair weather.

Time shall moult away his wings,   5
    Ere he shall discover
In the whole wide world again
    Such a constant lover.

But the spite on 't is, no praise
    Is due at all to me: 10
Love with me had made no stays
    Had it any been but she.

Had it any been but she,
    And that very face,

Sir John Suckling (1609–1642)

QUESTIONS

1. What figures of speech are used in stanzas 2 and 4?

2. Traditionally, lovers vow to be faithful forever to their sweethearts. Burns, in "A Red, Red Rose" (page 111), declares he will love his sweetheart "till a' the seas gang dry." Suckling's lover, on the other hand, *complains* that he has been faithful for three whole days and may be so for three more. The discrepancy between our expectation (aroused by the title) and this fulfillment constitutes a form of irony. Is this irony employed ultimately for the purpose of making a cynical observation about love or of paying an exaggerated compliment to the lady in question? In what respect does the speaker pay his sweetheart a greater compliment than does the lover who vows to be faithful forever?

3. Does the lover's complaint in the first stanza support his assertion in the third that no praise is due at all to him for this constancy?

MY LAST DUCHESS

Ferrara

That's my last Duchess painted on the wall,
Looking as if she were alive. I call
That piece a wonder, now; Fra Pandolf's hands
Worked busily a day, and there she stands.
Will 't please you sit and look at her? I said   5
"Fra Pandolf" by design, for never read
Strangers like you that pictured countenance,
The depth and passion of its earnest glance,
But to myself they turned (since none puts by
The curtain I have drawn for you, but I)   10
And seemed as they would ask me, if they durst,
How such a glance came there; so, not the first
Are you to turn and ask thus. Sir, 'twas not
Her husband's presence only, called that spot
Of joy into the Duchess' cheek; perhaps   15
Fra Pandolf chanced to say, "Her mantle laps
Over my lady's wrist too much," or, "Paint
Must never hope to reproduce the faint

131

Half-flush that dies along her throat." Such stuff
Was courtesy, she thought, and cause enough   20
For calling up that spot of joy. She had
A heart—how shall I say?—too soon made glad,
Too easily impressed; she liked whate'er
She looked on, and her looks went everywhere.
Sir, 'twas all one! My favor at her breast,   25
The dropping of the daylight in the West,
The bough of cherries some officious fool
Broke in the orchard for her, the white mule
She rode with round the terrace—all and each
Would draw from her alike the approving speech,   30
Or blush, at least. She thanked men—good! but thanked
Somehow—I know not how—as if she ranked
My gift of a nine-hundred-years-old name
With anybody's gift. Who'd stoop to blame
This sort of trifling? Even had you skill   35
In speech—which I have not—to make your will
Quite clear to such an one, and say, "Just this
Or that in you disgusts me; here you miss,
Or there exceed the mark"—and if she let
Herself be lessoned so, nor plainly set   40
Her wits to yours, forsooth, and made excuse—
E'en then would be some stooping; and I choose
Never to stoop. Oh, sir, she smiled, no doubt,
Whene'er I passed her; but who passed without
Much the same smile? This grew; I gave commands;   45
Then all smiles stopped together. There she stands
As if alive. Will 't please you rise? We'll meet
The company below, then. I repeat,
The Count your master's known munificence
Is ample warrant that no just pretense   50
Of mine for dowry will be disallowed;
Though his fair daughter's self, as I avowed
At starting, is my object. Nay, we'll go
Together down, sir. Notice Neptune, though,
Taming a sea-horse, thought a rarity,   55
Which Claus of Innsbruck cast in bronze for me!

Robert Browning (*1812–1889*)

1. Vocabulary: *officious* (27), *munificence* (49).

2. Ferrara is in Italy. The time is during the Renaissance, probably the sixteenth century. To whom is the Duke speaking? What is the occasion? Are the Duke's remarks about his last Duchess a digression, or do they have some relation to the business at hand?

3. Characterize the Duke as fully as you can. How does your characterization differ from the Duke's opinion of himself? What kind of irony is this?

4. Why was the Duke dissatisfied with his last Duchess? Was it sexual jealousy? What opinion do you get of the Duchess's personality, and how does it differ from the Duke's opinion?

5. What characteristics of the Italian Renaissance appear in the poem (marriage customs, social classes, art)? What is the Duke's attitude toward art? Is it insincere?

6. What happened to the Duchess? Should we have been told?

◊ **DISINHERITED**

Thy father all from thee, by his last will,
Gave to the poor. Thou hast good title still.

John Donne (1573–1631)

QUESTION

The situation in this poem might be called either paradoxical or ironical. Explain.

◊ **EARTH**

"A planet doesn't explode of itself," said drily
The Martian astronomer, gazing off into the air—
"That they were able to do it is proof that highly
Intelligent beings must have been living there."

John Hall Wheelock (b. 1886)

Allusion

The famous English diplomat and letter writer Lord Chesterfield was once invited to a great dinner given by the Spanish ambassador. At the conclusion of the meal the host rose and proposed a toast to his master, the king of Spain, whom he compared to the sun. The French ambassador followed with a health to the king of France, whom he likened to the moon. It was then Lord Chesterfield's turn. "Your excellencies have taken from me," he said; "all the greatest luminaries of heaven, and the stars are too small for me to make a comparison of my royal master; I therefore beg leave to give your excellencies—Joshua!"*

For a reader familiar with the Bible—that is, for one who recognizes the Biblical allusion—Lord Chesterfield's story will come as a stunning revelation of his wit. For an ALLUSION—a reference to something in history or previous literature—is, like a richly connotative word or a symbol, a means of suggesting far more than it says. The one word "Joshua," in the context of Chesterfield's toast, calls up in the reader's mind the whole Biblical story of how the Israelite captain stopped the sun and the moon in order that the Israelites might finish a battle and conquer their enemies before nightfall.† The force of the toast lies in its extreme economy; it says so much in so little, and it exercises the mind of the reader to make the connection for himself.

The effect of Chesterfield's allusion is chiefly humorous or witty, but allusions may also have a powerful emotional effect. The essayist William Hazlitt writes of addressing a fashionable audience about the lexicog-

*Samuel Shellabarger, *Lord Chesterfield and His World* (Boston: Little, Brown, 1951), p. 132.

†Joshua 10:12–14.

rapher Samuel Johnson. Speaking of Johnson's great heart and of his charity to the unfortunate, Hazlitt recounted how, finding a drunken prostitute lying in Fleet Street late at night, Johnson carried her on his broad back to the address she managed to give him. The audience, unable to face the picture of the famous dictionary-maker doing such a thing, broke out in titters and expostulations. Whereupon Hazlitt simply said: "I remind you, ladies and gentlemen, of the parable of the Good Samaritan." The audience was promptly silenced.*

Allusions are a means of reinforcing the emotion or the ideas of one's own work with the emotion or ideas of another work or occasion. Because they are capable of saying so much in so little, they are extremely useful to the poet.

"OUT, OUT—"

The buzz-saw snarled and rattled in the yard
And made dust and dropped stove-length sticks of wood,
Sweet-scented stuff when the breeze drew across it.
And from there those that lifted eyes could count
Five mountain ranges one behind the other   5
Under the sunset far into Vermont.
And the saw snarled and rattled, snarled and rattled,
As it ran light, or had to bear a load.
And nothing happened: day was all but done.
Call it a day, I wish they might have said   10
To please the boy by giving him the half hour
That a boy counts so much when saved from work.
His sister stood beside them in her apron
To tell them "Supper." At the word, the saw,
As if to prove saws knew what supper meant,   15
Leaped out at the boy's hand, or seemed to leap—
He must have given the hand. However it was,
Neither refused the meeting. But the hand!
The boy's first outcry was a rueful laugh,
As he swung toward them holding up the hand   20
Half in appeal, but half as if to keep
The life from spilling. Then the boy saw all—
Since he was old enough to know, big boy

*Jacques Barzun, *Teacher in America* (Boston: Little, Brown, 1945), p. 160.

Doing a man's work, though a child at heart—
He saw all spoiled. "Don't let him cut my hand off—   25
The doctor, when he comes. Don't let him, sister!"
So. But the hand was gone already.
The doctor put him in the dark of ether.
He lay and puffed his lips out with his breath.
And then—the watcher at his pulse took fright.   30
No one believed. They listened at his heart.
Little—less—nothing!—and that ended it.
No more to build on there. And they, since they
Were not the one dead, turned to their affairs.

Robert Frost (1874–1963)

QUESTIONS

1. How does this poem differ from a newspaper account that might have dealt with the same incident?

2. To whom does *they* (33) refer? The boy's family? The doctor and hospital attendants? Casual onlookers? Need we assume that all these people—whoever they are—turned immediately "to their affairs"? Does the ending of this poem seem to you callous or merely realistic? Would a more tearful and sentimental ending have made the poem better or worse?

3. What figure of speech is used in lines 21–22?

Allusions vary widely in the amount of reliance that the poet puts on them to convey his meaning. Lord Chesterfield risked his whole meaning on his hearers' recognizing his allusion. Robert Frost in "Out, Out—" makes his meaning entirely clear even for the reader who does not recognize the allusion contained in his title. His theme is the uncertainty and unpredictability of life, which may be accidentally ended at any moment, and the tragic waste of human potentiality which takes place when such premature deaths occur. A boy who is already "doing a man's work" and gives every promise of having a useful life ahead of him is suddenly wiped out. There seems no rational explanation for either the accident or the death. The only comment to be made is, "No more to build on there."

Frost's title, however, is an allusion to one of the most famous passages in all English literature, and it offers a good illustration of how a poet may use allusion not only to reinforce emotion but also to help define his theme. The passage is that in *Macbeth* in which Macbeth has just been informed of his wife's death. A good many readers will recall the key phrase, "Out, out, brief candle!" with its underscoring of the tragic brevity and uncertainty of life that can be snuffed out at any moment. For some readers, however, the allusion will summon up the whole passage in act V, scene 5, in which this phrase occurs. Macbeth's words are:

> She should have died hereafter;
> There would have been a time for such a word.
> To-morrow, and to-morrow, and to-morrow
> Creeps in this petty pace from day to day
> To the last syllable of recorded time; 5
> And all our yesterdays have lighted fools
> The way to dusty death. Out, out, brief candle!
> Life's but a walking shadow, a poor player,
> That struts and frets his hour upon the stage
> And then is heard no more. It is a tale 10
> Told by an idiot, full of sound and fury,
> Signifying nothing.

Macbeth's first words underscore the theme of premature death. The boy also "should have died hereafter." The rest of the passage, with its marvelous evocation of the vanity and meaninglessness of life, expresses neither Shakespeare's philosophy nor, ultimately, Frost's, but it is Macbeth's philosophy at the time of his bereavement, and it is likely to express the feelings of us all when such tragic accidents occur. Life does indeed seem cruel and meaningless, a tale told by an idiot, signifying nothing, when human life and potentiality are thus without explanation so suddenly ended.

Allusions vary widely in the number of readers to whom they will be familiar. The poet, in using an allusion as in using a figure of speech, is always in danger of not being understood. In appealing powerfully to one reader, he may lose another reader altogether. But the poet must assume a certain fund of common experience with his readers. He could not even write about the ocean unless he could assume that his reader had seen the ocean or pictures of it. In the same way he will assume a certain common fund of literary experience. He is often justified in expecting a rather wide range of literary experience in his readers, for the people who read poetry for pleasure are generally people of good minds and good education who have read widely. But, obviously, beginning readers will not have this range, just as they will not know the meanings of as many words as will maturer readers. The student ought therefore to be prepared to look up certain allusions, just as he should be eager to look up in his dictionary the meanings of unfamiliar words. He will find that every increase in knowledge will broaden his base for understanding both literature and life.

IN JUST-*

in Just-
spring   when the world is mud-
luscious the little
lame balloonman

whistles   far   and wee   5

and eddieandbill come
running from marbles and
piracies and it's
spring

when the world is puddle-wonderful   10

the queer
old balloonman whistles
far   and   wee
and bettyandisbel come dancing

from hop-scotch and jump-rope and   15

it's
spring
and
     the

goat-footed   20

*Mr. Cummings recorded "in Just-" (78 rpm, Linguaphone Institute, HBC).

                balloonMan   whistles
                far
                and
                wee

                                        e. e. cummings (1894–1962)

QUESTION

Why is the balloonman called *goat-footed*? How does the identification made by this mythological allusion enrich the meaning of the poem?

ON HIS BLINDNESS

When I consider how my light is spent
    Ere half my days in this dark world and wide,
    And that one talent which is death to hide
    Lodged with me useless, though my soul more bent
To serve therewith my Maker, and present   5
    My true account, lest he returning chide,
    "Doth God exact day-labor, light denied?"
    I fondly ask. But Patience, to prevent
That murmur, soon replies, "God doth not need
    Either man's work or his own gifts. Who best   10
    Bear his mild yoke, they serve him best. His state
Is kingly: thousands at his bidding speed,
    And post o'er land and ocean without rest;
    They also serve who only stand and wait."

                                        John Milton (1608–1674)

QUESTIONS

1. Vocabulary: *spent* (1), *fondly* (8), *prevent* (8), *post* (13).

2. What two meanings has *talent* (3)? What is Milton's "one talent"?

3. The poem is unified and expanded in its dimensions by a Biblical allusion that Milton's original readers would have recognized immediately. What is it? If you do not know, look up Matthew 25:14–30. In what ways is the situation in the poem similar to that in the parable? In what ways is it different?

4. What is the point of the poem?

◉ LAST STAND

When the alarm came
He saddled up his fence,
Took the bit in his teeth
And mounted.
Closing his eyes
He put his ear to the ground
And waited, trembling, for the sound
Of the approaching windmills.

Keith Jennison (b. 1911)

QUESTIONS

1. This poem is full of trite phrases, either used entire or alluded to. Identify them. Do they add up to a trite poem? Explain.

2. Is the image created by these trite metaphors visually consistent? Poetically valid? Explain.

3. Behind two of the trite phrases are respectively a historical allusion and a literary allusion. How does the subject of the poem resemble and how does it differ from the subject of the literary allusion? Are these allusions used directly or ironically?

LEDA AND THE SWAN

A sudden blow: the great wings beating still
Above the staggering girl, her thighs caressed
By the dark webs, her nape caught in his bill,
He holds her helpless breast upon his breast.

How can those terrified vague fingers push   5
The feathered glory from her loosening thighs?
And how can body, laid in that white rush,
But feel the strange heart beating where it lies?

A shudder in the loins engenders there
The broken wall, the burning roof and tower   10
And Agamemnon dead.
          Being so caught up,
So mastered by the brute blood of the air,
Did she put on his knowledge with his power
Before the indifferent beak could let her drop?

William Butler Yeats (1865–1939)

QUESTIONS

1. What is the connection between Leda and "the broken wall, the burning roof and tower / And Agamemnon dead"? If you do not know, look up the myth of Leda, and, if necessary, the story of Agamemnon.

2. What is the significance of the question asked in the last two lines?

THE SHIELD OF ACHILLES

She looked over his shoulder
    For vines and olive trees,
Marble well-governed cities,
    And ships upon untamed seas,
But there on the shining metal   5
    His hands had put instead
An artificial wilderness
    And a sky like lead.

A plain without a feature, bare and brown,
    No blade of grass, no sign of neighborhood,   10
Nothing to eat and nowhere to sit down,
    Yet, congregated on its blankness, stood
    An unintelligible multitude.
A million eyes, a million boots in line,
Without expression, waiting for a sign.   15

Out of the air a voice without a face
    Proved by statistics that some cause was just
In tones as dry and level as the place:
    No one was cheered and nothing was discussed;
    Column by column in a cloud of dust   20
They marched away enduring a belief
Whose logic brought them, somewhere else, to grief.

She looked over his shoulder
    For ritual pieties,
White flower-garlanded heifers,   25
    Libation and sacrifice,
But there on the shining metal
    Where the altar should have been,
She saw by his flickering forge-light
    Quite another scene.   30

Barbed wire enclosed an arbitrary spot
    Where bored officials lounged (one cracked a joke)
And sentries sweated, for the day was hot:
    A crowd of ordinary decent folk
    Watched from without and neither moved nor spoke   35
As three pale figures were led forth and bound
To three posts driven upright in the ground.

The mass and majesty of this world, all
    That carries weight and always weighs the same,
Lay in the hands of others; they were small   40
    And could not hope for help and no help came:
    What their foes like to do was done, their shame
Was all the worst could wish; they lost their pride
And died as men before their bodies died.

            She looked over his shoulder   45
                For athletes at their games,
            Men and women in a dance
                Moving their sweet limbs
            Quick, quick, to music,
                But there on the shining shield   50
            His hands had set no dancing-floor
                But a weed-choked field.

A ragged urchin, aimless and alone,
    Loitered about that vacancy; a bird
Flew up to safety from his well-aimed stone: 55
    That girls are raped, that two boys knife a third,
    Were axioms to him, who'd never heard
Of any world where promises were kept
Or one could weep because another wept.

            The thin-lipped armorer,   60
                Hephaestos, hobbled away;
            Thetis of the shining breasts
                Cried out in dismay
            At what the god had wrought
                To please her son, the strong   65
            Iron-hearted man-slaying Achilles
                Who would not live long.

W. H. Auden (b. 1907)

1. Vocabulary: *libation* (26).

2. The description of Achilles' shield, made for him at the request of his mother Thetis by Hephaestos, god of the forge, is one of the most famous passages in the *Iliad* (Book XVIII). On the shield Hephaestos depicted scenes from the Hellenic world. From what world do the three scenes in the poem come? Comment specifically on each and on the contrast between each and the expectation of Thetis preceding it.

3. What possible allusion is made in lines 36–37, and what is its purpose?

4. What figure of speech occurs in line 14? What meanings has *arbitrary* (31)?

THE CARPENTER'S SON

[handwritten margin note: allusion of Christ — possible speech Christ might have made.]

"Here the hangman stops his cart:
Now the best of friends must part.
Fare you well, for ill fare I:
Live, lads, and I will die.

"Oh, at home had I but stayed   5
'Prenticed to my father's trade,
Had I stuck to plane and adze,
I had not been lost, my lads.

"Then I might have built perhaps
Gallow-trees for other chaps,   10
Never dangled on my own,
Had I but left ill alone.

"Now, you see, they hang me high,
And the people passing by
Stop to shake their fists and curse;   15
So 'tis come from ill to worse.

"Here hang I, and right and left
Two poor fellows hang for theft:
All the same's the luck we prove,
Though the midmost hangs for love.   20

"Comrades all, that stand and gaze,
Walk henceforth in other ways;
See my neck and save your own:
Comrades all, leave ill alone.

"Make some day a decent end, 25
Shrewder fellows than your friend.
Fare you well, for ill fare I:
Live, lads, and I will die." *Christ died to save mankind
You are living through my glass.*
A. E. Housman (1859–1936)

QUESTIONS

1. With whom is the speaker being implicitly compared and contrasted? How do you know?

2. In what sense is the speaker being hanged "for love"? In what sense was his prototype?

3. What is the import of "Live, lads, and I will die" in the mouth of the speaker as contrasted with its traditional import in the story of his prototype?

4. What meaning has the speaker's advice to "leave ill alone" when transferred to the story of his prototype? What general meanings are implicit in the poem?

SIX POETS IN SEARCH OF A LAWYER

Finesse be first, whose elegance deplores
All things save beauty, and the swinging doors;
Whose cleverness in writing verse is just
Exceeded by his lack of taste and lust;
Who lives off lady lovers of his verse   5
And thanks them by departing with their purse;
Who writes his verse in order to amaze,
To win the Pulitzer, or *Time*'s sweet praise;
Who will endure a moment, and then pass,
As hopeless as an olive in his glass.   10

Dullard be second, as he always will,
From lack of brains as well as lack of skill.
Expert in some, and dilettante in all
The ways of making poems gasp and fall,
He teaches at a junior college where   15
He's recognized as Homer's son and heir.
Respectable, brown-suited, it is he
Who represents on forums poetry,
And argues to protect the libeled Muse,
Who'd tear his flimsy tongue out, could she choose.   20

His opposite is anarchistic *Bomb,*
Who writes a manifesto with aplomb.
Revolt! Revolt! No matter why or when,
It's novelty, old novelty again.
Yet *Bomb* if read intently may reveal   25
A talent not to murder but to steal;
First from old *Gone*, whose fragmentary style
Disguised his sawdust Keats a little while;
And now from one who writes at very best
What ne'er was thought and much the less expressed.   30

Lucre be next, who takes to poetry
The businessman he swore he would not be.
Anthologies and lecture tours and grants
Create a solvency which disenchants.
He writes his poems now to suit his purse,   35
Short-lined and windy, and reserves his curse
For all the little magazines so fine
That offer only fifty cents a line.
He makes his money, certainly, to write,
But writes for money. Such is appetite.   40

Of *Mucker* will I tell, who tries to show
He is a kind of poet men don't know.
To shadow box at literary teas
And every girl at Bennington to seize,
To talk of baseball rather than of Yeats,   45
To drink straight whisky while the bard creates—
This is his pose, and so his poems seem
Incongruous in proving life a dream.
Some say, with Freud, that *Mucker* has a reason
For acting virile in and out of season.   50

Scoundrel be last. Be deaf, be dumb, be blind,
Who writes satiric verses on his kind.

Donald Hall (b. 1928)

QUESTIONS

1. Vocabulary: *dilettante* (13).
2. The title conceals a literary allusion. What is it, and what are its
implications? Why are the six poets in search of a lawyer?

3. Does the author include himself in the satire? Where?

4. Why does the author's curse on *Scoundrel* take the form of "Be deaf, be dumb, be blind"? What allusion is made here?

5. Explain the allusions in lines 30 and 49–50. Are there other allusions in the poem?

6. Discuss the figures of speech used in lines 10, 14, 20, 24, 26, 28, 30, and 32. Are *Finesse, Dullard, Bomb,* and the rest examples of personification or of metonymy?

CHILDREN OF LIGHT

Our fathers wrung their bread from stocks and stones
And fenced their gardens with the Redman's bones;
Embarking from the Nether Land of Holland,
Pilgrims unhouseled by Geneva's night,
They planted here the Serpent's seeds of light;   5
And here the pivoting searchlights probe to shock
The riotous glass houses built on rock,
And candles gutter by an empty altar,
And light is where the landless blood of Cain
Is burning, burning the unburied grain.   10

Robert Lowell (b. 1917)

QUESTIONS

1. Vocabulary: *stocks* (1), *Nether* (3), *unhouseled* (4).

2. In structure the poem divides into two parts. Where does the division occur? How is it marked? How do the parts differ and compare? What is the connection between them?

3. What is the geographical locus of "here" (6)?

4. Examine the various uses of light and dark in the poem. How is the word "light" principally used? (The last line refers to the burning of "excess" grain to keep up market prices.)

5. Robert Lowell is a New Englander (descended through his mother from one of the Pilgrim fathers) and a converted Roman Catholic. How does this information contribute to your understanding of the poem?

6. The title derives from the parable of the unjust steward, Luke 18:1–12. "Stocks and stones" (1) echoes Milton's sonnet "On the Late Massacre in Piemont" (page 330). *Geneva* (4) is connected with the life of John Calvin, whose religious doctrines underlie Puritan beliefs. "Built on rock" (7) echoes Christ's words to Peter, Matthew 18:16. "Burning, burning"

(10) echoes T. S. Eliot's "The Waste Land," part III, and Buddha's Fire Sermon. "The unburied grain" (10) may suggest Christ's words in John 12:24. What other historical or Biblical references do you recognize in the poem? How much and in what ways do these allusions contribute to its force?

IN THE GARDEN

In the garden there strayed
A beautiful maid
As fair as the flowers of the morn;
The first hour of her life
She was made a man's wife,
And was buried before she was born.

Anonymous

QUESTION
Resolve the paradox by identifying the allusion.

QUATRAIN

Jack, eating rotten cheese, did say,
Like Samson I my thousands slay;
I vow, quoth Roger, so you do.
And with the self-same weapon too.

Benjamin Franklin (1706–1790)

DRINK TO ME ONLY

Drink to me only with thine eyes—
That's one way to economize.

Anonymous

Meaning
and Idea

Little Jack Horner
Sat in a corner
Eating a Christmas pie.
He stuck in his thumb
And pulled out a plum
And said, "What a good boy am I!"

Anonymous

The meaning of a poem is the experience it expresses—nothing less. But the reader who, baffled by a particular poem, asks perplexedly, "What does it *mean*?" is usually after something more specific than this. He wants something that he can grasp entirely with his mind. We may therefore find it useful to make a distinction between the TOTAL MEANING of a poem—that which it communicates (and which can be communicated in no other way)—and its PROSE MEANING—the ingredient that can be separated out in the form of a prose paraphrase. If we make this distinction, however, we must be careful not to confuse the two kinds of meaning. The prose meaning is no more the poem than a plum is a pie or than a prune is a plum.

The prose meaning will not necessarily or perhaps even usually be an idea. It may be a story, it may be a description, it may be a statement of emotion, it may be a presentation of human character, or it may be some combination of these. "The Mill" (page 34) tells a story; "The Eagle" (page 5) is primarily descriptive; "A Red, Red Rose" (page 111) is an expression of emotion; "My Last Duchess" (page 131) is an account of human character. None of these poems is directly concerned with ideas. The message-hunter will be baffled and disappointed by poetry of this kind, for he will not find what he is looking for, and he may attempt to read some idea into the poem that is really not there. Yet ideas are also part of human experience, and therefore many poems are concerned, at least partially, with presenting ideas. But with these poems message-hunting is an even more dangerous activity. For the message-hunter is likely to think that the whole object of reading the poem is to find the message—that the idea is really the only important thing in it. Like Little Jack Horner, he will reach in and pluck it out and say, "What a good boy am I!" as if the pie existed for the plum.

The idea in a poem is only part of the total experience it communicates. The value and worth of the poem are determined by the value of the total experience, not by the truth or the nobility of the idea itself. This is not to say that the truth of the idea is unimportant, or that its validity should not be examined and appraised. But a good idea will not make a good poem, nor need an idea with which the reader does not agree ruin one. The good reader of poetry will be a reader receptive to all kinds of experience. He will be able to make that "willing suspension of disbelief" that Coleridge characterized as constituting poetic faith. When one attends a performance of *Hamlet* he is willing to forget for the time being that such a person as Hamlet never existed and that the events on the stage are fictions. The reader of poetry should also be willing to enter imaginatively, for the time being, into ideas he objectively regards as untrue. It is one way of understanding these ideas better and of enlarging his own experience. The Christian should be able to enjoy a good poem expressing atheistic ideas, and the atheist a good poem in praise of God. The optimist by temperament should be able to find pleasure in pessimistic poetry, and the pessimist in optimistic poetry. The teetotaler should be able to enjoy "The Rubáiyát of Omar Khayyám," and the winebibber a good poem in praise of austerity. The primary value of a poem depends not so much on the truth of the idea presented as on the power with which it is communicated and on its being made a convincing part of a meaningful total experience. We must feel that the idea has been truly and deeply *felt* by the poet and that he is doing something more than merely moralizing. The plum must be made part of a pie. If the plum is properly combined with other ingredients and if the pie is well cooked, it should be enjoyable even for persons who do not care for the brand of plums it is made of. Let us consider, for instance, the following two poems.

BARTER

Life has loveliness to sell,
    All beautiful and splendid things,
Blue waves whitened on a cliff,
    Soaring fire that sways and sings,
And children's faces looking up,   5
Holding wonder like a cup.

Life has loveliness to sell,
    Music like a curve of gold,
Scent of pine trees in the rain,
    Eyes that love you, arms that hold,   10
And for your spirit's still delight,
Holy thoughts that star the night.

Spend all you have for loveliness,
    Buy it and never count the cost;
For one white singing hour of peace   15
    Count many a year of strife well lost,
And for a breath of ecstasy
Give all you have been, or could be.

Sara Teasdale (1884–1933)

STOPPING BY WOODS ON A SNOWY EVENING*

Whose woods these are I think I know.
His house is in the village though;
He will not see me stopping here
To watch his woods fill up with snow.

*Mr. Frost recorded "Stopping by Woods on a Snowy Evening" (LP, National Council of Teachers of English, RL 20-1; or LP, Yale, YP 320; or LP, Library of Congress, PL 20).

My little horse must think it queer   5
To stop without a farmhouse near
Between the woods and frozen lake
The darkest evening of the year.

He gives his harness bells a shake
To ask if there is some mistake.   10
The only other sound's the sweep
Of easy wind and downy flake.

The woods are lovely, dark and deep,
But I have promises to keep,
And miles to go before I sleep,   15
And miles to go before I sleep.

Robert Frost (1874–1963)

QUESTIONS

1. How do these two poems differ in idea?
2. What contrasts are suggested between the speaker in the second poem and (a) his horse and (b) the owner of the woods?

Both of these poems present ideas, the first more or less explicitly, the second symbolically. Perhaps the best way to get at the idea of the second poem is to ask two questions. First, why does the speaker stop? Second, why does he go on? He stops, we answer, to watch the woods fill up with snow—to observe a scene of natural beauty. He goes on, we answer, because he has "promises" to keep, that is, he has obligations to fulfill. He is momentarily torn between his love of beauty and these other various and complex claims that life has upon him. The small conflict in the poem is symbolical of a larger conflict in life. One part of the sensitive thinking man would like to give up his life to the enjoyment of beauty and art. But another part is aware of larger duties and responsibilities—responsibilities owed, at least in part, to other human beings. The speaker in the poem would like to satisfy both impulses. But when the two come into conflict, he seems to suggest, the "promises" must be given precedence.

The first poem also presents a philosophy but an opposed one. For this poet, beauty is of such supreme value that any conflicting demand should be sacrificed to it. "Spend all you have for loveliness, / Buy it and never count the cost . . . And for a breath of ecstasy / Give all you have been, or could be." The reader, if he is a thinking person, will have to choose between these two philosophies—to commit himself to one or the other. But if he is a good reader of poetry, this commitment should not destroy for him his enjoyment of either poem. If it does, he is reading for plums and not for pies.

Nothing so far said in this chapter should be construed as meaning that the truth or falsity of the idea in a poem is a matter of no importance. *Other things being equal*, the good reader naturally will, and properly should, value more highly the poem whose idea he feels to be maturer and nearer to the heart of human experience. There may be some ideas, moreover, that he feels to be so vicious or so foolish or so beyond the pale of normal human decency as to discredit *by themselves* the poems in which he finds them. A rotten plum may spoil a pie. But a good reader will always be a person of considerable intellectual flexibility and tolerance, able to entertain sympathetically ideas other than his own. He will often like a poem whose idea he disagrees with better than one with an idea he accepts. And, above all, he will not confuse the prose meaning of any poem with its total meaning. He will not mistake plums for pies.

SONG

The year's at the spring,
And day's at the morn;
Morning's at seven;
The hillside's dew-pearled;
The lark's on the wing;
The snail's on the thorn;
God's in his heaven—
All's right with the world!

Robert Browning (1812–1889)

DIRGE

Rough wind, that moanest loud
Grief too sad for song;

Wild wind, when sullen cloud
　　Knells all the night long;
Sad storm, whose tears are vain,
Bare woods, whose branches strain,
Deep caves and dreary main,—
　　Wail, for the world's wrong!

Percy Bysshe Shelley (1792–1822)

QUESTIONS

　1. In what ways are these two poems alike? In what ways are they
different?

　2. How would you evaluate the two comments made on the world? Is it
possible to justify both? Should you be surprised to learn that the first poet
was a tremendous admirer of the second poet?

TO A WATERFOWL

　　Whither, midst falling dew,
While glow the heavens with the last steps of day,
Far, through their rosy depths, dost thou pursue
　　Thy solitary way?

　　Vainly the fowler's eye   5
Might mark thy distant flight to do thee wrong,
As, darkly seen against the crimson sky,
　　Thy figure floats along.

　　Seek'st thou the plashy brink
Of weedy lake, or marge of river wide,   10
Or where the rocking billows rise and sink
　　On the chafed ocean side?

　　There is a Power whose care
Teaches thy way along that pathless coast—
The desert and illimitable air—   15
　　Lone wandering, but not lost.

　　All day thy wings have fanned,
At that far height, the cold, thin atmosphere,
Yet stoop not, weary, to the welcome land,
　　Though the dark night is near.   20

And soon that toil shall end;
Soon shalt thou find a summer home, and rest,
And scream among thy fellows; reeds shall bend,
    Soon, o'er thy sheltered nest.

Thou'rt gone, the abyss of heaven   25
Hath swallowed up thy form; yet, on my heart
Deeply has sunk the lesson thou hast given,
    And shall not soon depart.

He who, from zone to zone,
Guides through the boundless sky thy certain flight,   30
In the long way that I must tread alone,
    Will lead my steps aright.

William Cullen Bryant (1794–1878)

DESIGN*

I found a dimpled spider, fat and white,
On a white heal-all, holding up a moth
Like a white piece of rigid satin cloth—
Assorted characters of death and blight
Mixed ready to begin the morning right,   5
Like the ingredients of a witches' broth—
A snow-drop spider, a flower like a froth,
And dead wings carried like a paper kite.

What had that flower to do with being white,
The wayside blue and innocent heal-all?   10
What brought the kindred spider to that height,
Then steered the white moth thither in the night?
What but design of darkness to appall?—
If design govern in a thing so small.

Robert Frost (1874–1963)

[Handwritten annotation: Like as a disasterous design - killing each other off. All white "irony". All things God creates isn't good.]

QUESTIONS

1. Vocabulary: *characters* (4).
2. The heal-all is a wildflower, usually blue or violet but occasionally white, found blooming along roadsides in the summer. It was once supposed to have healing qualities, hence its name. Of what significance, scientific and poetic, is the fact that the spider, the heal-all, and the moth are all white?

*Mr. Frost recorded "Design" (LP, Yale, YP 320).

Of what poetic significance is the fact that the spider is "dimpled" and "fat" and like a "snow-drop," and that the flower is "innocent" and named "heal-all"?

3. The "argument from design," as it was called, was a favorite eighteenth-century argument for the existence of God. What twist does Frost give the argument? What questions does the poem pose?

4. Contrast Frost's poem in content with "To a Waterfowl." Is it possible to admire both?

FAREWELL, LOVE

Farewell, love, and all thy laws for ever,
Thy baited hooks shall tangle me no more;
Senec and Plato call me from thy lore
To perfect wealth, my wit for to endeavor;°   to exert my mind
In blind error when I did persever,   5
Thy sharp repulse that pricketh aye so sore
Hath taught me to set in trifles no store,
And scape forth, since liberty is lever.°   preferable
Therefore, farewell! Go trouble younger hearts,
And in me claim no more authority;   10
With idle youth go use thy property,
And thereon spend thy many brittle darts.
For hitherto though I have lost my time,
Me lusteth° no longer rotten boughs to climb.   I desire

Thomas Wyatt (1503?–1542)

QUESTION

Senec (3) is Seneca, the Roman Stoic philosopher, who taught that man's felicity lies in liberating oneself from bondage to the passions and appetites; Plato (3) likewise believed that man's highest good is to be found in the mind rather than in sensual satisfactions. What evaluation of love is made by Wyatt, both through his metaphors and in literal statement?

THE SPUR

You think it horrible that lust and rage
Should dance attention upon my old age;
They were not such a plague when I was young;
What else have I to spur me into song?

William Butler Yeats (1865–1939)

1. How do Yeats's metaphors for "lust and rage" resemble, and differ from, Wyatt's metaphors for love? How does his evaluation of sensuality and passion differ from Wyatt's? His view of youth and age?

2. Wyatt turns to philosophy; Yeats wishes to continue with poetry (4). Does this difference help to explain their different attitudes toward sensuality and love? Why?

THE APPARITION ✓

The Parthenon uplifted on its rock
first challenging the view on the approach to Athens

Abrupt the supernatural Cross,
    Vivid in startled air,
Smote the Emperor Constantine
And turned his soul's allegiance there.

With other power appealing down,   5
    Trophy of Adam's best!
If cynic minds you scarce convert,
You try them, shake them, or molest.

Diogenes, that honest heart,
    Lived ere your date began;   10
Thee had he seen, he might have swerved
In mood nor barked so much at Man.

Herman Melville (1819–1891)

QUESTIONS

1. Vocabulary: *cynic* (7).

2. Constantine I, Roman emperor 306–337, is said to have been converted to Christianity after beholding a fiery cross in the heavens. With what "other power" (5) does the apparition of the Parthenon smite the eyes of the traveler approaching Athens?

3. For what is "Adam" (6) a metonymy? What is the meaning of "Adam's best"?

4. Diogenes (412?–323 B.C.), Greek Cynic philosopher, persistently inveighed against the vices and follies of men and is said to have spent his life looking for an honest man—without success. (Melville is mistaken in saying he lived before the building of the Parthenon.) What is implied by Melville's calling Diogenes "that honest heart" (9)? How is the allusion to Diogenes related to the allusion to Constantine?

WHEN SERPENTS BARGAIN FOR THE RIGHT TO SQUIRM*

when serpents bargain for the right to squirm
and the sun strikes to gain a living wage—
when thorns regard their roses with alarm
and rainbows are insured against old age

when every thrush may sing no new moon in   5
if all screech-owls have not okayed his voice
—and any wave signs on the dotted line
or else an ocean is compelled to close

when the oak begs permission of the birch
to make an acorn—valleys accuse their   10
mountains of having altitude—and march
denounces april as a saboteur

then we'll believe in that incredible
unanimal mankind (and not until)

e. e. cummings (1894–1962)

QUESTIONS

1. What characteristics do the various activities not engaged in by nature have in common? What qualities of thought and feeling or kinds of behavior ought to replace these activities, in the poet's view?

2. What does the poet imply by calling man an *unanimal* (14)? What is the precise force here of *incredible* (13)?

3. How does the view of man implied in this poem differ from that implied in the preceding poem? Which of the two poems is *satirical* (see page 113)?

THE CAGED SKYLARK

As a dare-gale skylark scanted in a dull cage
    Man's mounting spirit in his bone-house, mean house, dwells—
    That bird beyond the remembering his free fells;
This in drudgery, day-laboring-out life's age.

*Mr. Cummings recorded "when serpents bargain for the right to squirm"
(LP, Caedmon, TC 1017).

Though aloft on turf or perch or poor low stage,   5
   Both sing sometimes the sweetest, sweetest spells,
   Yet both droop deadly sometimes in their cells
Or wring their barriers in bursts of fear or rage.

Not that the sweet-fowl, song-fowl, needs no rest—
Why, hear him, hear him babble and drop down to his nest,   10
   But his own nest, wild nest, no prison.

Man's spirit will be flesh-bound when found at best,
But uncumbered: meadow-down is not distressed
   For a rainbow footing it nor he for his bones risen.

Gerard Manley Hopkins (1844–1889)

QUESTIONS

1. Vocabulary: *scanted* (1), *fells* (3). What meanings of *mean* (2) are appropriate here? *Turf* (5) is a piece of sod placed in a cage.

2. This poem, written by a poet-priest, expresses his belief in the orthodox Roman Catholic doctrine of the resurrection of the body. According to this belief man's immortal spirit, after death, will be ultimately reunited with his body; this body, however, will be a weightless, perfected, glorified body, not the gross imperfect body of mortal life. Express the analogy in the poem as a pair of mathematical statements of proportion (in the form $a{:}b = c{:}d$, and $e{:}f = g{:}h = i{:}j$), using the following terms: caged skylark, mortal body, meadow-down, cage, rainbow, spirit-in-life, nest, immortal spirit, wild skylark, resurrected body.

3. Discuss the image of the last two lines as a figure for weightlessness. Why would not a shadow have been equally apt as a rainbow for this comparison?

THE IMMORTAL PART

When I meet the morning beam
Or lay me down at night to dream,
I hear my bones within me say,
"Another night, another day.

"When shall this slough of sense be cast,   5
This dust of thoughts be laid at last,
The man of flesh and soul be slain
And the man of bone remain?

"This tongue that talks, these lungs that shout,
These thews that hustle us about,   10
This brain that fills the skull with schemes,
And its humming hive of dreams,—

"These to-day are proud in power
And lord it in their little hour:
The immortal bones obey control   15
Of dying flesh and dying soul.

" 'Tis long till eve and morn are gone:
Slow the endless night comes on,
And late to fulness grows the birth
That shall last as long as earth.   20

"Wanderers eastward, wanderers west,
Know you why you cannot rest?
'Tis that every mother's son
Travails with a skeleton.

"Lie down in the bed of dust;   25
Bear the fruit that bear you must;
Bring the eternal seed to light,
And morn is all the same as night.

"Rest you so from trouble sore,
Fear the heat o' the sun no more,   30
Nor the snowing winter wild,
Now you labor not with child.

"Empty vessel, garment cast,
We that wore you long shall last.
—Another night, another day."   35
So my bones within me say.

Therefore they shall do my will
To-day while I am master still,
And flesh and soul, now both are strong,
Shall hale the sullen slaves along,   40

Before this fire of sense decay,
This smoke of thought blow clean away,
And leave with ancient night alone
The stedfast and enduring bone.

A. E. Housman (1859–1936)

1. Vocabulary: *slough* (5), *thews* (10), *travails* (24), *hale* (40).

2. Discuss the figures of speech in lines 3–16, 12, 19–27, 41–42, 43.

3. Do you recognize the allusion in stanza 8? If not, refer to page 342. How is the allusion appropriate here?

4. Contrast the meaning of the word *soul* in this poem with its meaning in "The Caged Skylark." How do the two poems differ in idea? Is there any pronounced difference between them in poetic merit?

ARS POETICA*

A poem should be palpable and mute
As a globed fruit,

Dumb
As old medallions to the thumb,

Silent as the sleeve-worn stone   5
Of casement ledges where the moss has grown—

A poem should be wordless
As the flight of birds.

      *

A poem should be motionless in time
As the moon climbs,   10

Leaving, as the moon releases
Twig by twig the night-entangled trees,

Leaving, as the moon behind the winter leaves,
Memory by memory the mind—

A poem should be motionless in time   15
As the moon climbs.

      *

A poem should be equal to:
Not true.

For all the history of grief
An empty doorway and a maple leaf.   20

For love
The leaning grasses and two lights above the sea—

*Mr. MacLeish recorded "Ars Poetica" (78 rpm, Harvard Vocarium, P–1220; or LP, Library of Congress, PL 29).

A poem should not mean
But be.

Archibald MacLeish (b. 1892)

QUESTIONS

1. How can a poem be "wordless" (7)? How can it be "motionless in time" (15)?

2. The Latin title, literally translatable as "The Art of Poetry," is a traditional title for works on the philosophy of poetry. What is *this* poet's philosophy of poetry? What does he mean by saying that a poem should not *mean* and should not be *true*?

Tone

Tone, in literature, may be defined as the writer's or speaker's attitude toward his subject, his audience, or himself. It is the emotional coloring, or the emotional meaning, of the work and is an extremely important part of the full meaning. In spoken language it is indicated by the inflections of the speaker's voice. If, for instance, a friend tells you, "I'm going to get married today," the facts of his statement are entirely clear. But the emotional meaning of his statement may vary widely according to the tone of voice with which he utters it. He may be ecstatic ("Hooray! I'm going to get married today!"); he may be incredulous ("I can't believe it! I'm going to get married today"); he may be resigned ("Might as well face it. I'm going to get married today"); he may be in despair ("Horrors! I'm going to get married today!"). Obviously, a correct interpretation of his tone will be an important part of understanding his full meaning. It may even have rather important consequences. If someone calls you a fool, your interpretation of his tone may determine whether you roll up your sleeves for a fight or walk off with your arm around his shoulder. If a girl says "No" to your proposal of marriage, your interpretation of her tone may determine whether you ask her again and win her or start going with someone else.

In poetry tone is likewise important. We have not really understood a poem unless we have accurately sensed whether the attitude it manifests is playful or solemn, mocking or reverent, calm or excited. But the correct determination of tone in literature is a much more delicate matter than it is with spoken language, for we do not have the speaker's voice to guide us. We must learn to recognize tone by other means. Almost all the elements of poetry go into indicating its tone: connotation, imagery, and metaphor; irony and understatement; rhythm, sentence construction, and formal pattern. There is therefore no simple formula for recognizing tone. It is an end product of all the elements in a poem. The best we can do is illustrate.

Robert Frost's "Stopping by Woods on a Snowy Evening" (page 150) seems a simple poem, but it has always afforded trouble to beginning readers. A very good student, asked to interpret it, once wrote this: "The poem means that we are forever passing up pleasures to go onward to what we wrongly consider our obligations. We would like to watch the snow fall on the peaceful countryside, but we always have to rush home to supper and other engagements. Mr. Frost feels that the average man considers life too short to stop and take time to appreciate true pleasures." This student did a good job in recognizing the central conflict of the poem. He went astray in recognizing its tone. Let's examine why.

In the first place, the fact that the speaker in the poem *does* stop to watch the snow fall in the woods immediately establishes him as a human being with more sensitivity and feeling for beauty than most. He is not one of the people of Wordsworth's sonnet who, "getting and spending," have laid waste their powers and lost the capacity to be stirred by nature. Frost's speaker is contrasted with his horse, who, as a creature of habit and an animal without esthetic perception, cannot understand the speaker's reason for stopping. There is also a suggestion of contrast with the "owner" of the woods, who, if he saw the speaker stopping, might be as puzzled as the horse. (Who most truly "profits" from the woods—its absentee owner or the person who can enjoy its beauty?) The speaker goes on because he has "promises to keep." But the word *promises*, though it may here have a wry ironic undertone of regret, has a favorable connotation: people almost universally agree that promises ought to be kept. If the poet had used a different term, say, "things to do," or "business to attend to," or "financial affairs to take care of," or "money to make," the connotations would have been quite different. As it is, the tone of the poem tells us that the poet is sympathetic to the speaker, is endorsing rather than censuring his action. Perhaps we may go even further. In the concluding two lines, because of their climactic position, because they are repeated, and because "sleep" in poetry is often used figuratively to refer to death, there is a suggestion of symbolic interpretation: "and many years to live before I die." If we accept this interpretation, it poses a parallel between giving oneself up to contemplation of the woods and dying. The poet's total implication would seem to be that beauty is a distinctively human value that deserves its place in a full life but that to devote one's life to its pursuit, at the expense of other obligations and duties, is tantamount to one's death as a responsible being. The poet therefore accepts the choice the speaker makes, though not without a touch of regret.

Differences in tone, and their importance, can perhaps be studied best in poems with similar content. Consider, for instance, the following pair.

THE VILLAIN

While joy gave clouds the light of stars,
    That beamed where'er they looked;
And calves and lambs had tottering knees,
    Excited, while they sucked;
While every bird enjoyed his song,   5
Without one thought of harm or wrong—
I turned my head and saw the wind,
    Not far from where I stood,
Dragging the corn by her golden hair,
    Into a dark and lonely wood.   10

W. H. Davies (1871–1940)

QUESTIONS

1. Vocabulary: *corn* (9).

2. From what realm of experience is the image in the title and the last two lines taken? What implications does your answer have for the way this image should be taken—that is, for its relation to reality?

APPARENTLY WITH NO SURPRISE

Apparently with no surprise
To any happy flower,
The frost beheads it at its play

In accidental power.
The blond assassin passes on,
The sun proceeds unmoved
To measure off another day
For an approving God.

Emily Dickinson (1830–1886)

QUESTIONS
1. What is the "blond assassin"?
2. What ironies are involved in this poem?

Both of these poems are concerned with nature; both use contrast as their basic organizing principle—a contrast between innocence and evil, joy and tragedy. But in tone the two poems are sharply different. The first is light and fanciful; its tone is one of delight or delighted surprise. The second, though superficially fanciful, is basically grim, almost savage; its tone is one of horror. Let's examine the difference.

In "The Villain" the images of the first six lines all suggest joy and innocence. The last four introduce the sinister. The poet, on turning his head, sees a villain dragging a beautiful maiden toward a dark wood to commit there some unmentionable deed, or so his metaphor tells us. But our response is one not of horror but of delight, for we realize that the poet does not mean us to take his metaphor seriously. He has actually seen only the wind blowing through the wheat and bending its golden tops gracefully toward a shady wood. The beauty of the scene has delighted him, and he has been further delighted by the fanciful metaphor which he has found to express it. The reader shares his delight both in the scene and in the metaphor.

The second poem makes the same contrast of joyful innocence (the "happy flower . . . at its play") with the sinister ("the blond assassin"). The chief difference would seem to be that the villain is this time the frost rather than the wind. But this time the poet, though her metaphor is no less fanciful, is earnest in what she is saying. For the frost actually *does* kill the flower. What makes the horror of the killing even worse is that nothing else in nature is disturbed over it or seems even to notice it. The sun "proceeds unmoved / To measure off another day." Nothing

165

in nature stops or pauses. The flower itself is not surprised. And even God—the God who we have all been told is benevolent and concerned over the least sparrow's fall—seems to approve of what has happened, for he shows no displeasure, and it was he who created the frost as well as the flower. Further irony lies in the fact that the "assassin" (the word's connotations are of terror and violence) is not dark but "blond," or white (the connotations here are of innocence and beauty). The destructive agent, in other words, is among the most exquisite creations of God's handiwork. The poet, then, is shocked at what has happened, and is even more shocked that nothing else in nature is shocked. What has happened seems inconsistent with a rule of benevolence in the universe. In her ironic reference to an "approving God," therefore, the poet is raising a dreadful question: are the forces that created and govern the universe actually benevolent? And if we think that the poet is unduly disturbed over the death of a flower, we may consider that what is true for the flower is true throughout nature. Death—even early or accidental death, in terrible juxtaposition with beauty—is its constant condition; the fate that befalls the flower befalls us all.

These two poems, then, though superficially similar, are basically as different as night and day. And the difference is primarily one of tone.

Accurate determination of tone, therefore, is extremely important, whether in the reading of poetry or the interpretation of a woman's "No." For the good reader it will be instinctive and automatic. For the beginning reader it will require study. But beyond the general suggestions for reading that have already been made, no specific instructions can be given. Recognition of tone requires an increasing familiarity with the meanings and connotations of words, alertness to the presence of irony and other figures, and, above all, careful reading. Poetry cannot be read as one would skim a newspaper or a mystery novel, looking merely for facts.

EXERCISES

1. Marvell's "To His Coy Mistress" (page 77) and Herrick's "To the Virgins, to Make Much of Time" (page 90) both treat a traditional poetic theme known as the *carpe diem* ("seize the day") theme. They differ, however, in tone. Characterize the tone of each, and point out the

differences in poetic management that account for the difference in tone.

2. Shakespeare (page 11), Hopkins (page 60), and Nashe (page 334) have all written poems entitled "Spring." Describe and account for the differences in tone among them.

3. Describe and account for the differences of tone in each of the following pairs: (a) "Song" and "Dirge" (page 152); (b) "Ulysses" and "Curiosity" (pages 96, 99); (c) "The Unknown Citizen" and "Departmental" (pages 127, 129).

THE COMING OF WISDOM WITH TIME ✓

Though leaves are many, the root is one;
Through all the lying days of my youth
I swayed my leaves and flowers in the sun;
Now I may wither into the truth.

William Butler Yeats (1865–1939)

QUESTION
Is the poet exulting over a gain or lamenting over a loss?

SINCE THERE'S NO HELP

Since there's no help, come let us kiss and part;
Nay, I have done, you get no more of me,
And I am glad, yea, glad with all my heart
That thus so cleanly I myself can free;
Shake hands forever, cancel all our vows,   5
And when we meet at any time again,
Be it not seen in either of our brows
That we one jot of former love retain.
Now at the last gasp of Love's latest breath,
When, his pulse failing, Passion speechless lies,   10
When Faith is kneeling by his bed of death,
And Innocence is closing up his eyes,
Now, if thou wouldst, when all have given him over,
From death to life thou mightst him yet recover.

Michael Drayton (1563–1631)

1. What difference in tone do you find between the first eight lines and the last six? What differences in rhythm and the kind of language used help to establish this difference in tone?

2. How many figures are there in the allegorical scene in lines 9–12? Why is "Love" dying?

3. Define the dramatic situation as precisely as possible, taking into consideration both the man's attitude and the woman's.

ELEGY FOR WILLIAM HUBBARD*

Hubbard is dead, the old plumber;
who will mend our burst pipes now,
the tap that has dripped all the summer,
testing the sink's overflow?

No other like him. Young men with knowledge   5
of new techniques, theories from books,
may better his work straight from college,
but who will challenge his squint-eyed looks

in kitchen, bathroom, under floorboards,
rules of thumb which were often wrong;   10
seek as erringly stopcocks in cupboards,
or make a job last half as long?

He was a man who knew the ginnels,°   gutters
alleyways, streets—the whole district,
family secrets, minor annals,   15
time-honored fictions fused to fact.

Seventy years of gossip muttered
under his cap, his tufty thatch,
so that his talk was slow and clotted,
hard to follow, and too much.   20

As though nothing fell, none vanished,
and time were the maze of Cheetham Hill,
in which the dead—with jobs unfinished—
waited to hear him ring the bell.

For much he never got round to doing,   25
but meant to, when weather bucked up,

*Mr. Connor recorded "Elegy for William Hubbard" (LP, Argo, RG 454).

or worsened, or when his pipe was drawing,
or when he'd finished this cup.

I thought time, he forgot so often,
had forgotten him, but here's Death's pomp   30
over his house, and by the coffin
the son who will inherit his blowlamp,

tools, workshop, cart, and cornet
(pride of Cheetham Prize Brass Band),
and there's his mourning widow, Janet,   35
stood at the gate he promised to mend.

Soon he will make his final journey;
shaved and silent, strangely trim,
with never a pause to talk to any-
body: how arrow-like, for him!   40

In St. Mark's church, whose dismal tower
he pointed and painted when a lad,
they will sing his praises amidst flowers
while, somewhere, a cellar starts to flood,

and the housewife banging his front-door knocker   45
is not surprised to find him gone,
and runs for Thwaite, who's a better worker,
and sticks at a job until it's done.

Tony Connor (b. 1930)

QUESTIONS

1. Characterize Hubbard. How does this *elegy* differ from the *eulogy*
that will be said for him in St. Mark's Church (41–43)? Compose his eulogy.

2. What is the poet's attitude toward his subject?

JOHN ANDERSON

John Anderson, a scholarly gentleman
advancing with his company in the attack
received some bullets through him as he ran.

So his creative brain whirled, and he fell back
in the bloody dust (it was a fine day there   5
and warm). Blood turned his tunic black

while past his desperate final stare
the other simple soldiers run
and leave the hero unaware.

Apt epitaph or pun   10
he could not hit upon, to grace
a scholar's death; he only eyed the sun.

But I think, the last moment of his gaze
beheld the father of gods and men,
Zeus, leaning from heaven as he dies,   15

whom in his swoon he hears again
summon Apollo in the Homeric tongue:
Descend Phoebus and cleanse the stain

of dark blood from the body of John Anderson.
Give him to Death and Sleep,   20
who'll bear him as they can

out of the range of darts to the broad vale
of Lycia; there lay him in a deep
solemn content on some bright dale.

And the brothers, Sleep and Death   25
lift up John Anderson at his last breath.

Keith Douglas (1920–1944)

QUESTIONS

1. Vocabulary: *tunic* (6), *simple* (8). *Lycia* (23) was in ancient times a region of southwest Asia Minor bordering on the Mediterranean; Apollo was supposed to have had his winter palace there.

2. What kind of person is John Anderson? Why is Phoebus Apollo the god summoned by Zeus to descend to him? Why is Zeus—not Jehovah—the god he "sees"? (The author, an English poet, wrote this poem at Oxford in 1940. He was himself later killed in the invasion of Normandy.)

3. "Elegy for William Hubbard" implied a contrast between the real William Hubbard and the character he would be given in the funeral eulogy. Is any contrast implied in this poem? What is the precise force of the word *hero* (9)? At whose expense is any irony possibly latent in the word?

4. Why does the poet (or Zeus) consign John Anderson to both Sleep and Death, not Death alone?

5. What is the poet's attitude toward John Anderson? Compare or contrast the tone of this poem with that of "Elegy for William Hubbard."

CROSSING THE BAR ✓

Sunset and evening star,
   And one clear call for me!
And may there be no moaning of the bar
   When I put out to sea,

But such a tide as moving seems asleep,   5
   Too full for sound and foam,
When that which drew from out the boundless deep
   Turns again home.

Twilight and evening bell,
   And after that the dark!   10
And may there be no sadness of farewell
   When I embark;

For though from out our bourne of Time and Place
   The flood may bear me far,
I hope to see my Pilot face to face   15
   When I have crossed the bar.

Alfred, Lord Tennyson (1809–1892)

QUESTIONS

1. Vocabulary: *bourne* (13).
2. What two sets of figures does Tennyson use for approaching death? What is the precise moment of death in each set?
3. In troubled weather the wind and waves above the sandbar across a harbor's mouth make a moaning sound. What metaphorical meaning has the "moaning of the bar" here (3)? For what kind of death is the poet wishing? Why does he want "no sadness of farewell" (11)?
4. What is "that which drew from out the boundless deep" (7)? What is "the boundless deep"? To what is it opposed in the poem? Why is "Pilot" (15) capitalized?

THE OXEN ✓

Christmas Eve, and twelve of the clock.
   "Now they are all on their knees,"
An elder said as we sat in a flock
   By the embers in hearthside ease.

We pictured the meek mild creatures where   5
    They dwelt in their strawy pen,
Nor did it occur to one of us there
    To doubt they were kneeling then.

So fair a fancy few would weave
    In these years! Yet, I feel,   10
If someone said on Christmas Eve,
    "Come; see the oxen kneel

"In the lonely barton° by yonder coomb°   farm; valley
    Our childhood used to know,"
I should go with him in the gloom,   15
    Hoping it might be so.

Thomas Hardy (1840–1928)

QUESTIONS

1. Is the simple superstition referred to in the poem here opposed to, or identified with, religious faith? With what implications for the meaning of the poem?

2. What are "these years" (10) and how do they contrast with the years of the poet's boyhood? What event in intellectual history between 1840 and 1915 (the date of composition of this poem) was most responsible for the change?

3. Both "Crossing the Bar" and "The Oxen" in their last lines use a form of the verb *hope*. By full discussion of tone, establish the precise meaning of hope in each poem. What degree of expectation does it imply? How should the word be handled in reading Tennyson's poem aloud?

GO WEST YOUNG MAN

Yessir they're all named
either Ken or Stan or Don
every one of them and

those aren't just nick-
names either no they're   5
really christened like

that just Ken or Stan or
Don and you shake hands
with anybody you run into

no matter who the hell 10
it is and say "glad to
know you Ken glad to

know you Don" and then
two minutes later (you
may not have said ten 15

words to the guy) you
shake hands again and
say "glad to have met

you Stan glad to" and
they haven't heard much 20
about Marx and the class

struggle because they
haven't had to and by
god it makes a country

that is fit to live in 25
and by god I'm glad to
know you Don I'm glad!

James Laughlin (b. 1914)

QUESTIONS

1. Does the tone of this poem mainly undercut or support the assertion made in lines 23–25? Explain.
2. Explain the title.

YES; I WRITE VERSES

Yes; I write verses now and then,
But blunt and flaccid is my pen,
No longer talked of by young men
    As rather clever;
In the last quarter are my eyes, 5
You see it by their form and size;
Is it not time then to be wise?
    Or now or never.

Fairest that ever sprang from Eve!
While Time allows the short reprieve,   10
Just look at me! would you believe
    'Twas once a lover?
I cannot clear the five-bar gate,
But, trying first its timbers' state,
Climb stiffly up, take breath, and wait   15
    To trundle over.

Through gallopade I cannot swing
The entangling blooms of Beauty's spring;
I cannot say the tender thing,
    Be't true or false,   20
And am beginning to opine
Those girls are only half-divine
Whose waists yon wicked boys entwine
    In giddy waltz.

I fear that arm above that shoulder,   25
I wish them wiser, graver, older,
Sedater, and no harm if colder,
    And panting less.
Ah! people were not half so wild
In former days, when, starchly mild,   30
Upon her high-heeled Essex smiled
    The brave Queen Bess.

                    Walter Savage Landor (1775–1864)

QUESTIONS

1. Vocabulary: *flaccid* (2), *trundle* (16), *gallopade* (17).
2. Identify and explain the figures of speech in lines 2, 5, 9, and 18 and the allusion in lines 31–32.

TO AGE

Welcome, old friend! These many years
    Have we lived door by door;
The Fates have laid aside their shears
    Perhaps for some few more.

I was indocile at an age   5
   When better boys were taught,
But thou at length hast made me sage,
   If I am sage in aught.

Little I know from other men,
   Too little they from me,   10
But thou hast pointed well the pen
   That writes these lines to thee.

Thanks for expelling Fear and Hope,
   One vile, the other vain;
One's scourge, the other's telescope,   15
   I shall not see again.

Rather what lies before my feet
   My notice shall engage—
He who hath braved Youth's dizzy heat
   Dreads not the frost of Age.   20

Walter Savage Landor (1775–1864)

QUESTIONS

   1. Vocabulary: *indocile* (5), *scourge* (15).
   2. Identify and explain the figures of speech in lines 1–2, 11, 13–16, and 19–20 and the allusion in lines 3–4.
   3. Define the poet's attitude toward himself and advancing old age in this poem and in the preceding one. (He was 71 when "Yes; I Write Verses" was published, 78 when "To Age" was published.) What are the apparent differences? Try to account for them.
   4. Describe the difference in tone between the two poems.

SONG

Love is a sickness full of woes,
   All remedies refusing;
A plant that with most cutting grows,
   Most barren with best using.
      Why so?   5

175

More we enjoy it, more it dies;
If not enjoyed, it sighing cries,
    Heigh-ho!

Love is a torment of the mind,
    A tempest everlasting;   10
And Jove hath made it of a kind
    Not well, nor full, nor fasting.
    Why so?
More we enjoy it, more it dies;
If not enjoyed, it sighing cries,   15
    Heigh-ho!

Samuel Daniel (1562–1619)

QUESTIONS

1. Identify and explain the paradoxes in the poem. How many of them would also have to be classified as metaphors?
2. A dictionary defines *heigh-ho* (8) as "an exclamation of surprise, exultation, melancholy, or weariness." Which is it here?
3. The same dictionary gives *hī′hō* and *hä′hō* as alternate pronunciations. How would you pronounce it here? Why?

LOVE

There's the wonderful love of a beautiful maid,
    And the love of a staunch true man,
And the love of a baby that's unafraid—
    All have existed since time began.
But the most wonderful love, the Love of all loves,
    Even greater than the love for Mother,
Is the infinite, tenderest, passionate love
    Of one dead drunk for another.

Anonymous

QUESTION

The radical shift in tone makes "Love" come off. If such a shift were unintentional in a poem, what would our view be?

Musical
Devices

It is obvious to the most uninitiated reader that poetry makes a greater use of the "music" of language than does language that is not poetry. The poet, unlike the man who uses language to convey only information, chooses his words for sound as well as for meaning, and he uses the sound as a means of reinforcing his meaning. So prominent is this musical quality of poetry that some writers have made it the distinguishing term in their definitions of poetry. Edgar Allan Poe, for instance, describes poetry as "music . . . combined with a pleasurable idea." Whether or not it deserves this much importance, verbal music, like connotation, imagery, and figurative language, is one of the important resources that enable the poet to do something more than communicate mere information. The poet may indeed sometimes pursue verbal music for its own sake; more often, at least in first-rate poetry, it is an adjunct to the total meaning or communication of the poem.

There are two broad ways by which the poet achieves his musical quality: by his choice and arrangement of sounds and by his arrangement of accents. In this chapter we will consider one aspect of the first of these.

An essential element in all music is repetition. In fact, we might say that all art consists of giving structure to two elements: repetition and variation. All things we enjoy greatly and lastingly have these two elements. We enjoy the sea endlessly because it is always the same yet always different. We enjoy a baseball game because it contains the same complex combination of pattern and variation. Our love of art, then, is rooted in human psychology. We like the familiar, we like variety, but we like them combined. If we get too much sameness, the result is monotony and tedium; if we get too much variety, the result is bewilderment and confusion. The composer of music, therefore, repeats certain musical tones; he repeats them in certain combinations, or chords; and he repeats them in certain patterns, or melodies. The poet likewise repeats certain sounds in certain combinations and arrangements, and thus gives organization and structure to his verse. Consider the following short example.

THE TURTLE

The turtle lives 'twixt plated decks
Which practically conceal its sex.
I think it clever of the turtle
In such a fix to be so fertile.

Ogden Nash (b. 1902)

Here is a little joke, a paradox of animal life to which the author has cleverly drawn our attention. An experiment will show us, however, that much of its appeal lies not so much in what it says as in the manner in which it says it. If, for instance, we recast the verse as prose: "The turtle lives in a shell which almost conceals its sex. It is ingenious of the turtle, in such a situation, to be so prolific," the joke falls flat. Some of its appeal must lie in its metrical form. So now we cast it in unrimed verse:

Because he lives between two decks,
It's hard to tell a turtle's gender.
The turtle is a clever beast
In such a plight to be so fertile.

Here, perhaps, is *some* improvement, but still the piquancy of the original is missing. Much of that appeal must have consisted in the use of rime—the repetition of sound in *decks* and *sex*, *turtle* and *fertile*. So we try once more:

The turtle lives 'twixt plated decks
Which practically conceal its sex.
I think it clever of the turtle
In such a plight to be so fertile.

But for the perceptive reader there is still something missing—he does not at first see what—but some little touch that makes the difference between a good piece of verse and a little masterpiece in its kind. And then he sees it: *plight* has been substituted for *fix*.

But why should *fix* make such a difference? Its meaning is little different from that of *plight*; its only important difference is in sound. But there we are. The final *x* in *fix* catches up the concluding consonant sound in *sex*, and its initial *f* is repeated in the initial consonant sound of *fertile*. Not only do these sound recurrences provide a subtle gratification to the ear, but they also give the verse structure; they emphasize and draw together the key words of the piece: *sex*, *fix*, and *fertile*.

The poet may repeat any unit of sound from the smallest to the largest. He may repeat individual vowel and consonant sounds, whole syllables, words, phrases, lines, or groups of lines. In each instance, in a good poem, the repetition will serve several purposes: it will please the ear, it will emphasize the words in which the repetition occurs, and it will give structure to the poem. The popularity and initial impressiveness of such repetitions is evidenced by their becoming in many instances embedded in the language as clichés like "wild and woolly," "first and foremost," "footloose and fancy-free," "penny-wise, pound-foolish," "dead as a doornail," "might and main," "sink or swim," "do or die," "pell-mell," "helter-skelter," "harum-scarum," "hocus-pocus." Some of these kinds of repetition have names, as we will see.

A syllable consists of a vowel sound that may be preceded or followed by consonant sounds. Any of these sounds may be repeated. The repetition of initial consonant sounds, as in "tried and true," "safe and sound," "fish or fowl," "rime or reason," is ALLITERATION. The repetition of vowel sounds, as in "mad as a hatter," "time out of mind," "free and easy," "slapdash," is ASSONANCE. The repetition of final consonant sounds, as in "first and last," "odds and ends," "short and sweet," "a stroke of luck," or Shakespeare's "struts and frets" (page 137) is CONSONANCE.*

*There is no established terminology for these various repetitions. *Alliteration* is used by some writers to mean any repetition of consonant sounds. *Assonance* has been used to mean the similarity as well as the identity of vowel sounds, or

Repetitions may be used alone or in combination. Alliteration and assonance are combined in such phrases as "time and tide," "thick and thin," "kith and kin," "alas and alack," "fit as a fiddle," and Edgar Allan Poe's famous line, "The viol, the violet, and the vine." Alliteration and consonance are combined in such phrases as "crisscross," "last but not least," "lone and lorn," "good as gold," Housman's "strangling in a string" (page 59), and Isabella Gardner's "the slap and slop of waves on little sloops" (page 230). The combination of assonance and consonance is rime.

RIME is the repetition of the accented vowel sound and all succeeding sounds. It is called MASCULINE when the rime sounds involve only one syllable, as in *decks* and *sex* or *support* and *retort*. It is FEMININE when the rime sounds involve two or more syllables, as in *turtle* and *fertile* or *spitefully* and *delightfully*. It is referred to as INTERNAL RIME when one or both riming words are *within* the line and as END RIME when both riming words are at the *ends* of lines. End rime is probably the most frequently used and most consciously sought-after sound repetition in English poetry. Because it comes at the end of the line, it receives emphasis as a musical effect and perhaps contributes more than any other musical resource except rhythm and meter to give poetry its musical effect as well as its structure. There exists, however, a large body of poetry that does not employ rime and for which rime would not be appropriate. Also, there has always been a tendency, especially noticeable in modern poetry, to substitute approximate rimes for perfect rimes at the ends of lines. APPROXIMATE RIMES include words with any kind of sound similarity, from close to fairly remote. Under approximate rime we include alliteration, assonance, and consonance or their combinations when used at the end of the line; half-rime (feminine rimes in which only half of the word rimes—the accented half, as in *lightly* and *frightful*, or the unaccented half, as in *yellow* and *willow*); and other simi-

---

even the similarity of any sounds whatever. *Consonance* has often been reserved for words in which both the initial *and* final consonant sounds correspond, as in *green* and *groan, moon* and *mine*. *Rime* (or rhyme) has been used to mean any sound repetition, including alliteration, assonance, and consonance. In the absence of clear agreement on the meanings of these terms, the terminology chosen here has appeared most useful, with support in usage. Labels are useful in analysis. The student should, however, learn to recognize the devices and, more important, to see their function, without worrying too much over nomenclature.

larities too elusive to name. "Dr. Sigmund Freud Discovers the Sea Shell" (page 68), "when serpents bargain for the right to squirm" (page 157), "Poem in October" (page 246), and "Vergissmeinicht" (page 313), among others, employ various kinds of approximate rime.

THAT NIGHT WHEN JOY BEGAN

That night when joy began
Our narrowest veins to flush,
We waited for the flash
Of morning's levelled gun.

But morning let us pass,   5
And day by day relief
Outgrew his nervous laugh,
Grows credulous of peace.

As mile by mile is seen
No trespasser's reproach,   10
And love's best glasses reach
No fields but are his own.

W. H. Auden (b. 1907)

QUESTIONS

1. What has been the past experience with love of the two people in the poem? What is their present experience? What precisely is the tone of the poem?

2. What basic metaphor underlies the poem? Work it out stanza by stanza. What is "the flash of morning's levelled gun"? Does line 10 mean that no trespasser reproaches the lovers or that no one reproaches the lovers for being trespassers? Does *glasses* (11) refer to spectacles, tumblers, or field glasses? Point out three personifications.

3. The rime pattern in this poem is intricate and exact. Work it out, considering alliteration, assonance, and consonance.

In addition to the repetition of individual sounds and syllables, the poet may repeat whole words, phrases, lines, or groups of lines. When such repetition is done according to some fixed pattern, it is called a REFRAIN. The refrain is especially common in songlike poetry. Examples are to be found in Shakespeare's "Winter" (page 6) and "Spring" (page 11).

It is not to be thought that we have exhausted the possibilities of sound repetition by giving names to a few of the more prominent kinds. The complete study of possible kinds of sound repetition in poetry would be so complex that it would break down under its own machinery. Some of the subtlest and loveliest effects escape our net of names. In as short a phrase as this from the prose of John Ruskin—"ivy as light and lovely as the vine"—we notice alliteration in *light* and *lovely*, assonance in *ivy, light,* and *vine,* and consonance in *ivy* and *lovely,* but we have no name to connect the *v* in *vine* with the *v*'s in *ivy* and *lovely,* or the second *l* in *lovely* with the first *l*, or the final syllables of *ivy* and *lovely* with each other; but these are all an effective part of the music of the line. Also contributing to the music of poetry is the use of related rather than identical sounds, such as *m* and *n* or *p* and *b* or the vowel sounds in *boat, boot,* and *book.*

These various musical repetitions, for a trained reader, will ordinarily make an almost subconscious contribution to his reading of the poem: the reader will feel their effect without necessarily being aware of what has caused it. There is value, however, in occasionally analyzing a poem for these devices in order to increase awareness of them. A few words of caution are necessary. First, the repetitions are entirely a matter of sound; spelling is irrelevant. *Bear* and *pair* are rimes, but *through* and *rough* are not. *Cell* and *sin, folly* and *philosophy* alliterate, but *sin* and *sugar, gun* and *gem* do not. Second, alliteration, assonance, consonance, and masculine rime are matters that ordinarily involve only stressed or accented syllables; for only such syllables ordinarily make enough impression on the ear to be significant in the sound pattern of the poem. We should hardly consider *which* and *its* in the second line of "The Turtle," for instance, as an example of assonance, for neither word is stressed enough in the reading to make it significant as a sound. Third, the words involved in these repetitions must be close enough together that the ear retains the sound, consciously or subconsciously, from its first occurrence to its second. This distance varies according to circumstances, but for alliteration, assonance, and consonance the words ordinarily have to be in the same line or adjacent lines. End rime bridges a longer gap.

A FORSAKEN GARDEN

In a coign of the cliff between lowland and highland,
    At the sea-down's edge between windward and lee,
Walled round with rocks as an inland island,
    The ghost of a garden fronts the sea.
A girdle of brushwood and thorn encloses   5
    The steep square slope of the blossomless bed
Where the weeds that grew green from the graves of its roses
    Now lie dead.

The fields fall southward, abrupt and broken,
    To the low last edge of the long lone land.   10
If a step should sound or a word be spoken,
    Would a ghost not rise at the strange guest's hand?
So long have the grey bare walks lain guestless,
    Through branches and briars if a man make way,
He shall find no life but the sea-wind's, restless   15
    Night and day.

The dense hard passage is blind and stifled
    That crawls by a track none turn to climb
To the strait waste place that the years have rifled
    Of all but the thorns that are touched not of time.   20
The thorns he spares when the rose is taken;
    The rocks are left when he wastes the plain.
The wind that waters, the weeds wind-shaken,
    These remain.

Not a flower to be pressed of the foot that falls not;   25
    As the heart of a dead man the seed-plots are dry;
From the thicket of thorns whence the nightingale calls not,
    Could she call, there were never a rose to reply.
Over the meadows that blossom and wither
    Rings but the note of a sea-bird's song;   30
Only the sun and the rain come hither
    All year long.

The sun burns sere and the rain dishevels
    One gaunt bleak blossom of scentless breath.
Only the wind here hovers and revels   35
    In a round where life seems barren as death.

Here there was laughing of old, there was weeping
   Haply, of lovers none ever will know,
Whose eyes went seaward a hundred sleeping
     Years ago.   40

Heart handfast in heart as they stood, "Look thither,"
   Did he whisper? "look forth from the flowers to the sea;
For the foam-flowers endure when the rose-blossoms wither,
   And men that love lightly may die—but we?"
And the same wind sang and the same waves whitened,   45
   And or ever the garden's last petals were shed,
In the lips that had whispered, the eyes that had lightened,
     Love was dead.

Or they loved their life through, and then went whither?
   And were one to the end—but what end who knows?   50
Love deep as the sea as a rose must wither,
   As the rose-red seaweed that mocks the rose.
Shall the dead take thought for the dead to love them?
   What love was ever as deep as a grave?
They are loveless now as the grass above them   55
     Or the wave.

All are at one now, roses and lovers,
   Not known of the cliffs and the fields and the sea.
Not a breath of the time that has been hovers
   In the air now soft with a summer to be.   60
Not a breath shall there sweeten the seasons hereafter
   Of the flowers or the lovers that laugh now or weep,
When as they that are free now of weeping and laughter
     We shall sleep.

Here death may deal not again for ever;   65
   Here change may come not till all change end.
From the graves they have made they shall rise up never,
   Who have left nought living to ravage and rend.
Earth, stones, and thorns of the wild ground growing,
   While the sun and the rain live, these shall be;   70
Till a last wind's breath upon all these blowing
     Roll the sea.

Till the slow sea rise and the sheer cliff crumble,
  Till the terrace and meadow the deep gulfs drink,
Till the strength of the waves of the high tides humble   75
  The fields that lessen, the rocks that shrink,
Here now in his triumph where all things falter,
  Stretched out on the spoils that his own hand spread,
As a god self-slain on his own strange altar,
  <u>Death lies dead.</u> *— Suggests immortality*   80

Algernon Charles Swinburne (1837–1909)

QUESTIONS   *advantageous position before*

1. Vocabulary: *coign* (1), *or* (46).
2. What meanings does the garden symbolize? What does the poem say or suggest about beauty? Love? Life? Does the poet believe in immortality?
3. What parts of the poem deal with the past? Which with the present? Which with the future? Why are all three necessary to the theme of the poem?
4. Explain the paradox in the last two lines.
5. Copy the first two stanzas (double-space if you typewrite), and, using different-colored pencils, encircle and tie together all examples of alliteration, assonance, consonance, alliteration combined with assonance, alliteration combined with consonance, internal rime, internal half-rime, masculine end rime, and feminine end rime. In addition, point out notable examples of assonance and of alliteration in stanza 3, of word repetition in stanza 7. Do these exhaust the kinds of musical repetition used in the poem?
6. The short final line brings each stanza effectively to an end. Does it differ from the other lines only in length, or is it also rhythmically different?
7. What are the primary sources of the appeal of this poem?

We should not leave the impression that the use of these musical devices is necessarily or always valuable. Like the other resources of poetry, they can be judged only in the light of the poem's total intention. Many of the greatest works of English poetry—for instance, *Hamlet* and *King Lear* and *Paradise Lost*—do not employ end rime. Both alliteration and rime, especially feminine rime, if used excessively or unskillfully, become humorous or silly. If the intention is humorous, the result is delightful; if not, fatal. Shakespeare, who knew how to use all these devices to the utmost advantage, parodied their unskillful use in lines like

"The preyful princess pierced and pricked a pretty pleasing pricket" in *Love's Labor's Lost* and

> Whereat with blade, with bloody, blameful blade,
> He bravely broached his boiling bloody breast

in *Midsummer Night's Dream*. Swinburne parodied his own highly alliterative style in "Nephelidia" with lines like "Life is the lust of a lamp for the light that is dark till the dawn of the day when we die." Used skillfully and judiciously, however, musical devices provide a palpable and delicate pleasure to the ear and, even more important, add dimension to meaning.

EXERCISES

Discuss the various ways in which the following poems make use of refrain:

1. "Winter," page 6.
2. "Spring," page 11.
3. "The House on the Hill," page 106.
4. "The Shield of Achilles," page 141.
5. "The Waking," page 208.
6. "Oh Who Is That Young Sinner," page 209.
7. "The Barrel-Organ," page 210.
8. "Boot and Saddle," page 227.
9. "Night of Spring," page 228.
10. "The Bench of Boors," page 233.
11. "Edward," page 250.
12. "Fugal Chorus," page 253.
13. "Cha Till Maccruimein," page 272.
14. "Spring," page 334.
15. "Do Not Go Gentle into That Good Night," page 348.

GOD'S GRANDEUR ✓

The world is charged with the grandeur of God.
    It will flame out, like shining from shook foil;
    It gathers to a greatness, like the ooze of oil
Crushed. Why do men then now not reck his rod?
Generations have trod, have trod, have trod;   5
    And all is seared with trade; bleared, smeared with toil;
    And wears man's smudge and shares man's smell: the soil
Is bare now, nor can foot feel, being shod.

And for all this, nature is never spent;

    There lives the dearest freshness deep down things;   10

And though the last lights off the black West went

    Oh, morning, at the brown brink eastward, springs—

Because the Holy Ghost over the bent

    World broods with warm breast and with ah! bright wings.

Gerard Manley Hopkins (1844–1889)

QUESTIONS

1. What is the theme of this sonnet?

2. The image in lines 3–4 refers probably to olive oil being collected in great vats from crushed olives. Explain the simile in line 2 and the symbols in lines 7–8 and 11–12.

3. Explain "reck his rod" (4), "spent" (9), "bent" (13).

4. Using different-colored pencils, encircle and connect examples of alliteration, assonance, consonance, and internal rime. Do these help to carry the meaning?

THE HARBOR

    Passing through huddled and ugly walls,

    By doorways where women haggard

    Looked from their hunger-deep eyes,

    Haunted with shadows of hunger-hands,

    Out from the huddled and ugly walls,   5

    I came sudden, at the city's edge,

    On a blue burst of lake—

    Long lake waves breaking under the sun

    On a spray-flung curve of shore;

    And a fluttering storm of gulls,   10

    Masses of great gray wings

    And flying white bellies

    Veering and wheeling free in the open.

Carl Sandburg (1878–1967)

QUESTIONS

1. Define as precisely as possible the contrast in content between the first five and the last seven lines of the poem. What qualities are symbolized by the gulls? What judgment is made by means of the contrast?

2. This poem is in free verse (without meter) and does not rime. But you should be able to find examples of assonance in almost every line. Underline or draw circles around the repeated vowels. What vowel sound dominates the first six lines? Does the pattern change in the last seven? If so, what function is served by this change?

3. What consonant sounds are most prominent in the first six lines? Is there a change in the last seven? Why?

I HEAR AN ARMY

I hear an army charging upon the land,
    And the thunder of horses plunging, foam about their knees:
Arrogant, in black armor, behind them stand,
    Disdaining the reins, with fluttering whips, the charioteers.

They cry unto the night their battle-name: 5
    I moan in sleep when I hear afar their whirling laughter.
They cleave the gloom of dreams, a blinding flame,
    Clanging, clanging upon the heart as upon an anvil.

They come shaking in triumph their long, green hair:
    They come out of the sea and run shouting by the shore.   10
My heart, have you no wisdom thus to despair?
    My love, my love, my love, why have you left me alone?

James Joyce (1882–1941)

QUESTIONS

1. What is the rime scheme of the poem? What kinds of rime does it employ?

2. Find examples of assonance, consonance, and alliteration in the poem: circle similar sounds and connect them. Do any of these sound correspondences seem to you to contribute to the meaning? Are there any other types of sound repetition in the poem?

3. What is the situation in the poem? (Who is the speaker? Where is he? Why is he in despair? What are the army and the charioteers?)

4. What different kinds of imagery are used in the poem? What figures of speech? How do they contribute to the meaning of the poem?

PARTING, WITHOUT A SEQUEL

She has finished and sealed the letter
    At last, which he so richly has deserved,

With characters venomous and hatefully curved,   *[handwritten: evil]*   *[handwritten: evil-like serpent]*
And nothing could be better.

But even as she gave it   5
Saying to the blue-capped functioner of doom,
"Into his hands," she hoped the leering groom
Might somewhere lose and leave it.

Then all the blood
Forsook the face. She was too pale for tears,   10
Observing the ruin of her younger years.
She went and stood

Under her father's vaunting oak
Who kept his peace in wind and sun, and glistened
Stoical in the rain; to whom she listened   15
If he spoke.

And now the agitation of the rain   *[handwritten: threadbare]*
Rasped his sere leaves, and he talked low and gentle
Reproaching the wan daughter by the lintel;
Ceasing and beginning again.   20

Away went the messenger's bicycle,
His serpent's track went up the hill forever,   *[handwritten: evil]*
And all the time she stood there hot as fever *[handwritten: — mad]*
And cold as any icicle. *[handwritten: — numb as to what she's done.]*

[handwritten left margin: Confusion]

John Crowe Ransom (b. 1888)

QUESTIONS

1. Identify the figures of speech in lines 3 and 22 and discuss their effectiveness. Are there traces of dramatic irony in the poem? Where?

2. Is the oak literal or figurative? Neither? Both? Discuss the meanings of *vaunting* (13), *stoical* (15), *sere* (18), and *lintel* (19). *[handwritten annotation above: ostentatious or bragging, boastful]*

3. Do you find any trite language in the poem? Where? What does it tell us about the girl's action?

4. W. H. Auden has defined poetry as "the clear expression of mixed feelings." Discuss the applicability of the definition to this poem. Try it out on other poems.

5. A feminine rime that involves two syllables is known also as a DOUBLE RIME. Find examples in the poem of both perfect and approximate

double rimes. A feminine rime that involves three syllables is a TRIPLE RIME. Find one example of a triple rime. Which lines employ masculine or SINGLE RIMES, either perfect or approximate?

WINTER OCEAN

Many-maned scud-thumper, tub
of male whales, maker of worn wood, shrub-
ruster, sky-mocker, rave!
portly pusher of waves, wind-slave.

John Updike (b. 1932)

QUESTIONS

1. The fun of this poem lies chiefly in two features: in its invention of elaborate epithets (descriptive names) for something familiar (in Old English poetry, partially imitated here, these descriptive names were called *kennings*), and in its equally elaborate sound correspondences. How apt are the names? List or chart the sound correspondences. Are they also appropriate?

2. What figure of speech is most central to the poem?

THE HUNT

The dog fox rolls on his lolling tongue
The frosty grape of the morning.
He points his nose to the scent of day,
He slits his eyes to the yellow sun,
He feels in his haunch a rising thunder   5
And his lifted ear takes warning:
   The horn blows true,
   The hounds break through,
   The hunter spreads,
   The huntsman rides,   10
And the red-tailed fox goes under.

The dog fox breaks to a hidden hole
And deep in the fern goes under.
He stiffens haunch and poises pads,
He gulps his spittle and drops his tail,   15

He downs his ears to the gathering thunder,
Crouching as they go over:
> Blowing horn,
> Baying hound,
> Shuddering hoof   20
> Shaking ground,
And the red-tailed fox goes under.

Heavy the huntsman will fall to bed
And heavily snore till morning.
The hunter will drowse and shake the stall   25
With a heavy hoof and hang his head.
The hound will whimper, and done with yawning,
Sleep as the moon goes under,
> And deep in the shade
> Of night will creep   30
> The fox to his feast
> On the feathered roost
And dine till the sun is dawning.

Louis Kent (b. 1910)

QUESTIONS

1. How do the three stanzas organize the poem? What are huntsman, hunter, hounds, and fox doing in each?

2. In each stanza the four short lines have a different syntactical pattern. Describe each.

3. Pick out the most prominent examples of alliteration, assonance, consonance, masculine rime, feminine rime, internal rime, approximate rime. Analyze the four short lines in each stanza for sound. What elements of refrain does the poem have? How much rime pattern does it have? Beyond their purely musical appeal, how do these sound repetitions contribute to the effectiveness of the poem?

THE CHANGELING

Toll no bell for me, dear Father, dear Mother,
> Waste no sighs;
There are my sisters, there is my little brother
> Who plays in the place called Paradise,

Your children all, your children for ever;
　　But I, so wild,
Your disgrace, with the queer brown face, was never,
　　Never, I know, but half your child!

In the garden at play, all day, last summer,
　　　　Far and away I heard   10
The sweet "tweet-tweet" of a strange new-comer,
　　The dearest, clearest call of a bird.
It lived down there in the deep green hollow,
　　My own old home, and the fairies say
The word of a bird is a thing to follow,   15
　　So I was away a night and a day.

One evening, too, by the nursery fire,
　　We snuggled close and sat round so still,
When suddenly as the wind blew higher,
　　Something scratched on the window-sill.   20
A pinched brown face peered in—I shivered;
　　No one listened or seemed to see;
The arms of it waved and the wings of it quivered,
　　Whoo—I knew it had come for me;
　　Some are as bad as bad can be!   25
All night long they danced in the rain,
Round and round in a dripping chain,
Threw their caps at the window-pane,
　　Tried to make me scream and shout
　　And fling the bedclothes all about: 30
I meant to stay in bed that night,
And if only you had left a light
　　They would never have got me out!

　　Sometimes I wouldn't speak, you see,
　　Or answer when you spoke to me,   35
Because in the long, still dusks of Spring
You can hear the whole world whispering:
　　The shy green grasses making love,
　　The feathers grow on the dear, grey dove,
　　The tiny heart of the redstart beat,   40
　　The patter of the squirrel's feet,
The pebbles pushing in the silver streams,

The rushes talking in their dreams,
　　The swish-swish of the bat's black wings,
　　The wild-wood bluebell's sweet ting-tings,　　　　　　　　　45
　　　　Humming and hammering at your ear,
　　　　Everything there is to hear
In the heart of hidden things,
　　But not in the midst of the nursery riot.
　　That's why I wanted to be quiet,　　　　　　　　　　　　50
　　　　Couldn't do my sums, or sing,
　　　　Or settle down to anything.
　　And when, for that, I was sent upstairs
　　I *did* kneel down to say my prayers;
But the King who sits on your high church steeple　　　　　55
Has nothing to do with us fairy people!

'Times I pleased you, dear Father, dear Mother,
　　Learned all my lessons and liked to play,
And dearly I loved the little pale brother
　　Whom some other bird must have called away.　　　　　60
Why did They bring me here to make me
　　Not quite bad and not quite good,
Why, unless They're wicked, do They want, in spite, to take me
　　Back to their wet, wild wood?
Now, every night I shall see the windows shining,　　　　　65
　　The gold lamp's glow, and the fire's red gleam,
While the best of us are twining twigs and the rest of us are whining
　　　　In the hollow by the stream.
Black and chill are Their nights on the wold;
　　And They live so long and They feel no pain:　　　　　　70
I shall grow up, but never grow old,
I shall always, always be very cold,
　　　　I shall never come back again!

Charlotte Mew (1869–1928)

　　1. Vocabulary: *redstart* (40), *wold* (69).
　　2. In fairy lore a changeling is a fairy child, usually defective in some way, that has been left in place of a stolen human baby. What kind of child is the speaker? What characteristics denote him as a changeling?
　　3. Two kinds of world are juxtaposed in the poem: the human world

and the fairy world. What kind of world is each? Does the contrast of the two, even though the fairy world is imaginary, help to illuminate the quality of the human world?

4. How does the speaker feel toward his family, the human world, and the fairy world? Which world does he prefer?

5. Take any ten or twelve lines of the poem and analyze them for internal rime, alliteration, assonance, consonance, masculine end rime, and feminine end rime. How is the effect of these devices different from their effect in the preceding poem?

AUTUMNUS *comparing seasons to cycles of life*

When the leaves in autumn wither,
    With a tawny tannèd face,
Warped and wrinkled-up together,
    The year's late beauty to disgrace: *aging, or old person*

There thy life's glass may'st thou find thee,
    Green now, gray now, gone anon;
    Leaving (worldling) of thine own,
Neither fruit, nor leaf behind thee. *person who hasn't done or accomplished anything*

Joshua Sylvester (1563–1618)

QUESTIONS

1. To whom is the poem addressed? What is the *glass* (5)?
2. Discuss the contribution of musical devices to the structure and meaning of the poem.

HOGAMUS, HIGAMUS

Hogamus, higamus,
Men are polygamous;
Higamus, hogamus,
Woman monogamous.

Anonymous

Rhythm
and Meter

Our love of rhythm and meter is rooted even deeper in us than our love for musical repetition. It is related to the beat of our hearts, the pulse of our blood, the intake and outflow of air from our lungs. Everything that we do naturally and gracefully we do rhythmically. There is rhythm in the way we walk, the way we swim, the way we ride a horse, the way we swing a golf club or a baseball bat. So native is rhythm to us that we read it, when we can, into the mechanical world around us. Our clocks go tick-tick-tick-tick, but we hear them go tick-tock, tick-tock in an endless trochaic. The click of railway wheels beneath us patterns itself into a tune in our heads. There is a strong appeal for us in language that is rhythmical.

The term RHYTHM refers to any wavelike recurrence of motion or sound. In speech it is the natural rise and fall of language. All language is to some degree rhythmical, for all language involves some kind of alternation between accented and unaccented syllables. Language varies considerably, however, in the degree to which it exhibits rhythm. In some forms of speech the rhythm is so unobtrusive or so unpatterned that we are scarcely, if at all, aware of it. In other forms of speech the rhythm is so pronounced that we may be tempted to tap our foot to it.

METER is the kind of rhythm we can tap our foot to. In language that is metrical the accents are so arranged as to occur at apparently equal intervals of time, and it is this interval we mark off with the tap of our foot. Metrical language is called VERSE. Nonmetrical language is

195

PROSE. Not all poetry is metrical, nor is all metrical language poetry. *Verse* and *poetry* are not synonymous terms, nor is a *versifier* necessarily a *poet.*

The study of meter is a fascinating but highly complex subject. It is by no means an absolute prerequisite to an enjoyment, even a rich enjoyment, of poetry. But a knowledge of its fundamentals does have certain values. It can make the beginning reader more aware of the rhythmical effects of poetry and of how poetry should be read. It can enable the more advanced reader to analyze how certain effects are achieved, to see how rhythm is adapted to thought, and to explain what makes one poem (in this respect) better than another. The beginning student ought to have at least an elementary knowledge of the subject. It is not so difficult as its terminology might suggest.

In every word of more than one syllable, one syllable is *accented* or *stressed*, that is, given more prominence in pronunciation than the rest.*
We say to*day*, to*mor*row, *yes*terday, *dai*ly, inter*vene*. If words of even one syllable are arranged into a sentence, we give certain words, or syllables, more prominence in pronunciation than the rest. We say: "He *went* to the *store*," or "*Jack* is *driv*ing his *car*." There is nothing mysterious about this; it is the normal process of language. The only difference between prose and verse is that in prose these accents occur more-or-less haphazardly; in verse the poet has arranged them to occur at regular intervals.

The word *meter* comes from a word meaning "measure." To measure something we must have a unit of measurement. For measuring length we use the inch, the foot, and the yard; for measuring time we use the second, the minute, and the hour. For measuring verse we use the foot, the line, and (sometimes) the stanza.

The basic metrical unit, the FOOT, consists normally of one accented syllable plus one or two unaccented syllables, though occasionally there may be no unaccented syllables, and very rarely there may be three. For diagramming verse, various systems of visual symbols have been invented.

*Though the words *accent* and *stress* are generally used interchangeably, as here, a distinction is sometimes made between them in technical discussions. *Accent*, the relative prominence given a syllable in relation to its neighbors, is then said to result from one or more of four causes: *stress*, or force of utterance, producing loudness; *duration; pitch;* and *juncture*, the manner of transition between successive sounds. Of these, *stress*, in English verse, is most important.

In this book we shall use a short curved line to indicate an unaccented syllable, a short horizontal line to indicate an accented syllable, and a vertical bar to indicate the division between feet. The basic kinds of feet are thus as follows:

Example	Name of foot	Name of meter*	
to-*day*	Iamb	Iambic	Duple meters
dai-ly	Trochee	Trochaic	
in-ter-*vene*	Anapest	Anapestic	Triple meters
yes-ter-day	Dactyl	Dactylic	
day-*break*	Spondee	(Spondaic)	
day	Monosyllabic foot		

The secondary unit of measurement, the LINE, is measured by naming the number of feet in it. The following names are used:

Monometer	one foot	Pentameter	five feet
Dimeter	two feet	Hexameter	six feet
Trimeter	three feet	Heptameter	seven feet
Tetrameter	four feet	Octameter	eight feet

The third unit, the STANZA, consists of a group of lines whose metrical pattern is repeated throughout the poem. Since not all verse is written in stanzas, we shall save our discussion of this unit till a later chapter.

The process of measuring verse is referred to as SCANSION. To *scan* any specimen of verse, we do three things: (1) we identify the prevailing foot, (2) we name the number of feet in a line—if this length follows any regular pattern, and (3) we describe the stanza pattern—if there is one. Suppose we try out our skill on the poem "To Lucasta, Going to the Wars" (page 119).

---

*In the spondee the accent is thought of as being distributed equally or almost equally over the two syllables and is sometimes referred to as a hovering accent. No whole poems are written in spondees or monosyllabic feet; hence there are only four basic meters: iambic, trochaic, anapestic, and dactylic. Iambic and trochaic are DUPLE METERS because they employ two-syllable feet; anapestic and dactylic are TRIPLE METERS because they employ three-syllable feet.

The first step in scanning a poem is to read it normally, listening to where the accents fall, and perhaps keeping time with your hand. In "To Lucasta" we immediately run into difficulty, for the first line is highly irregular and may leave us uncertain as to just where the accents fall. Let us pass over it, then, and look for easier lines. Though the second stanza, we discover, is more regular than the first, the third stanza is the most regular of the three. So let us begin with it. Lines 9, 11, and 12 go regularly, and we mark them as follows:

> ˘ — | ˘ — | ˘ — | ˘ — |
> Yet this in-con-stan-cy is such
>   As you too shall a-dore;   10
> ˘ — | ˘ — | ˘ — | ˘ — |
> I could not love thee, Dear, so much,
>   ˘ — | ˘ — | ˘ — |
>   Loved I not hon-or more.

Line 10 might also be marked regularly, but if we listen carefully we shall probably detect a slightly stronger stress on *too*, though it comes in an unstressed position, than on either of the adjacent syllables. So we'll mark it thus:

> ˘ — | — — | ˘ — |
> As you too shall a-dore.

We now see that this stanza is written in lines of alternating iambic tetrameter and iambic trimeter. Knowing this, we return to the first and second stanzas, expecting them, since they look similar, to conform to a similar pattern.

In the second stanza, lines 7 and 8 are perfectly regular, so we mark them confidently, but lines 5 and 6 offer some variation. Here is what we hear:

> — ˘ — — ˘ — ˘ —
> True, a new mis-tress now I chase,   5
> — — ˘ ˘ —
> The first foe in the field;
> ˘ — | ˘ — | ˘ — | ˘ — |
> And with a strong-er faith em-brace
> ˘ — | ˘ — | ˘ — |
> A sword, a horse, a shield.

Since we are expecting lines 5 and 6 to conform to the established pattern, we shall assume that they are respectively a tetrameter and a trimeter line, and we shall mark the divisions between the feet in such a way as to yield the maximum number of iambs. The result is as follows:

$\smile$ $\smile$|$\smile$ $\smile$|$\smile$ $\smile$|$\smile$ $\smile$|
True, a new mis-tress now I chase,   5
$\smile$ $\smile$|$\smile$ $\smile$|$\smile$ $\smile$|
The first foe in the field.

We are now ready for the difficult first stanza. Following the same process of first marking the accents where we hear them and then dividing the feet so as to yield tetrameter and trimeter lines with the maximum possible number of iambic feet, we get something like the following:

$\smile$ $\smile$|$\smile$ $\smile$ |$\smile$ $\smile$|$\smile$ $\smile$|
Tell me not, Sweet, I am un-kind,
$\smile$ $\smile$ |$\smile$ $\smile$|$\smile$ $\smile$|
That from the nun-ner-y
$\smile$ $\smile$|$\smile$ $\smile$ |$\smile$ $\smile$|$\smile$ $\smile$ |
Of thy chaste breast and qui-et mind
$\smile$ $\smile$|$\smile$ $\smile$ |$\smile$ $\smile$|
To war and arms I fly.

We are now ready to make a few generalizations about scansion.

1. A good reader will not ordinarily stop to scan a poem he is reading, and he certainly will not read a poem with the exaggerated emphasis on accented syllables that we sometimes give them in order to make the scansion more apparent. However, occasional scansion of a poem does have value. We hope to make this more apparent in the next chapter.

2. Scansion is at best a gross way of describing the rhythmical quality of a poem. It depends on classifying all syllables into either accented or unaccented categories and on ignoring the sometimes considerable difference between degrees of accent. Actually "accented" and "unaccented" are relative terms, and seldom will two syllables have exactly the same degree of accent. Whether we call a syllable accented or unaccented depends, moreover, on its degree of accent relative to the syllables on either side of it. In line 7 of "To Lucasta," for instance, the accent on *with* is not nearly so great as the accent on *strong*, and in line 2 the accent on the final *y* in *nunnery* is *lighter* than that on the *un*accented *thee* in line 11. Scansion therefore is incapable of dealing with the subtlest rhythmical effects in poetry. It is nevertheless a useful device, and probably any device more sensitive would be so complicated as to be no longer useful.

3. Scansion is not an altogether exact science. Within certain limits we may say that a certain scansion is right or wrong, but beyond these limits there is legitimate room for personal interpretation and disagreement between qualified readers. Lines 11 and 12 of "To Lucasta," for

instance, have been scanned above as perfectly regular. But a different reader might read line 11 thus:

$$- \cup \mid \cup \ - \mid \ - \quad - \mid \cup \ - \mid$$
I could not love thee, Dear, so much,

or line 12 thus:

$$- \ - \mid \ - \ - \mid \cup \ - \mid$$
Loved I not hon-or more.

The divisions between feet, moreover, are highly arbitrary and have little meaning except to help us name the meter of the poem. They correspond to no real divisions in the reading of the line, coming often, as they do, in the middle of a word. They are placed where they are usually only for the purpose of yielding the most possible of a single kind of foot. Accordingly, line 6 has been marked:

$$\cup \ - \mid - \ \cup \mid \cup \ - \mid$$
The first foe in the field,

though it might more plausibly have been marked:

$$\cup \ - \mid - \mid \cup \ \cup \ - \mid$$
The first foe in the field.

4. Finally—and this is the most important generalization of all— perfect regularity of meter is no criterion of merit. Beginning students sometimes get the notion that it is. If the meter is smooth and perfectly regular, they feel that the poet has handled his meter successfully and deserves all credit for it. Actually there is nothing easier than for any moderately talented versifier to make language go ta-*dum* ta-*dum* ta-*dum*. But there are two reasons why this is not generally desirable. The first is that, as we have said, all art consists essentially of repetition and variation. If a meter alternates too regularly between light and heavy beats, the result is to banish variation; the meter becomes mechanical and, for any sensitive reader, monotonous. The second is that, once a basic meter has been established, any deviations from it become highly significant and are the means by which the poet can use meter to reinforce meaning. If a meter is too perfectly regular, the probability is that the poet, instead of adapting rhythm to meaning, has simply forced his meaning into a metrical straitjacket.

Actually what gives the skillful use of meter its greatest effectiveness is that it consists, not of one rhythm, but of two. One of these is the *expected* rhythm. The other is the *heard* rhythm. Once we have determined the basic meter of a poem, say, iambic tetrameter, we have an expectation that this rhythm will continue. Thus a silent drumbeat is set up in our minds, and this drumbeat constitutes the expected rhythm. But the actual rhythm of the words—the heard rhythm—will sometimes confirm this expected rhythm and sometimes not. Thus the two rhythms are counterpointed against each other, and the appeal of the verse is magnified just as when two melodies are counterpointed against each other in music or as when we see two swallows flying together and around each other, following the same general course but with individual variations and making a much more eye-catching pattern than one swallow flying alone. If the heard rhythm conforms too closely to the expected rhythm, the meter becomes dull and uninteresting. If it departs too far from the expected rhythm, there ceases to be an expected rhythm. If the irregularity is too great, meter disappears, and the result is prose rhythm or free verse.

There are several ways by which variation can be introduced into the poet's use of meter. The most obvious way is by the substitution of different kinds of feet for regular feet. In our scansion of "To Lucasta," for instance, we noted one spondaic and two trochaic substitutions in the very first line. A less obvious but equally important means of variation is through simple phrasing and variation of degrees of accent. Lines 2, 4, 8, and 12 of "To Lucasta" have all been marked as regular, but actually there is considerable difference between them. Line 4 is quite regular, for the phrasing corresponds with the metrical pattern, and the line can be read ta-*dum* ta-*dum* ta-*dum*. Line 8 is even more regular, for the unaccented syllables are all *very* light, the accented syllables are all *very* strong, and the divisions between the feet are marked off by grammatical pauses indicated in the punctuation. This line goes ta-*dumm!* ta-*dumm!* ta-*dumm!* Line 12, on the other hand, is less regular, because the word *honor* cuts across the division between two feet. We should read it ta-*dum* ta-*dum*pty *dum*. And line 2 is even less regular because not only does *nunnery* cut across the division between two feet, but its final syllable is so lightly stressed as hardly to be accented at all. We should read this line something like ta-*dum* ta-*dum*pteree. Finally, variation can be introduced by grammatical and rhetorical pauses. Line 11 of "To Lucasta," though scanned as regular, actually introduces variation because of the pause indicated by the commas around *Dear*.

The uses of rhythm and meter are several. Like the musical repetitions of sound, the musical repetitions of accent can be pleasing for their own sake. In addition, rhythm works as an emotional stimulus and serves, when used skillfully, to heighten our attention and awareness to what is going on in a poem. Finally, by his choice of meter, and by his skillful use of variation within the metrical framework, the poet can adapt the sound of his verse to its content and thus make meter a powerful reinforcement of meaning. We should avoid, however, the notion that there is any mystical correspondence between certain meters and certain emotions. There are no "happy" meters and no "melancholy" ones. The poet's choice of meter is probably less important than how he handles it after he has chosen it. However, some meters are swifter than others, some slower; some are more lilting than others, some more dignified. The poet can choose a meter that is appropriate or one that is inappropriate to his content, and by his handling of it can increase the appropriateness or inappropriateness. If he chooses a swift, lilting meter for a serious and grave subject, the meter will probably act to keep the reader from feeling any really deep emotion. But if he chooses a more dignified meter, it will intensify the emotion. In all great poetry, meter works intimately with the other elements of the poem to produce the appropriate total effect.

We must not forget, of course, that poetry need not be metrical at all. Like alliteration and rime, like metaphor and irony, like even imagery, meter is simply one resource the poet may or may not use. His job is to employ his resources to the best advantage for the object he has in mind—the kind of experience he wishes to express. And on no other basis can we judge him.

EXERCISES

1. Two additional terms that every student should be familiar with and should be careful to discriminate between are *blank verse* and *free verse*. BLANK VERSE is a very specific meter: *iambic pentameter, unrimed*. It has a special name because it is the principal English meter, that is, the meter that has been used for a large proportion of the greatest English poetry, including the tragedies of Shakespeare and the epics of Milton. Iambic pentameter in English seems especially suitable for the serious treatment of serious themes. The natural movement of the English language tends to

be iambic. Lines shorter than pentameter tend to be songlike, not suited to sustained treatment of serious material. Lines longer than pentameter tend to break up into shorter units, the hexameter line being read as two three-foot units, the heptameter line as a four-foot and a three-foot unit, and so on. Rime, while highly appropriate to most short poems, often proves a handicap for a long and lofty work. (The word *blank* implies that the end of the line is "blank," that is, bare of rime.) The above generalizations of course represent tendencies, not laws.

FREE VERSE, by our definition, is not verse at all; that is, it is not metrical. It may be rimed or unrimed. The word *free* means that it is free of metrical restrictions. The only difference between free verse and rhythmical prose is that free verse introduces one additional rhythmical unit, the line. The arrangement into lines divides the material into rhythmical units or cadences. Beyond its line arrangement there are no necessary differences between it and rhythmical prose.

Of the following poems, some are in free verse (*F*), some in blank verse (*B*), and some in other (*O*) meters. Determine into which category each belongs and indicate by putting an *F*, *B*, or *O* after it.

a. "Dulce et Decorum Est," page 8.
b. "It Is Not Growing Like a Tree," page 29.
c. "Portrait d'une Femme," page 52.
d. "Driving to Town Late to Mail a Letter," page 63.
e. "Ulysses," page 96.
f. "Out, Out—," page 135.
g. "Go West Young Man," page 172.
h. "A Christmas Tree," page 256.
i. "City Life," page 328.
j. "There Was a Child Went Forth," page 349.

2. Another useful distinction is that between end-stopped lines and run-on lines. An END-STOPPED LINE is one in which the end of the line corresponds with a natural speech pause; a RUN-ON LINE is one in which the sense of the line hurries on into the next line. (There are, of course, all degrees of end-stop and run-on. A line ending with a period or semicolon is heavily end-stopped. A line without punctuation at the end but representing a slight pause between phrases or sense units would be lightly end-stopped.) The use of run-on lines is one way the poet can make use of grammatical or rhetorical pauses to vary his basic meter. Examine, for instance, Swift's "A Description of the Morning" (page 60) and Browning's "My Last Duchess" (page 131). Both of these poems are written in the same meter: iambic pentameter, rimed in couplets. Is their general rhythmical effect quite similar or markedly different? What accounts for the difference? Does this contrast support our statement that

the poet's choice of meter is probably less important than the way he handles it?

VIRTUE

Sweet day, so cool, so calm, so bright,
  The bridal of the earth and sky;
The dew shall weep thy fall to night,
  For thou must die.

Sweet rose, whose hue, angry and brave,   5
  Bids the rash gazer wipe his eye;
Thy root is ever in its grave,
  And thou must die.

Sweet spring, full of sweet days and roses,
  A box where sweets compacted lie;   10
My music shows ye have your closes,
  And all must die.

Only a sweet and virtuous soul,
  Like seasoned timber, never gives;
But though the whole world turn to coal,   15
  Then chiefly lives.

George Herbert (1593–1633)

QUESTIONS

1. Vocabulary: *brave* (5), *closes* (11).

2. How are the four stanzas interconnected? How do they build to a climax? How does the fourth contrast with the first three?

3. Scan the poem, identify its meter, and point out the principal variations from the expected rhythm.

THE OAK

Live thy Life,
  Young and old,
Like yon oak,
Bright in spring,
  Living gold;   5

Summer-rich
Then; and then
Autumn-changed,
Soberer-hued
Gold again.   10

All his leaves
Fall'n at length,
Look, he stands,
Trunk and bough,
Naked strength.   15

Alfred, Lord Tennyson (1809–1892)

QUESTIONS

1. Scan the poem without putting in the bar divisions. Should this poem be regarded as iambic or trochaic? Could it be either? Some metrists have discarded the traditional distinction between iambic and trochaic and between anapestic and dactylic as being artificial. The only real distinction, they feel, is between duple and triple meters. Does this poem support their claim?

2. With the above question in mind, turn to Donne's "Song: Go and Catch a Falling Star" (page 312) and scan it. How would you classify it?

THE "JE NE SAIS QUOI"

Yes, I'm in love, I feel it now,
    And Celia has undone me;
And yet I'll swear I can't tell how
    The pleasing plague stole on me.

'Tis not her face that love creates,   5
    For there no Graces revel;
'Tis not her shape, for there the Fates
    Have rather been uncivil.

'Tis not her air, for sure in that,
    There's nothing more than common;   10
And all her sense is only chat,
    Like any other woman.

Her voice, her touch, might give the alarm—
    'Tis both perhaps, or neither;

> In short, 'tis that provoking charm
>   Of Celia altogether.

William Whitehead (1715–1785)

QUESTIONS

1. *Je ne sais quoi* is a French expression meaning "I do not know what" —an indefinable something. Does the use of approximate rimes rather than perfect rimes in the even lines of this poem help to establish the quality of uncertainty which is the subject of the poem?

2. Find examples of OXYMORON (a compact paradox in which two successive words seemingly contradict each other) in the first and last stanzas. What broad paradox underlies the whole poem?

3. What is the reason for the capitalization and pluralization of grace and fate in the second stanza? What is the image here conveyed? Is *love* (5) the subject or object of the verb?

4. Because of the feminine rimes of the even-numbered lines, you will find, on scanning the poem, that there is an extra unaccented syllable left over in these lines. For instance, the first two lines may be scanned as follows:

> ˘   ‒ | ˘   ‒ | ˘ ‒ | ˘   ‒ |
> Yes, I'm in love, I feel it now,
> ˘   ‒ | ˘   ‒ | ˘   ‒ | ˘
> And Cel-ia has un-done me.

It will often happen that one or two unaccented syllables are left over—at the end of the line with iambic and anapestic meter, at the beginning of the line with trochaic and dactylic meter. Although we ignore these unaccented extras in naming the meter (the above poem is written in alternating iambic tetrameter and iambic trimeter), they make considerable difference in the rhythmical effect. They are another way the poet can vary his basic meter.

5. All the lines of Tennyson's "The Oak" begin and end with accented syllables (the rimes are masculine); half of the lines of "The 'Je Ne Sais Quoi'" begin and end with unaccented syllables (and have feminine rimes). Do you see any correlation between this metrical difference of the two poems and their difference of subject? Could the subject matter of either poem be treated as successfully in the meter of the other?

IF EVERYTHING HAPPENS THAT CAN'T BE DONE

> if everything happens that can't be done
>   (and anything's righter
>   than books
>   could plan)

the stupidest teacher will almost guess   5
(with a run
skip
around we go yes)
there's nothing as something as one

one hasn't a why or because or although   10
(and buds know better
than books
don't grow)
one's anything old being everything new
(with a what   15
which
around we come who)
one's everyanything so

so world is a leaf so tree is a bough
(and birds sing sweeter   20
than books
tell how)
so here is away and so your is a my
(with a down
up   25
around again fly)
forever was never till now

now i love you and you love me
(and books are shuter
than books   30
can be)
and deep in the high that does nothing but fall
(with a shout
each
around we go all)   35
there's somebody calling who's we

we're anything brighter than even the sun
(we're everything greater
than books
might mean)   40
we're everyanything more than believe

      (with a spin
      leap
      alive we're alive)
      we're wonderful one times one   45

                              e. e. cummings (1894–1962)

QUESTIONS

   1. Explain the last line. Of what very familiar idea is this poem a fresh treatment?

   2. The poem is based on a contrast between heart and mind, or love and learning. Which does the poet prefer? What symbols does he use for each?

   3. What is the tone of the poem?

   4. Which lines of each stanza regularly rime with each other (either perfect or approximate rime)? How does the poet link the stanzas together?

   5. What is the basic metrical scheme of the poem? What does the meter contribute to the tone? What line (in the fifth stanza) most clearly states the subject and occasion of the poem? How does meter underline its significance?

   6. Can you suggest any reason why the poet wrote lines 2–4 and 6–8 of each stanza as three lines rather than one? What metrical variations does the poet use in lines 6–8 of each stanza and with what effect?

THE WAKING*

      I wake to sleep, and take my waking slow.
      I feel my fate in what I cannot fear.
      I learn by going where I have to go.

      We think by feeling. What is there to know?
      I hear my being dance from ear to ear.   5
      I wake to sleep, and take my waking slow.

      Of those so close beside me, which are you?
      God bless the Ground! I shall walk softly there,
      And learn by going where I have to go.

      Light takes the Tree; but who can tell us how?   10
      The lowly worm climbs up a winding stair;
      I wake to sleep, and take my waking slow.

      Great Nature has another thing to do
      To you and me; so take the lively air,
      And, lovely, learn by going where to go.   15

   *Mr. Roethke recorded "The Waking" (LP, Folkways, FL 9736).

This shaking keeps me steady. I should know.
What falls away is always. And is near.
I wake to sleep, and take my waking slow.
I learn by going where I have to go.

Theodore Roethke (1908–1963)

QUESTIONS

1. The tone of this poem will probably become clear before its actual sense. If so, what assertion made by the poem does this fact support? What attitude does the poem express toward life and death?

2. The statements made in the poem seem disconnected rather than logically consecutive. Is their disconnectedness related or unrelated to the thought content? Is the poem as a whole coherent or incoherent? Discuss.

3. Identify and discuss the paradoxes of the poem. Why are they appropriate?

4. Much of the poem's appeal lies in its sound qualities and its pronounced, stately rhythm. Discuss both. What effect is produced by the heavily end-stopped lines? Does the poem anywhere vary from strict metrical regularity? What keeps its regularity from becoming tedious?

OH WHO IS THAT YOUNG SINNER

Oh who is that young sinner with the handcuffs on his wrists?
And what has he been after that they groan and shake their fists?
And wherefore is he wearing such a conscience-stricken air?
Oh they're taking him to prison for the color of his hair.

'Tis a shame to human nature, such a head of hair as his;   5
In the good old time 'twas hanging for the color that it is;
Though hanging isn't bad enough and flaying would be fair
For the nameless and abominable color of his hair.

Oh a deal of pains he's taken and a pretty price he's paid
To hide his poll or dye it of a mentionable shade;   10
But they've pulled the beggar's hat off for the world to see and stare,
And they're taking him to justice for the color of his hair.

Now 'tis oakum for his fingers and the treadmill for his feet,
And the quarry-gang on Portland in the cold and in the heat,
And between his spells of labor in the time he has to spare   15
He can curse the God that made him for the color of his hair.

A. E. Housman (1859–1936)

1. Vocabulary: *poll* (10), *oakum* (13). *Portland* (14), an English peninsula, is the site of a famous criminal prison.

2. What kind of irony does the poem exhibit? Explain.

3. What symbolical meanings are suggested by "the color of his hair"?

4. This poem represents a kind of meter that we have not yet discussed. It *may* be scanned as iambic heptameter:

> ˘ ‿ | ˘ ‿ | ˘ ‿ | ˘ ‿ | ˘ ‿ | ˘ ‿ | ˘ ‿ |
> Oh who is that young sin-ner with the hand-cuffs on his wrists?

But you will probably find yourself reading it as a four-beat line:

> ˘ ‿ | ˘ ˘ ˘ ‿ | ˘ ˘ ˘ ‿ | ˘ ˘ ˘ ‿ |
> Oh who is that young sin-ner with the hand-cuffs on his wrists?

Although the meter is duple insofar as there is an alternation between unaccented and accented syllables, there is also an alternation in the degree of stress on the accented syllables: the first, third, fifth, and seventh stresses being heavier than the second, fourth, and sixth; the result is that the two-syllable feet tend to group themselves into larger units. We may scan it as follows, using a short line for a light accent, a longer one for a heavy accent:

> ˘ —| ˘ ‿ ˘ —| ˘ ‿ ˘ —| ˘ ‿ ˘ — |
> Oh who is that young sin-ner with the hand-cuffs on his wrists?
> ˘ —| ˘ ‿ ˘ —| ˘ ‿ ˘ —| ˘ ‿ ˘ — |
> And what has he been af-ter that they groan and shake their fists?
> ˘ —| ˘ ‿ ˘ —| ˘ ‿ ˘ —| ˘ ‿ — |
> And where-fore is he wear-ing such a con-science-strick-en air?
> ˘ ˘ —| ˘ ‿ ˘ —| ˘ ‿ ˘ —| ˘ ‿ ˘ — |
> Oh they're tak-ing him to pris-on for the col-or of his hair.

This kind of meter, in which there is an alternation between heavy and light stresses, is known as DIPODIC (two-footed) VERSE. The alternation may not be perfect throughout, but it will be frequent enough to establish a pattern in the reader's mind. Now scan the last three stanzas.

5. For another example of dipodic verse, see "America for Me" (page 276).

THE BARREL-ORGAN

There's a barrel-organ carolling across a golden street
    In the City as the sun sinks low,
With a silvery cry of linnets in its dull mechanic beat,
    As it dies into the sunset glow;
And it pulses through the pleasures of the City and the pain
    That surround the singing organ like a large eternal light;   5

And they've given it a glory and a part to play again
  In the Symphony that rules the day and night.

And now it's marching onward through the realms of old romance,
  And trolling out a fond familiar tune,   10
And now it's roaring cannon down to fight the King of France,
  And now it's prattling softly to the moon,
And all around the organ there's a sea without a shore
  Of human joys and wonders and regrets,
To remember and to recompense the music evermore   15
  For what the cold machinery forgets. . . .

            Yes; as the music changes,
              Like a prismatic glass,
            It takes the light and ranges
              Through all the moods that pass;   20
            Dissects the common carnival
              Of passions and regrets,
            And gives the world a glimpse of all
              The colors it forgets.

            And there *La Traviata* sighs   25
              Another sadder song;
            And there *Il Trovatore* cries
              A tale of deeper wrong;
            And bolder knights to battle go
              With sword and shield and lance,   30
            Than ever here on earth below
              Have whirled into—*a dance!*—

Go down to Kew in lilac-time, in lilac-time, in lilac-time;
  Go down to Kew in lilac-time (it isn't far from London!)
And you shall wander hand in hand with love in summer's wonderland;   35
  Go down to Kew in lilac-time (it isn't far from London!)

The cherry-trees are seas of bloom and soft perfume and sweet perfume,
  The cherry-trees are seas of bloom (and oh, so near to London!)
And there they say, when dawn is high and all the world's a blaze of sky
  The cuckoo, though he's very shy, will sing a song for London.   40

The Dorian nightingale is rare and yet they say you'll hear him there
  At Kew, at Kew in lilac-time (and oh, so near to London!)

The linnet and the throstle, too, and after dark the long halloo
   And golden-eyed *tu-whit, tu-whoo* of owls that ogle London.

For Noah hardly knew a bird of any kind that isn't heard   45
   At Kew, at Kew in lilac-time (and oh, so near to London!)
And when the rose begins to pout and all the chestnut spires are out
   You'll hear the rest without a doubt, all chorusing for London:—

Come down to Kew in lilac-time, in lilac-time, in lilac-time;
   Come down to Kew in lilac-time (it isn't far from London!)   50
And you shall wander hand in hand with love in summer's wonderland;
   Come down to Kew in lilac-time (it isn't far from London!)

And then the troubadour begins to thrill the golden street,
   In the City as the sun sinks low;
And in all the gaudy busses there are scores of weary feet   55
Marking time, sweet time, with a dull mechanic beat,
And a thousand hearts are plunging to a love they'll never meet,
Through the meadows of the sunset, through the poppies and the wheat,
   In the land where the dead dreams go.

                    .   .   .   .

         So it's Jeremiah, Jeremiah,   60
            What have you to say
         When you meet the garland girls
            Tripping on their way?

         All around my gala hat
            I wear a wreath of roses   65
         (A long and lonely year it is
            I've waited for the May!)
         If any one should ask you,
            The reason why I wear it is—
         My own love, my true love   70
            Is coming home to-day.

      And it's buy a bunch of violets for the lady
         (*It's lilac-time in London; it's lilac-time in London!*)
      Buy a bunch of violets for the lady
         While the sky burns blue above: 75

      On the other side the street you'll find it shady
         (*It's lilac-time in London; it's lilac-time in London!*)

> But buy a bunch of violets for the lady,
>   And tell her she's your own true love.

There's a barrel-organ carolling across a golden street   80
    In the City as the sun sinks glittering and slow;
And the music's not immortal; but the world has made it sweet
And enriched it with the harmonies that make a song complete
In the deeper heavens of music where the night and morning meet,
    As it dies into the sunset-glow;   85
And it pulses through the pleasures of the City and the pain
    That surround the singing organ like a large eternal light,
And they've given it a glory and a part to play again
    In the Symphony that rules the day and night.

            And there, as the music changes,   90
                The song runs round again.
            Once more it turns and ranges
                Through all its joy and pain,
            Dissects the common carnival
                Of passions and regrets;   95
            And the wheeling world remembers all
                The wheeling song forgets.

            Once more *La Traviata* sighs
                Another sadder song:
            Once more *Il Trovatore* cries   100
                A tale of deeper wrong;
            Once more the knights to battle go
                With sword and shield and lance
            Till once, once more, the shattered foe
                Has whirled into—*a dance!*   105

Come down to Kew in lilac-time, in lilac-time, in lilac-time;
    Come down to Kew in lilac-time (it isn't far from London!)
And you shall wander hand in hand with love in summer's wonderland;
    Come down to Kew in lilac-time (it isn't far from London!)

                                    Alfred Noyes (1880–1958)

QUESTIONS

    1. A barrel-organ is a mechanical hand organ played by turning a crank.
The City is the business section of London. Kew, a suburb of London, is

famous for its large public gardens. *La Traviata* and *Il Trovatore* are popular operas by Verdi. What precisely is the hour of the day in the poem?

2. The poem describes the music of the barrel-organ and its effect on the people on the street. Lines 17–52, 60–79, and 90–109 represent melodies played by the organ. How many different melodies are metrically indicated? What effect does the music have on the people? Do the people have any effect on the music?

3. The four-line refrain with which the poem ends is about as appealing for pure melodiousness as anything in poetry. Analyze the musical devices which it makes use of and try to account for its effectiveness.

4. The narrative stanzas and two of the songs are in dipodic verse* and illustrate additional varieties of dipodic feet. Notice that a dipodic foot (like a spondee in duple meter) *may* have no unaccented syllables at all:

$$\_ \; \breve{} \_\_ | \_ \; \breve{} \_\_ | \_ \; \breve{} \_\_ \; \breve{} \; \_\_ |$$
There's a bar-rel-or-gan car-ol-ling a-cross a gold-en street
$$\breve{} \; \breve{} \; \_\_ | \breve{} \_ \; \breve{} \_\_ | \_ \; \breve{} \_\_ |$$
In the Cit-y as the sun sinks low.

An additional variation is the metrical pause or rest. Unlike grammatical and rhetorical pauses, the metrical pause affects the scansion. If you beat out the rhythm of lines 72–75 with your hand, you will find that some of the beats fall *between* syllables. The METRICAL PAUSE, then, is a pause that replaces an accented syllable. It is usually found in verse that has a pronounced lilt or swing. We have represented it in the scansion with an *x*:

$$\breve{} \; \breve{} \; \_\_ | \breve{} \_ \; \breve{} \_\_ | \breve{} \; \breve{} \_\_ \breve{} | \breve{}_x$$
And it's buy a bunch of vi-o-lets for the la-dy
$$\breve{} \_\_ | \breve{} \_ \; \breve{} \_\_ | \breve{}_x \breve{} \_\_ | \breve{} \_ \; \breve{} \_\_ | \breve{}_x$$
(*It's li-lac-time in Lon-don; it's li-lac-time in Lon-don!*)
$$\_\_ | \_ \; \breve{} \_\_ \breve{} \_\_ | \breve{}_x$$
Buy a bunch of vi-o-lets for the la-dy
$$\breve{} \; \breve{} \_\_ | \_ \; \_\_ |_x \breve{} \_\_ |$$
While the sky burns blue a-bove.

Scan the rest of this song, and also the song before it, looking out for metrical pauses.

METRICAL FEET

$$\_ \; \breve{} \; \breve{} \; \_ \; \breve{} \; \_\_$$
Trochee trips from long to short.

From long to long in solemn sort
$$\_ \_ \_ \_ \_ \_$$
Slow Spondee stalks; strong foot! yet ill able

*See question 4 to "Oh Who Is That Young Sinner" (page 210) for definition of dipodic.

‾ ◡ ◡   ‾   ◡   ◡   ◡   ‾ ◡ ◡   ‾ ◡ ◡
Ever to come up with Dactyl trisyllable.

◡ ‾ ◡   ‾   ◡   ‾ ◡   ‾
Iambics march from short to long;—

◡ ◡ ‾   ◡ ◡   ‾   ◡ ◡   ‾ ◡ ◡   ‾
With a leap and a bound the swift Anapests throng.

Samuel Taylor Coleridge (1772–1834)

QUESTION

If you have trouble remembering the metrical feet, memorize this.

HAD I THE CHOICE

Had I the choice to tally greatest bards,
To limn their portraits, stately, beautiful, and emulate at will,
Homer with all his wars and warriors—Hector, Achilles, Ajax,
Or Shakespeare's woe-entangled Hamlet, Lear, Othello—Tennyson's fair
   ladies,
Meter or wit the best, or choice conceit to wield in perfect rhyme, delight of
   singers;
These, these, O sea, all these I'd gladly barter,
Would you the undulation of one wave, its trick to me transfer,
Or breathe one breath of yours upon my verse,
And leave its odor there.

Walt Whitman (1819–1892)

QUESTIONS

   1. Vocabulary: *limn* (2), *conceit* (5).
   2. What poetic qualities does Whitman propose to barter and in exchange for what? What qualities do the sea and its waves symbolize?
   3. What kind of "verse" is this? Why does Whitman prefer it to "meter" and "perfect rhyme"?

Sound
and Meaning

Rhythm and sound cooperate to produce what we call the music of poetry. This music, as we have pointed out, may serve two general functions: it may be enjoyable in itself; it may be used to reinforce meaning and intensify the communication.

Pure pleasure in sound and rhythm exists from a very early age in the human being—probably from the age the baby first starts cooing in its cradle, certainly from the age that children begin chanting nursery rimes and skipping rope. The appeal of the following verse, for instance, depends almost entirely on its "music":

Pease por-ridge hot,
Pease por-ridge cold,
Pease por-ridge in the pot
Nine days old.

There is very little sense here; the attraction comes from the emphatic rhythm, the emphatic rimes (with a strong contrast between the short vowel and short final consonant of *hot-pot* and the long vowel and long final consonant combination of *cold-old*), and the heavy alliteration (exactly half the words begin with *p*). From nonsense rimes such as this, many of us graduate into a love of more meaningful poems whose appeal resides largely in the sound they make. Much of the pleasure that we find in Swinburne's "A Forsaken Garden" (page 183) lies in its musical quality. Other famous examples are Vachel Lindsay's "The Congo," Edgar Allan Poe's "The Bells," and Alfred Noyes's "The Barrel-Organ" (page 210).

The peculiar function of poetry as distinguished from music, however, is to convey not sounds but meaning or experience *through* sounds. In third- and fourth-rate poetry sound and rhythm sometimes distract attention from sense. In first-rate poetry the sound exists, not for its own sake, not for mere decoration, but as a medium of meaning. Its function is to support the leading player, not to steal the scene.

There are numerous ways in which the poet may reinforce meaning through sound. Without claiming to exhaust them, perhaps we can include most of the chief means under four general headings.

First, the poet can choose words whose sound in some degree suggests their meaning. In its narrowest sense this is called onomatopoeia. ONOMATOPOEIA, strictly defined, means the use of words which, at least supposedly, sound like what they mean, such as *hiss, snap,* and *bang.*

SONG: HARK, HARK!

Hark, hark!
  Bow-wow.
The watch-dogs bark!
  Bow-wow.
Hark, hark! I hear
The strain of strutting chanticleer
Cry, "Cock-a-doodle-doo!"

William Shakespeare (1564–1616)

In this lyric, *bark, bow-wow,* and *cock-a-doodle-doo* are onomatopoetic words. In addition Shakespeare has reinforced the onomatopoetic effect with the repeated use of *hark,* which sounds like *bark.* The usefulness of onomatopoeia, of course, is strictly limited, because it can be used only where the poet is describing sound, and most poems do not describe sound. And the use of pure onomatopoeia, as in the above example, is likely to be fairly trivial except as it forms an incidental part of a more complex poem. But by combining onomatopoeia with other devices that help convey meaning, the poet can achieve subtle and beautiful effects whose recognition is one of the keenest pleasures in reading poetry.

217

In addition to onomatopoetic words there is another group of words, sometimes called PHONETIC INTENSIVES, whose sound, by a process as yet obscure, to some degree suggests their meaning. An initial *fl-* sound, for instance, is often associated with the idea of moving light, as in *flame, flare, flash, flicker, flimmer*. An initial *gl-* also frequently accompanies the idea of light, usually unmoving, as in *glare, gleam, glint, glow, glisten*. An initial *sl-* often introduces words meaning "smoothly wet," as in *slippery, slick, slide, slime, slop, slosh, slobber, slushy*. Short *-i-* often goes with the idea of smallness, as in *inch, imp, thin, slim, little, bit, chip, sliver, chink, slit, sip, whit, tittle, snip, wink, glint, glimmer, flicker, pigmy, midge, chick, kid, kitten, minikin, miniature*. Long *-o-* or *-oo-* may suggest melancholy or sorrow, as in *moan, groan, woe, mourn, forlorn, toll, doom, gloom, moody*. Medial and final *-are* sometimes goes with the idea of a big light or noise, as *flare, glare, stare, blare*. Medial *-att-* suggests some kind of particled movement, as in *spatter, scatter, shatter, chatter, rattle, prattle, clatter, batter*. Final *-er* and *-le* indicate repetition, as in *glitter, flutter, shimmer, whisper, jabber, chatter, clatter, sputter, flicker, twitter, mutter*, and *ripple, bubble, twinkle, sparkle, rattle, rumble, jingle*. None of these various sounds is invariably associated with the idea that it seems to suggest, and, in fact, a short *-i-* is found in *thick* as well as *thin*, in *big* as well as *little*. Language is a complex phenomenon. But there is enough association between these sounds and ideas to suggest some sort of intrinsic if obscure relationship, and a word like *flicker*, though not onomatopoetic, for it does not refer to sound, would seem somehow to suggest its sense, the *fl-* suggesting moving light, the *-i-* suggesting smallness, the *-ck-* suggesting sudden cessation of movement (as in *crack, peck, pick, hack*, and *flick*), and the *-er* suggesting repetition. The above list of sound-idea correspondences is only a very partial one. A complete list, though it would involve only a small proportion of words in the language, would probably be a longer list than that of the more strictly onomatopoetic words, to which they are related.

SPLINTER

The voice of the last cricket
across the first frost

is one kind of good-by.
It is so thin a splinter of singing.

Carl Sandburg (1878–1967)

QUESTIONS

1. Why is "so thin a splinter" a better choice of metaphor than "so small an atom" or "so meager a morsel"?

2. How does the poet intensify the effect of the two phonetic intensives in line 4?

Second, the poet can choose sounds and group them so that the effect is smooth and pleasant sounding (*euphonious*) or rough and harsh sounding (*cacophonous*). The vowels are in general more pleasing than the consonants, for the vowels are musical tones, whereas the consonants are merely noises. A line with a high percentage of vowel sounds in proportion to consonant sounds will therefore tend to be more melodious than one in which the proportion is low. The vowels and consonants themselves differ considerably in quality. The "long" vowels, such as those in *fate, reed, rime, coat, food,* and *dune* are fuller and more resonant than the "short" vowels, as in *fat, red, rim, cot, foot,* and *dun.* Of the consonants, some are fairly mellifluous, such as the "liquids," *l, m, n,* and *r;* the soft *v* and *f* sounds; the semi-vowels *w* and *y;* and such combinations as *th* and *wh.* Others, such as the "explosives," *b, d, g, k, p,* and *t,* are harsher and sharper in their effect. These differences in sound are the poet's materials. However, he will not necessarily seek out the sounds that are pleasing and attempt to combine them in melodious combinations. Rather, he will use euphonious and cacophonous combinations as they are appropriate to his content. Consider, for instance, the following poem.

UPON JULIA'S VOICE

So smooth, so sweet, so silv'ry is thy voice,
As, could they hear, the Damned would make no noise,
But listen to thee (walking in thy chamber)
Melting melodious words to Lutes of Amber.

Robert Herrick (1591–1674)

Literally, an amber lute is as nonsensical as a silver voice. What connotations
do *Amber* and *silv'ry* have that contribute to the meaning of this poem?

There are no strictly onomatopoetic words in this poem, and yet the
sound seems marvelously adapted to the sense. Especially remarkable are
the first and last lines, those most directly concerned with Julia's voice.
In the first line the sounds that most strike the ear are the unvoiced *s*'s
and the soft *v*'s, supported by *th*: "So smooth, so sweet, so silv'ry is thy
voice." In the fourth line the predominating sounds are the liquid consonants *m*, *l*, and *r*, supported by a *w*: "Melting melodious words to Lutes
of Amber." The least euphonious line in the poem, on the other hand, is
the second, where the subject is the tormented in hell, not Julia's voice.
Here the prominent sounds are the *d*'s, supported by a voiced *s* (a voiced
s buzzes, unlike the unvoiced *s*'s in line 1), and two *k* sounds: "As,
could they hear, the damned would make no noise." Throughout the
poem there is a remarkable correspondence between the pleasant-sound-
ing and the pleasant in idea, the unpleasant-sounding and the unpleasant
in idea.

A third way in which a poet can reinforce meaning through sound
is by controlling the speed and movement of his lines by his choice and
use of meter, by his choice and arrangement of vowel and consonant
sounds, and by his disposition of pauses. In meter the unaccented syllables go faster than the accented syllables; hence the triple meters are
swifter than the duple. But the poet can vary the tempo of any meter
by the use of substitute feet. Whenever two or more unaccented syllables
come together, the effect will be to speed up the pace of the line; when
two or more accented syllables come together, the effect will be to slow
it down. This pace will also be affected by the vowel lengths and by
whether the sounds are easily run together. The long vowels take longer
to pronounce than the short ones. Some words are easily run together,
while others demand that the position of the mouth be re-formed before
the next word is uttered. It takes much longer, for instance, to say,
"Watch dogs catch much meat" than to say, "My aunt is away," though
the number of syllables is the same. And finally the poet can slow down
the speed of a line through the introduction of grammatical and rhetorical pauses. Consider lines 54–56 from Tennyson's "Ulysses" (page 97):

~ _ | ~ _ | ~ _ | ~ _ | ~ _ |
ᐯ The lights be-gin to twin-kle from the rocks;

~ _ | _ _ | ~ _ | _ _ | ~ _ |
The long day wanes; the slow moon climbs; the deep

_ _ | ~ _ | ~ _ | ~ _ | ~
Moans round with man-y voi-ces. . . .

In these lines Tennyson wished the movement to be slow, in accordance with the slow waning of the long day and the slow climbing of the moon. His meter is iambic pentameter. This is not a swift meter, but in lines 55–56 he slows it down, (1) by introducing three spondaic feet, thus bringing three accented syllables together in three separate places; (2) by choosing for his accented syllables words that have long vowel sounds or diphthongs that the voice hangs on to: *long, day, wanes, slow, moon, climbs, deep, moans, round*; (3) by choosing words that are not easily run together (except for *day* and *slow*, each of these words begins and ends with consonant sounds that demand varying degrees of readjustment of the mouth before pronunciation is continued); (4) by introducing two grammatical pauses, after *wanes* and *climbs*, and a rhetorical pause after *deep*. The result is an extremely effective use of the movement of the verse to accord with the movement suggested by the words.*

A fourth way for a poet to fit sound to sense is to control both sound and meter in such a way as to put emphasis on words that are important in meaning. He can do this by marking out such words by alliteration, assonance, consonance, or rime; by placing them before a pause; or by skillfully placing or displacing them in the metrical pattern. Look again at Shakespeare's "Spring" (page 11):

/ ~ _ | _ _ | ~ _ | ~ _ |
ᐯ When dai-sies pied and vio-lets blue

~ _ | ~ _ | ~ _ | ~ _ |
And la-dy-smocks all sil-ver-white

~ _ | ~ _ | ~ _ | ~ _ |
And cuck-oo-buds of yel-low hue

~ _ | ~ _ | ~ _ | ~ _ |
Do paint the mea-dows with de-light,

~ _ | ~ _ | ~ _ | ~ _ |
The cuck-oo then, on ev-ery tree,

_ _ | ~ _ | ~ _ | ~ _ |
Mocks mar-ried men; for thus sings he,

"Cuckoo!

Cuckoo, cuckoo!" O, word of fear,

Unpleasing to a married ear!

*In addition, Tennyson uses one onomatopoetic word (*moans*) and one phonetic intensive (*twinkle*).

The scansion is regular until the beginning of the sixth line: there we find a spondaic substitution in the first foot. In addition, the first three words in this line are heavily alliterated, all beginning with *m*. And further, each of these words ends in a consonant, thus preventing their being run together. The result is to throw heavy emphasis on these three words: to give them, one might almost say, a tone of solemnity, or mock-solemnity. Whether or not the solemnity is in the sound, the emphasis on these three words is appropriate, for it serves to signal the shift in tone that takes place at this point. The first five lines have contained nothing but delightful images; the concluding four introduce the note of irony.

Just as Shakespeare uses metrical irregularity, plus alliteration, to give emphasis to important words, Tennyson, in the concluding line of "Ulysses," uses marked regularity, plus skillful use of grammatical pause, to achieve the same effect:

> Though much is ta-ken, much a-bides; and though
> We are not now that strength which in old days
> Moved earth and heav-en, that which we are, we are:
> One e-qual tem-per of he-ro-ic hearts,
> Made weak by time and fate, but strong in will
> To strive, to seek, to find, and not to yield.

The blank verse rhythm throughout "Ulysses" is remarkably subtle and varied, but the last line is not only regular in its scansion but heavily regular, for a number of reasons. First, all the words are monosyllables: no words cross over the divisions between feet. Second, the unaccented syllables are all very small and unimportant words—four *to*'s and one *and*, whereas the accented syllables consist of four important verbs and a very important *not*. Third, each of the verbs is followed by a grammatical pause pointed off by a mark of punctuation. The result is to cause a pronounced alternation between light and heavy syllables that brings the accent down on the four verbs and the *not* with sledge-hammer blows. The line rings out like a challenge, which it is.

THE SPAN OF LIFE

The old dog barks backward without getting up.
I can remember when he was a pup.

Robert Frost (1874–1963)

QUESTIONS

1. Is the dog a dog only or also a symbol?
2. The first line presents a visual and auditory image; the second line makes a comment. But does the second line *call up* images? Does it suggest more than it says? Would the poem have been more or less effective if the second line had been, "He was frisky and lively when he was a pup"?

We may well conclude our discussion of the adaptation of sound to sense by analyzing this very brief poem. It consists of one riming anapestic tetrameter couplet. Its content is a contrast between the decrepitude of an old dog and his friskiness as a pup. The scansion is as follows:

The old dog barks back-ward with-out get-ting up.
I can re-mem-ber when he was a pup.

How is sound fitted to sense? In the first place, the triple meter chosen by the poet is a swift meter, but in the first line he has jammed it up in a remarkable way by substituting a kind of foot so rare that we do not even have a name for it. It might be called a triple spondee: at any rate it is a foot in which the accent is distributed over three syllables. This foot, following the accented syllable in the first foot, creates a situation where four accented syllables are pushed up together. In addition, each of these accented syllables begins and ends with a strong consonant sound or cluster of consonant sounds, so that they cannot be run together in pronunciation: the mouth must be re-formed between each syllable: "The *old dog barks backward*." The result is to slow down the line drastically, to almost destroy its rhythmical quality, and to make it difficult to utter. Indeed, the line is as decrepit as the old dog who turns his head but does not get up. When we get to the second line, however, the contrast is startling. The rhythm is swift and regular, the syllables end in vowels or liquid consonants and are easily run together, the whole line ripples fluently off the tongue. In addition, where the first line has a high proportion of explosive and cacophonous consonants—"The *old dog barks backward* without *getting up*"—the second line contains predominantly consonants which are smoother and more graceful—"I *can remember when he was* a pup." Thus the motion and the sound of the lines are remarkably in accord with the visual images they suggest. In addition, in the first line the poet has supported the onomatopoetic word *barks* with a near echo *back,* so that the sound reinforces the auditory image. If the poem does a great deal in just two lines, this skillful adaptation of sound to sense is one very important reason.

In analyzing verse for correspondence between sound and sense, we need to be very cautious not to make exaggerated claims. A great deal of nonsense has been written about the moods of certain meters and the effects of certain sounds, and it is easy to suggest correspondences that exist really only in our imaginations. Nevertheless, the first-rate poet has nearly always an instinctive tact about handling his sound so that it in some degree supports his meaning; the inferior poet is usually obtuse to these correspondences. One of the few absolute rules that can be applied to the judgment of poetry is that the form should be adequate to the content. This rule does not mean that there must always be a close and easily demonstrable correspondence. It does mean that there will be no glaring discrepancies. Poor poets, and even good poets in their third-rate work, sometimes go horribly wrong.

The two selections we introduced this chapter with illustrate, first, the use of sound in verse almost purely for its own sake ("Pease porridge hot"), and second, the use of sound in verse almost purely to *imitate* meaning ("Hark, hark! Bow-wow"), and they are, as significant poetry, perhaps the most trivial pieces in the whole book. But in between these extremes there is an abundant range of poetic possibilities where sound is pleasurable for itself without violating meaning and where sound to varying degrees corresponds with and corroborates meaning; and in this rich middle range, for the reader who can learn to perceive them, lie many of the greatest pleasures of reading poetry.

EXERCISES

In which of the following pairs of quotations is sound more successfully adapted to sense? As precisely as possible, explain why. (The poet whose name is given is in each case the author of the superior version.)

1. a. Go forth—and Virtue, ever in your sight,
      Shall be your guide by day, your guard by night.

   b. Go forth—and Virtue, ever in your sight,
      Shall point your way by day, and keep you safe at night.

Charles Churchill

2. a. How charming is divine philosophy!
      Not harsh and rough as foolish men suppose
      But musical as is the lute of Phoebus.

   b. How charming is divine philosophy!
      Not harsh and crabbed as dull fools suppose
      But musical as is Apollo's lute.

Milton

3. a. All day the fleeing crows croak hoarsely over the snow.

   b. All day the out-cast crows croak hoarsely across the whiteness.

Elizabeth Coatsworth

4. a. Your talk attests how bells of singing gold
      Would sound at evening over silent water.

   b. Your low voice tells how bells of singing gold
      Would sound at twilight over silent water.

Edwin Arlington Robinson

5. a. A thousand streamlets flowing through the lawn,
      The moan of doves in gnarled ancient oaks,
      And quiet murmuring of countless bees.

   b. Myriads of rivulets hurrying through the lawn,
      The moan of doves in immemorial elms,
      And murmuring of innumerable bees.

Tennyson

6. a. It is the lark that sings so out of tune,
      Straining harsh discords and unpleasing sharps.

   b. It is the lark that warbles out of tune
      With harsh discordant voice and hateful flats.

Shakespeare

7. a. "Artillery" and "armaments" and "implements of war"
      Are phrases too severe to please the gentle Muse.

   b. Bombs, drums, guns, bastions, batteries, bayonets, bullets,—
      Hard words, which stick in the soft Muses' gullets.

Byron

8. a. The hands of the sisters Death and Night incessantly softly wash
      again, and ever again, this soiled world.

   b. The hands of the soft twins Death and Night repeatedly wash again,
      and ever again, this dirty world.

Whitman

9. a. The curfew sounds the knell of parting day,
      The lowing cattle slowly cross the lea,
      The plowman goes wearily plodding his homeward way,
      Leaving the world to the darkening night and me.

   b. The curfew tolls the knell of parting day,
      The lowing herd wind slowly o'er the lea,
      The plowman homeward plods his weary way,
      And leaves the world to darkness and to me.

Thomas Gray

10. a. Let me chastise this odious, gilded bug,
       This painted son of dirt, that smells and bites.

    b. Yet let me flap this bug with gilded wings,
       This painted child of dirt, that stinks and stings.

Pope

SOUND AND SENSE

True ease in writing comes from art, not chance,
As those move easiest who have learned to dance.
'Tis not enough no harshness gives offense,
The sound must seem an echo to the sense:
Soft is the strain when Zephyr gently blows,   5
And the smooth stream in smoother numbers flows;
But when loud surges lash the sounding shore,
The hoarse, rough verse should like the torrent roar;
When Ajax strives some rock's vast weight to throw,
The line too labors, and the words move slow;   10
Not so, when swift Camilla scours the plain,
Flies o'er the unbending corn, and skims along the main.
Hear how Timotheus' varied lays surprise,
And bid alternate passions fall and rise!

Alexander Pope (1688–1744)

QUESTIONS

1. Vocabulary: *numbers* (6), *lays* (13).

2. This excerpt is from a long poem (called *An Essay on Criticism*) on the arts of writing and judging poetry. Which line is the topic sentence of the passage?

3. There are four classical allusions: *Zephyr* (5) was god of the west wind; *Ajax* (9), a Greek warrior noted for his strength; *Camilla* (11), a legendary queen reputedly so fleet of foot that she could run over a field of corn without bending the blades or over the sea without wetting her feet; *Timotheus* (13), a famous Greek rhapsodic poet. Does the use of these allusions enable Pope to achieve greater economy?

4. Copy the passage and scan it. Then, considering both meter and sounds, show how Pope practices what he preaches. (Incidentally, on which syllable should *alternate* in line 14 be accented?)

✓BOOT AND SADDLE

Boot, saddle, to horse, and away!
Rescue my castle before the hot day
Brightens to blue from its silvery gray.
    Chorus: Boot, saddle, to horse, and away!

Ride past the suburbs, asleep as you'd say;   5
Many's the friend there, will listen and pray,
"God's luck to gallants that strike up the lay—
    Chorus: Boot, saddle, to horse, and away!"

Forty miles off, like a roebuck at bay,
Flouts Castle Brancepeth the Roundheads' array;   10
Who laughs, "Good fellows ere this, by my fay,°   faith
    Chorus: Boot, saddle, to horse, and away?"

Who? My wife Gertrude; that, honest and gay,
Laughs when you talk of surrendering, "Nay!
I've better counselors; what counsel they?   15
    Chorus: Boot, saddle, to horse, and away!"

Robert Browning (1812–1889)

QUESTIONS

1. Vocabulary: *lay* (7).

2. The historical setting for this song is the English Civil War (1642–1649) between the Royalists (Cavaliers) and the Puritans (Roundheads). Who is the speaker? What is the situation? Who is imagined to be speaking in the three passages between quotation marks?

3. Comment on the choice of meter in relation to the subject, especially on the handling of the meter in the refrain.

NIGHT OF SPRING

Slow, horses, slow,
As through the wood we go—
We would count the stars in heaven,
Hear the grasses grow:

Watch the cloudlets few   5
Dappling the deep blue,
In our open palms outspread
Catch the blessèd dew.

Slow, horses, slow,
As through the wood we go—   10
We would see fair Dian rise
With her huntress bow:

We would hear the breeze
Ruffling the dim trees,
Hear its sweet love-ditty set   15
To endless harmonies.

Slow, horses, slow,
As through the wood we go—
All the beauty of the night
We would learn and know!   20

Thomas Westwood (1814–1888)

QUESTIONS

1. Vocabulary: *Dian* (11).

2. Compare and contrast this poem with the preceding poem in subject and situation, and in adaptation of sound to sense, especially in the refrain.

3. Find phonetic intensives in stanzas 2 and 4. How do the rimes function in stanza 4?

I LIKE TO SEE IT LAP THE MILES

I like to see it lap the miles,
And lick the valleys up,
And stop to feed itself at tanks;
And then, prodigious, step

Around a pile of mountains,   5
And, supercilious, peer
In shanties by the sides of roads;
And then a quarry pare

To fit its ribs,
And crawl between,   10
Complaining all the while
In horrid, hooting stanza;
Then chase itself down hill

And neigh like Boanerges;
Then, punctual as a star,   15
Stop—docile and omnipotent—
At its own stable door.

                              Emily Dickinson (1830–1886)

QUESTIONS

1. Vocabulary: *prodigious* (4), *supercilious* (6). *Boanerges* (14), literally "Sons of Thunder," was possibly the name of a famous horse at the time this poem was written. It commonly refers to a declamatory or vociferous preacher, from Christ's having used it of James and John (Mark 3:17).

2. What basic metaphor underlies the poem? What additional figures do you find in lines 8, 12, 15, 16, and 17? Explain their appropriateness. Is this poem about a locomotive only or a whole train?

3. Point out examples of alliteration, assonance, and consonance. Does this poem have a rime scheme?

4. Considering such matters as sounds and sound repetitions, grammatical pauses, run-on lines, monosyllabic and polysyllabic words, onomatopoeia, and meter, explain in detail how sound is fitted to sense in this poem.

HEAVEN-HAVEN

A Nun Takes the Veil

I have desired to go
        Where springs not fail,
To fields where flies no sharp and sided hail
        And a few lilies blow.

And I have asked to be
        Where no storms come,

Where the green swell is in the havens dumb,
        And out of the swing of the sea.

Gerard Manley Hopkins (1844–1889)

QUESTIONS

1. Who is the speaker and what is the situation? Explain the metaphors that form the substance of the poem. What things are being compared?

2. Comment on the meaning of *springs* (2) and on the effectiveness of the poet's choice of *lilies* (4).

3. How do the sound repetitions of the title reinforce the meaning? Are there other instances in the poem where sound reinforces meaning?

4. Scan the poem. (The meter is basically iambic, but there is a great deal of variation.) How does the meter reinforce meaning, especially in the last line? What purpose is served by the displacement of *not* (2) from its normal order?

SUMMER REMEMBERED

Sounds sum and summon the remembering of summers.
The humming of the sun
The mumbling in the honey-suckle vine
The whirring in the clovered grass
The pizzicato plinkle of ice in an auburn   5
uncle's amber glass.
The whing of father's racquet and the whack
of brother's bat on cousin's ball
and calling voices call-
ing voices spilling voices . . .   10

The munching of saltwater at the splintered dock
the slap and slop of waves on little sloops
The quarreling of oarlocks hours across the bay
The canvas sails that bleat as they
are blown. The heaving buoy bell-   15
ing HERE I am
HERE you are HEAR HEAR

listen listen listen
The gramophone is wound
the music goes round and around   20

BYE   BYE BLUES   LINDY'S COMING
voices calling   calling   calling
"Children! Children! Time's Up
Time's Up"
Merrily sturdily wantonly the familial voices   25
cheerily chidingly call to the children TIME'S UP
and the mute children's unvoiced clamor sacks the summer air
crying Mother   Mother   are you there?

Isabella Gardner (b. 1915)

QUESTIONS

1. In terms of what two things or activities are past summers "remembered" in the poem?

2. "Bye, Bye Blues" and "Lindy's Coming" (21) were popular songs of the 1920s. How do these titles, the title of the poem, and the parents' call to the children point to the true subject of the poem? What has happened in the last two lines?

3. List the onomatopoetic words used. How does the poet reinforce their effect? In what other ways does she use sound to convey or reinforce meaning?

IN MEMORIAM, VII

Dark house, by which once more I stand
    Here in the long unlovely street,
    Doors, where my heart was used to beat
So quickly, waiting for a hand,

A hand that can be clasped no more—   5
    Behold me, for I cannot sleep,
    And like a guilty thing I creep
At earliest morning to the door.

He is not here; but far away
    The noise of life begins again   10
    And ghastly through the drizzling rain
On the bald street breaks the blank day.

Alfred, Lord Tennyson (1809–1892)

1. *In Memoriam* is a sequence of poems composed after the death at the age of twenty-two of the poet's closest friend. Whose is the "dark house" (1)? What is the situation?

2. What function is served by the imagery of the last two lines?

3. Demonstrate how the poet uses sound and meter to reinforce his meaning.

IN MEMORIAM, XXVIII

The time draws near the birth of Christ:
    The moon is hid; the night is still;
    The Christmas bells from hill to hill
Answer each other in the mist.

Four voices of four hamlets round,   5
    From far and near, on mead and moor,
    Swell out and fail, as if a door
Were shut between me and the sound:

Each voice four changes on the wind,
    That now dilate, and now decrease,   10
    Peace and goodwill, goodwill and peace,
Peace and goodwill, to all mankind.

This year I slept and woke with pain,
    I almost wished no more to wake,
    And that my hold on life would break   15
Before I heard those bells again:

But they my troubled spirit rule,
    For they controlled me when a boy;
    They bring me sorrow touched with joy,
The merry merry bells of Yule.   20

Alfred, Lord Tennyson (1809–1892)

QUESTIONS

1. How does the mood of this section differ from that of VII? Why?

2. How does Tennyson, without using onomatopoeia, nevertheless give something of a bell-like sound to this section?

3. How does this section, though written in the same meter as VII, differ in rhythmical effect? How does this difference contribute to the difference in mood? Study especially the placement of grammatical pauses.

4. Contrast the last lines of VII and XXVIII.

ALL DAY I HEAR

All day I hear the noise of waters
    Making moan,
Sad as the sea-bird is, when going
    Forth alone,
He hears the winds cry to the waters'   5
    Monotone.

The grey winds, the cold winds are blowing
    Where I go.
I hear the noise of many waters
    Far below.   10
All day, all night, I hear them flowing
    To and fro.

James Joyce (1882–1941)

QUESTIONS

1. What is the central purpose of the poem? Is it primarily descriptive?
2. What kinds of imagery does the poem contain?
3. Discuss the adaptation of sound to meaning, commenting on the use of onomatopoeia, phonetic intensives, alliteration, consonance, rime, vowel quality, stanzaic structure, the counterpointing of the rhythmically varied long lines with the rhythmically regular short lines.

✓ THE BENCH OF BOORS

In bed I muse on Teniers' boors,
Embrowned and beery losels all:
    A wakeful brain
    Elaborates pain:
Within low doors the slugs of boors   5
Laze and yawn and doze again.

In dreams they doze, the drowsy boors,
Their hazy hovel warm and small:
    Thought's ampler bound
    But chill is found: 10
Within low doors the basking boors
Snugly hug the ember-mound.

Sleepless, I see the slumberous boors
Their blurred eyes blink, their eyelids fall:
    Thought's eager sight   15
    Aches—overbright!
Within low doors the boozy boors
Cat-naps take in pipe-bowl light.

Herman Melville (1819–1891)

QUESTIONS

1. Vocabulary: *boors* (title), *losels* (2), *slugs* (5).
2. David Teniers, the Younger, a seventeenth-century Flemish painter, was famous for his genre paintings of peasant life. What was the essential characteristic of this life according to the poem? What symbolism do you find in the fifth line of each stanza?
3. What is the relation of the third and fourth lines of each stanza to the speaker? To the boors? How does the form of the stanza emphasize the contrast in thought?
4. Comment on other correspondences between sound and meaning.

THE DANCE*

In Breughel's great picture, The Kermess,
the dancers go round, they go round and
around, the squeal and the blare and the
tweedle of bagpipes, a bugle and fiddles
tipping their bellies (round as the thick-   5
sided glasses whose wash they impound)
their hips and their bellies off balance
to turn them. Kicking and rolling about
the Fair Grounds, swinging their butts, those

*Dr. Williams recorded "The Dance" (LP, *Pleasure Dome*, Columbia ML-4259).

shanks must be sound to bear up under such   10
rollicking measures, prance as they dance
in Breughel's great picture, The Kermess.

William Carlos Williams (1883–1963)

QUESTIONS

1. Peter Breughel, the Elder, was a sixteenth-century Flemish painter of peasant life. A kermess is an annual outdoor festival or fair. How do the form, the meter, and the sounds of this poem reinforce its content?

2. Explore the similarities and differences between this poem and the preceding, both as to form and content.

LITTLE DICKY DILVER

Little Dicky Dilver
Had a wife of silver;
He took a stick and broke her back
And sold her to the miller;
The miller wouldn't have her
So he threw her in the river.

Mother Goose Rhyme

QUESTION

Comment on sound and meaning in the title and in the one line that doesn't rime (at least approximately) with the others.

Pattern

Art, ultimately, is organization. It is a searching after order, after form. The primal artistic act was God's creation of the universe out of chaos, shaping the formless into form; and every artist since, on a lesser scale, has sought to imitate Him—by selection and arrangement to reduce the chaotic in experience to a meaningful and pleasing order. For this reason we evaluate a poem partially by the same criteria that an English instructor uses to evaluate a theme— by its unity, its coherence, and its proper placing of emphasis. In a well-constructed poem there is neither too little nor too much; every part of the poem belongs where it is and could be placed nowhere else; any interchanging of two stanzas, two lines, two words, or even two accents, would to some extent damage the poem and make it less effective. We come to feel, with a truly first-rate poem, that the choice and placement of every word is inevitable, that it could not be otherwise.

In addition to the internal ordering of materials, images, ideas, and sounds, the poet may also impose some external pattern on his poem, may give it not only an inside logical order but an outside symmetry. In doing so, he appeals to the human instinct for design, the instinct that makes primitive men tattoo and paint their bodies, later men to decorate their swords and shields with beautiful and complex designs, and modern men to choose patterned ties, carpets, curtains, and wallpapers. The poet appeals to our love of the shapely.

In general, there are three broad kinds of form into which the poet may cast his work: continuous form, stanzaic form, and a fixed form.

In CONTINUOUS FORM, as illustrated by "Had I the Choice" (page 215), "Dover Beach" (page 299), "Ulysses" (page 96), and "My Last

Duchess" (page 131), the element of formal design is slight. The lines follow each other without formal grouping, the only breaks being dictated by units of meaning, as paragraph breaks are in prose. Even here there are degrees of formal pattern. The free verse "Had I the Choice" has neither regular meter nor rime. "Dover Beach," on the other hand, is metrical; it has no regularity in length of line, but the meter is prevailingly iambic. "Ulysses" is regular in both meter and length of line; it is unrimed iambic pentameter, or blank verse. And to these regularities "My Last Duchess" adds regularity of rime, for it is written in riming iambic pentameter couplets. Thus, in increasing degrees, the authors of "Dover Beach," "Ulysses," and "My Last Duchess" have chosen a predetermined pattern in which to cast their work.

In STANZAIC FORM the poet writes in a series of STANZAS, that is, repeated units having the same number of lines, the same metrical pattern, and often an identical rime scheme. The poet may choose some traditional stanza pattern (for poetry, like college, is rich in tradition) or invent his own. The traditional stanza patterns (for example, terza rima, ballad meter, rime royal, Spenserian stanza) are many, and the student specializing in literature will wish to familiarize himself with some of them; the general student should know that they exist. Often the use of one of these traditional stanza forms constitutes a kind of literary allusion. The reader who is conscious of its traditional use or of its use by a previous great poet will be aware of subtleties in the communication that a less well read reader may miss.

As with continuous form, there are degrees of formal pattern in stanzaic form. In "Poem in October" (page 246), for instance, the stanzas are alike in length of line but are without a regular pattern of rime. In "To Lucasta" (page 119), a rime pattern is added to a metrical pattern. In Shakespeare's "Winter" (page 6) and "Spring" (page 11), a refrain is employed in addition to the patterns of meter and rime. The following poem illustrates additional elements of design:

THE GREEDY THE PEOPLE

the greedy the people
(as if as can yes)
they sell and they buy

237

and they die for because
though the bell in the steeple   5
says Why

the chary the wary
(as all as can each)
they don't and they do
and they turn to a which   10
though the moon in her glory
says Who

the busy the millions
(as you're as can i'm)
they flock and they flee   15
through a thunder of seem
though the stars in their silence
say Be

the cunning the craven
(as think as can feel)   20
they when and they how
and they live for until
though the sun in his heaven
says Now

the timid the tender   25
(as doubt as can trust)
they work and they pray
and they bow to a must
though the earth in her splendor
says May   30

e. e. cummings (1894–1962)

QUESTIONS

1. This poem is a constellation of interlocking patterns. To appreciate
them fully, read it first in the normal fashion, one line after another; then
read all the first lines of the stanzas, followed by the second lines, the third
lines, and so on. Having done this, describe (a) the rime scheme; (b) the
metrical design; (c) the sound pattern (How are the two main words in
each of the first lines related?); (d) the syntactical pattern. Prepare a model
of the poem in which the recurring words are written out, blanks are left
for varying words, and recurring parts of speech are indicated in parentheses.

The model for the third lines would be: *they [verb] and they [verb]*. Describe the pattern of meaning. How do the first four lines of each stanza relate to the last two? What blanks in your model are to be filled in by words related in meaning?

2. A trademark of e. e. cummings as a poet is his imaginative freedom with parts of speech. For instance, in line 21 he uses conjunctions as verbs. What different parts of speech does he use as nouns in the fourth line of each stanza? Can you see meanings for these unusual nouns? Explain the contrast between the last words in the fourth and sixth lines of each stanza. What two meanings has the final word of the poem?

3. Sum up briefly the meaning of the poem.

A stanza form may be described by designating four things: the rime scheme (if there is one), the position of the refrain (if there is one), the prevailing metrical foot, and the number of feet in each line. Rime scheme is traditionally designated by using letters of the alphabet to indicate the riming lines, and x for unrimed lines. Refrain lines may be indicated by a capital letter, and the number of feet in the line by a numerical exponent after the letter. Thus the stanza pattern of Browning's "Meeting at Night" (page 55) is iambic tetrameter *abccba* (or iambic *abccba*⁴); that of cummings' "if everything happens that can't be done" (page 206) is anapestic $a^4x^2x^1a^1b^4x^1x^1b^2a^3$; that of Shakespeare's "Spring" (page 11) is iambic $ababcc^4X^1DD^4$.

A FIXED FORM is a traditional pattern that applies to a whole poem. In French poetry many fixed forms have been widely used: rondeaus, roundels, villanelles, triolets, sestinas, ballades, double ballades, and others. In English poetry, though most of the fixed forms have been experimented with, perhaps only two—the limerick and the sonnet—have really taken hold.

The LIMERICK, though really a subliterary form, will serve to illustrate the fixed form in general. Its pattern is anapestic $aa^3bb^2a^3$:

> There was a young la-dy of Ni-ger
> Who smiled as she rode on a ti-ger;
> They re-turned from the ride
> With the la-dy in-side,
> And the smile on the face of the ti-ger.

Anonymous

The limerick form is used exclusively for humorous and nonsense verse, for which, with its swift catchy meter, short lines, and emphatic rimes, it is particularly suitable. By trying to recast these little jokes and bits of nonsense in a different meter and pattern or into prose, we may discover how much of their effect they owe particularly to the limerick form. There is, of course, no magical or mysterious identity between certain forms and certain types of content, but there may be more or less correspondence. A form may be appropriate or inappropriate. The limerick form is apparently inappropriate for the serious treatment of serious material.

The SONNET is less rigidly prescribed than the limerick. It must be fourteen lines in length, and it almost always is iambic pentameter, but in structure and rime scheme there may be considerable leeway. Most sonnets, however, conform more or less closely to one of two general models or types, the Italian and the English.

The ITALIAN or *Petrarchan* SONNET (so called because the Italian poet Petrarch practiced it so extensively) is divided usually between eight lines called the octave, using two rimes arranged *abbaabba*, and six lines called the sestet, using any arrangement of either two or three rimes: *cdcdcd* and *cdecde* are common patterns. Usually in the Italian sonnet, corresponding to the division between octave and sestet indicated by the rime scheme (and sometimes marked off in printing by a space), there is a division in thought. The octave presents a situation and the sestet a comment, or the octave an idea and the sestet an example, or the octave a question and the sestet an answer.

ON FIRST LOOKING INTO CHAPMAN'S HOMER

> Much have I travelled in the realms of gold,
>> And many goodly states and kingdoms seen;
>> Round many western islands have I been
> Which bards in fealty to Apollo hold.
>> Oft of one wide expanse had I been told   5
>> That deep-browed Homer ruled as his demesne;
> Yet did I never breathe its pure serene
> Till I heard Chapman speak out loud and bold:
> Then felt I like some watcher of the skies
>> When a new planet swims into his ken;   10

> Or like stout Cortez when with eagle eyes
> He stared at the Pacific—and all his men
> Looked at each other with a wild surmise—
> Silent, upon a peak in Darien.

John Keats (1795–1821)

QUESTIONS

1. Vocabulary: *fealty* (4), *Apollo* (4), *demesne* (6), *ken* (10), *Darien* (14).

2. John Keats, at twenty-one, could not read Greek, and was probably acquainted with Homer's *Iliad* and *Odyssey* only through the translations of Alexander Pope, which to him would have seemed prosy and stilted. Then one day he and a friend found a vigorous poetic translation by the Elizabethan poet George Chapman. Keats and his friend, enthralled, sat up late at night excitedly reading aloud to each other from Chapman's book. Toward morning Keats walked home and, before going to bed, wrote the above sonnet and sent it to his friend. What common ideas underlie the three major figures of speech in the poem?

3. What is the rime scheme? What division of thought corresponds to the division between octave and sestet?

4. Balboa, not Cortez, discovered the Pacific. Does this mistake seriously detract from the value of the poem? Why or why not?

The ENGLISH or *Shakespearean* SONNET (invented by the English poet Surrey and made famous by Shakespeare) is composed of three quatrains and a concluding couplet, riming *abab cdcd efef gg*. Again, there is usually a correspondence between the units marked off by the rimes and the development of the thought. The three quatrains, for instance, may present three examples and the couplet a conclusion or (as in the following example) three metaphorical statements of one idea plus an application.

THAT TIME OF YEAR

> That time of year thou mayst in me behold
> When yellow leaves, or none, or few, do hang
> Upon those boughs which shake against the cold,
> Bare ruined choirs where late the sweet birds sang.
> In me thou see'st the twilight of such day   5

As after sunset fadeth in the west,
Which by and by black night doth take away,
Death's second self, that seals up all in rest.
In me thou see'st the glowing of such fire,
That on the ashes of his youth doth lie   10
As the deathbed whereon it must expire,
Consumed with that which it was nourished by.
This thou perceivest, which makes thy love more strong,
To love that well which thou must leave ere long.

William Shakespeare (1564–1616)

QUESTIONS

1. What are the three major images introduced by the three quatrains? What do they have in common? Can you see any reason for presenting them in this particular order, or might they be rearranged without loss?

2. Each of the images is to some degree complicated rather than simple. For instance, what additional image is introduced by "bare ruined choirs" (4)? Explain its appropriateness.

3. What additional comparisons are introduced in the second and third quatrains?

4. Explain line 12.

At first glance it may seem absurd that a poet should choose to confine himself in an arbitrary fourteen-line mold with prescribed meter and rime scheme. He does so partly from the desire to carry on a tradition, as all of us carry out certain traditions for their own sake, else why should we bring a tree indoors at Christmas time? But, in addition, the tradition of the sonnet has proved a useful one for, like the limerick, it seems effective for certain types of subject matter and treatment. Though this area cannot be as narrowly limited or as rigidly described as for the limerick, the sonnet is usually most effective when used for the serious treatment of love but has also been used for the discussion of death, religion, political situations, and related subjects. Again, there is no magical affinity between form and subject, or treatment, and excellent sonnets have been written outside these traditional areas. The sonnet tradition has also proved useful because it has provided a challenge to the poet. The inferior poet, of course, is often defeated by that challenge: he will use unnecessary words to fill out his meter or inappropriate words for the sake of his rime. The good poet is inspired by the challenge: it will call forth ideas and images that might not otherwise have come. He will subdue his form rather than be subdued by it; he will make it do his will. There is no doubt that the presence of a net makes good tennis players more precise in their shots than they otherwise would be. And finally, there is in all form the pleasure of form itself.

EXERCISES

1. There are three examples in this book of the French fixed form known as the villanelle. After reading "The House on the Hill" (page 106), "The Waking" (page 208), and "Do Not Go Gentle into That Good Night" (page 348), frame a definition for the villanelle.

2. Most of "John Anderson" (page 169) is written in the stanzaic form known as *terza rima* (most famous for its use by Dante in *The Divine Comedy*). Read the poem and describe *terza rima*.

3. How many sonnets can you find in this book? List them by page number and designate each as English or Italian, noting any irregularities. Can you make any generalizations from them about the nature or subject matter of sonnets?

A HANDFUL OF LIMERICKS*

I sat next the Duchess at tea.
It was just as I feared it would be:
    Her rumblings abdominal
    Were simply abominable,
And everyone thought it was me.

There was a young lady of Lynn
Who was so uncommonly thin
    That when she essayed
    To drink lemonade
She slipped through the straw and fell in.

*Most limericks are anonymous. If not written anonymously, they soon become so, unfortunately for the glory of their authors, because of repeated oral transmission and reprinting without accreditation.

A tutor who tooted the flute
Tried to tutor two tooters to toot.
    Said the two to the tutor,
      "Is it harder to toot or
To tutor two tooters to toot?"

There was a young maid who said, "Why
Can't I look in my ear with my eye?
    If I put my mind to it,
    I'm sure I can do it.
You never can tell till you try."

There was an old man of Peru
Who dreamt he was eating his shoe.
    He awoke in the night
    In a terrible fright,
And found it was perfectly true!

A decrepit old gas man named Peter,
While hunting around for the meter,
    Touched a leak with his light.
    He arose out of sight,
And, as anyone can see by reading this, he
      also destroyed the meter.

Well, it's partly the shape of the thing
That gives the old limerick wing;
    These accordion pleats
    Full of airy conceits
Take it up like a kite on a string.

HUNTING SONG

The fox came lolloping, lolloping,
Lolloping. His tongue hung out
And his ears were high.
He was like death at the end of a string
When he came to the hollow
Log. Ran in one side
And out of the other. O
He was sly.

5

The hounds came tumbling, tumbling,
Tumbling. Their heads were low   10
And their eyes were red.
The sound of their breath was louder than death
When they came to the hollow
Log. They held at one end
But a bitch found the scent. O   15
They were mad.

The hunter came galloping, galloping,
Galloping. All damp was his mare
From her hooves to her mane.
His coat and his mouth were redder than death   20
When he came to the hollow
Log. He took in the rein
And over he went. O
He was fine.

The log, he just lay there, alone in   25
The clearing. No fox nor hound
Nor mounted man
Saw his black round eyes in their perfect disguise
(As the ends of a hollow
Log). He watched death go through him,   30
Around him and over him. O
He was wise.

Donald Finkel (b. 1929)

QUESTIONS

1. Delight in pattern is clearly a major attraction of this poem. Point out all the elements of pattern, including stanza organization, meter, rime, repeated words, and grammatical structures.

2. Chart the elements that are constant throughout the four stanzas of the poem, then those that are alike in three stanzas but not in all four. Can you find justification or compensation for the variations?

POEM IN OCTOBER*

It was my thirtieth year to heaven
Woke to my hearing from harbor and neighbor wood
And the mussel pooled and the heron
Priested shore
The morning beckon   5
With water praying and call of seagull and rook
And the knock of sailing boats on the net webbed wall
Myself to set foot
That second
In the still sleeping town and set forth.   10

My birthday began with the water-
Birds and the birds of the winged trees flying my name
Above the farms and the white horses
And I rose
In rainy autumn   15
And walked abroad in a shower of all my days.
High tide and the heron dived when I took the road
Over the border
And the gates
Of the town closed as the town awoke.   20

A springful of larks in a rolling
Cloud and the roadside bushes brimming with whistling
Blackbirds and the sun of October
Summery
On the hill's shoulder,   25
Here were fond climates and sweet singers suddenly
Come in the morning where I wandered and listened
To the rain wringing
Wind blow cold
In the woods faraway under me.   30

Pale rain over the dwindling harbor
And over the sea wet church the size of a snail
With its horns through mist and the castle
Brown as owls
But all the gardens   35

*Mr. Thomas recorded "Poem in October" (LP, *Pleasure Dome*, Columbia, ML-4259).

Of spring and summer were blooming in the tall tales
Beyond the border and under the lark full cloud.
         There could I marvel
            My birthday
     Away but the weather turned around.   40

         It turned away from the blithe country
And down the other air and the blue altered sky
         Streamed again a wonder of summer
            With apples
         Pears and red currants   45
And I saw in the turning so clearly a child's
Forgotten mornings when he walked with his mother
         Through the parables
            Of sun light
     And the legends of the green chapels   50

         And the twice told fields of infancy
That his tears burned my cheeks and his heart moved in mine.
         These were the woods the river and sea
            Where a boy
         In the listening   55
Summertime of the dead whispered the truth of his joy
To the trees and the stones and the fish in the tide.
         And the mystery
            Sang alive
     Still in the water and singingbirds.   60

         And there could I marvel my birthday
Away but the weather turned around. And the true
         Joy of the long dead child sang burning
            In the sun.
         It was my thirtieth   65
Year to heaven stood there then in the summer noon
Though the town below lay leaved with October blood.
         O may my heart's truth
            Still be sung
     On this high hill in a year's turning.   70

Dylan Thomas (*1914–1953*)

1. The setting is a small fishing village on the coast of Wales. The poet's first name in Welsh means "water" (12). Trace the poet's walk in relation to the village, the weather, and the time of day.

2. "The weather turned around" is an expression indicating a change in the weather or the direction of the wind. In what psychological sense does the weather turn around during the poet's walk? Who is "the long dead child" (63), and what kind of child was he? With what wish does the poem close?

3. Explain "thirtieth year to heaven" (1), "horns" (33), "tall tales" (36), "green chapels" (50), "October blood" (67).

4. The elaborate stanza pattern in this poem is based not on the meter (which is very free) but on a syllable count. How many syllables are there in each line of the stanza? (In line 1 *thirtieth* is counted as only two syllables.) Notice that the stanzas 1 and 3 consist of exactly one sentence each.

5. The poem makes a considerable use of approximate rime, though not according to a regular pattern. Point out examples.

THE SONNET

A Sonnet is a moment's monument—*a*
Memorial from the Soul's eternity *b*
To one dead deathless hour. Look that it be, *b*
Whether for lustral rite or dire portent, *a*
Of its own arduous fullness reverent: *a*   5
Carve it in ivory or in ebony, *b*
As Day or Night may rule; and let Time see *b*
Its flowering crest impearled and orient. *a*

A Sonnet is a coin; its face reveals *c*
The Soul—its converse, to what Power 'tis due:—*d*   10
Whether for tribute to the august appeals *c*
Of Life, or dower in Love's high retinue, *d*
It serve; or, 'mid the dark wharf's cavernous breath, *e*
In Charon's palm it pay the toll to Death. *e*

Dante Gabriel Rossetti (1828–1882)

1. Vocabulary: *lustral* (4), *portent* (4), *arduous* (5), *orient* (8), *retinue* (12), *Charon* (14). The Greeks buried their dead with coins over their eyes or in their mouths to pay for their passage to the underworld.

2. Rossetti "defines" the sonnet and gives advice about writing it. What characteristics of the Italian sonnet does Rossetti bring out?

3. What is Rossetti's advice for writing the sonnet? Keats once advised poets to "rift every vein with ore." Is Rossetti's advice similar or different?

4. This sonnet consists essentially of two extended metaphors, one in the octave and one in the sestet. Trace the development and implications of each. Which is the more consistently and remarkably worked out?

FROM **ROMEO AND JULIET**

ROMEO	If I profane with my unworthiest hand	
	This holy shrine, the gentle sin is this;	
	My lips, two blushing pilgrims, ready stand	
	To smooth that rough touch with a tender kiss.	
JULIET	Good pilgrim, you do wrong your hand too much,	5
	Which mannerly devotion shows in this;	
	For saints have hands that pilgrims' hands do touch,	
	And palm to palm is holy palmers' kiss.	
ROMEO	Have not saints lips, and holy palmers too?	
JULIET	Ay, pilgrim, lips that they must use in prayer.	10
ROMEO	O! then, dear saint, let lips do what hands do;	
	They pray, Grant thou, lest faith turn to despair.	
JULIET	Saints do not move,° though grant for prayers' sake,	propose,
ROMEO	Then move not, while my prayers' effect I take.	instigate

William Shakespeare (1564–1616)

QUESTIONS

1. These fourteen lines have been lifted out of Act I, scene 5, of Shakespeare's play. They are the first words exchanged between Romeo and Juliet, who are meeting, for the first time, at a masquerade ball given by her father. Romeo is dressed as a pilgrim. Struck by Juliet's beauty, he has come up to greet her. What stage action accompanies this passage?

2. What is the basic metaphor employed? How does it affect the tone of the relationship between Romeo and Juliet?

3. What play on words do you find in lines 8 and 13–14? What two meanings has line 11?

4. By meter and rime scheme, these lines form a sonnet. Do you think this was coincidental or intentional on Shakespeare's part? Discuss.

THE TROLL'S NOSEGAY

A simple nosegay! was that much to ask?
(Winter still nagged, with scarce a bud yet showing.)
He loved her ill, if he resigned the task.
"Somewhere," she cried, "there *must* be blossom blowing."
It seems my lady wept and the troll swore   5
By Heaven he hated tears: he'd cure her spleen—
Where she had begged one flower he'd shower fourscore,
A bunch fit to amaze a China Queen.

Cold fog-drawn Lily, pale mist-magic Rose
He conjured, and in a glassy cauldron set   10
With elvish unsubstantial Mignonette
And such vague bloom as wandering dreams enclose.
But she?
     Awed,
          Charmed to tears,
               Distracted,
                    Yet—
Even yet, perhaps, a trifle piqued—who knows?

Robert Graves (b. 1895)

QUESTIONS

   1. Vocabulary: *troll* and *nosegay* (title), *blowing* (4), *spleen* (6).
   2. Graves uses a fairytale tradition to point up a truth about human nature. Explain the tradition. What is the truth?
   3. Comment on "China Queen" (8). From what tradition does it come? What meanings does it suggest here?
   4. Comment on the adjectives used in lines 9–12. What is their effect?
   5. How does the word *yet* change between lines 13 and 14?
   6. Comment on the form of the poem.

EDWARD

"Why dois° your brand° sae drap wi bluid,   does; sword
       Edward, Edward,
Why dois your brand sae drap wi bluid,
   And why sae sad gang° yee O?"   go

"O I hae killed my hauke sae guid,   5
          Mither, mither,
O I hae killed my hauke sae guid,
     And I had nae mair bot hee O."

"Your haukis bluid was nevir sae reid,
          Edward, Edward,   10
Your haukis bluid was nevir sae reid,
     My deir son I tell thee O."
"O I hae killed my reid-roan steid,
          Mither, mither,
O I hae killed my reid-roan steid,   15
     That erst° was sae fair and frie° O."   formerly; spirited

"Your steid was auld, and ye hae got mair,
          Edward, Edward,
Your steid was auld, and ye hae got mair,
     Sum other dule° ye drie° O."   grief; suffer 20
"O I hae killed my fadir deir,
          Mither, mither,
O I hae killed my fadir deir,
     Alas, and wae is mee O!"

"And whatten penance wul ye drie for that,   25
          Edward, Edward,
And whatten penance wul ye drie for that?
     My deir son, now tell me O."
"Ile set my feit in yonder boat,
          Mither, mither,   30
Ile set my feit in yonder boat,
     And Ile fare ovir the sea O."

"And what wul ye doe wi your towirs and your ha,°   hall
          Edward, Edward,
And what wul ye doe wi your towirs and your ha,   35
     That were sae fair to see O?"
"Ile let thame stand tul they doun fa,°   fall
          Mither, mither,
Ile let thame stand tul they doun fa,
     For here nevir mair maun° I bee O."   must   40

251

"And what wul ye leive to your bairns° and your wife,   children
            Edward, Edward,
And what wul ye leive to your bairns and your wife,
    Whan ye gang ovir the sea O?"   44
"The warldis° room, late them beg thrae° life,   world's; through
            Mither, mither,
The warldis room, late them beg thrae life,
    For thame nevir mair wul I see O."

"And what wul ye leive to your ain mither deir,
            Edward, Edward?   50
And what wul ye leive to your ain mither deir?
    My deir son, now tell me O."
"The curse of hell frae me sall ye beir,
            Mither, mither,
The curse of hell frae me sall ye beir,   55
    Sic° counseils ye gave to me O."   Such

Anonymous

QUESTIONS

1. What has Edward done and why? Where do the two climaxes of the poem come?

2. Tell as much as you can about Edward and his feelings toward what he has done. From what class of society is he? Why does he at first give false answers to his mother's questions? What reversal of feelings and loyalties has he undergone? Do his answers about his hawk and steed perhaps indicate his present feelings toward his father? How do you explain his behavior to his wife and children? What are his present feelings toward his mother?

3. Tell as much as you can about Edward's mother. Why does she ask what Edward has done—doesn't she already know? Is there any clue as to the motivation of her deed? How skillful is she in her questioning? What do we learn about her from her dismissal of Edward's steed as "auld" and only one of many (17)? From her asking Edward what penance *he* will do for his act (25)? From her reference to herself as Edward's "ain mither deir" (49)?

4. Structure and pattern are both important in this poem. Could any of the stanzas be interchanged without loss, or do they build up steadily to the two climaxes? What effect has the constant repetition of the two short refrains, "Edward, Edward" and "Mither, mither"? What is the effect of the final "O" at the end of each speech? Does the repetition of each question and

answer simply waste words or does it add to the suspense and emotional intensity? (Try reading the poem omitting the third and seventh lines of each stanza. Is it improved or weakened?)

5. Much of what happened is implied, much is omitted. Does the poem gain anything in power from what is *not* told?

FUGAL-CHORUS

Great is Caesar: He has conquered Seven Kingdoms.
The First was the Kingdom of Abstract Idea:
Last night it was Tom, Dick and Harry; tonight it is S's with P's;
Instead of inflexions and accents
There are prepositions and word-order;   5
Instead of aboriginal objects excluding each other
There are specimens reiterating a type;
Instead of wood-nymphs and river-demons,
There is one unconditioned ground of Being.
Great is Caesar: God must be with Him.   10

Great is Caesar: He has conquered Seven Kingdoms.
The Second was the Kingdom of Natural Cause:
Last night it was Sixes and Sevens; tonight it is One and Two;
Instead of saying, "Strange are the whims of the Strong,"
We say "Harsh is the Law but it is certain";   15
Instead of building temples, we build laboratories;
Instead of offering sacrifices, we perform experiments;
Instead of reciting prayers, we note pointer-readings;
Our lives are no longer erratic but efficient.
Great is Caesar: God must be with Him.   20

Great is Caesar: He has conquered Seven Kingdoms.
The Third was the Kingdom of Infinite Number:
Last night it was Rule-of-Thumb, tonight it is To-a-T;
Instead of Quite-a-lot, there is Exactly-so-many;
Instead of Only-a-few, there is Just-these;   25
Instead of saying, "You must wait until I have counted,"
We say, "Here you are. You will find this answer correct";
Instead of a nodding acquaintance with a few integers
The Transcendentals are our personal friends.
Great is Caesar: God must be with Him.   30

Great is Caesar: He has conquered Seven Kingdoms.
The Fourth was the Kingdom of Credit Exchange:
Last night it was Tit-for-Tat, tonight it is C.O.D.;
When we have a surplus, we need not meet someone with a deficit;
When we have a deficit, we need not meet someone with a surplus; 35
Instead of heavy treasures, there are paper symbols of value;
Instead of Pay at Once, there is Pay when you can;
Instead of My Neighbor, there is Our Customers;
Instead of Country Fair, there is World Market.
Great is Caesar: God must be with Him. 40

Great is Caesar: He has conquered Seven Kingdoms.
The Fifth was the Kingdom of Inorganic Giants:
Last night it was Heave-Ho, tonight it is Whee-Spree;
When we want anything, They make it;
When we dislike anything, They change it; 45
When we want to go anywhere, They carry us;
When the Barbarian invades us, They raise immovable shields;
When we invade the Barbarian, They brandish irresistible swords;
Fate is no longer a fiat of Matter, but a freedom of Mind.
Great is Caesar: God must be with Him. 50

Great is Caesar: He has conquered Seven Kingdoms.
The Sixth was the Kingdom of Organic Dwarfs:
Last night it was Ouch-Ouch, tonight it is Yum-Yum;
When diseases waylay us, They strike them dead;
When worries intrude on us, They throw them out; 55
When pain accosts us, They save us from embarrassment;
When we feel like sheep, They make us lions;
When we feel like geldings, They make us stallions;
Spirit is no longer under Flesh, but on top.
Great is Caesar: God must be with Him. 60

Great is Caesar: He has conquered Seven Kingdoms.
The Seventh was the Kingdom of Popular Soul:
Last night it was Order-Order, tonight it is Hear-Hear;
When he says, You are happy, we laugh;
When he says, You are wretched, we cry; 65
When he says, It is true, everyone believes it;
When he says, It is false, no one believes it;
When he says, This is good, this is loved;

When he says, That is bad, that is hated.
Great is Caesar: God must be with Him.   70

W. H. Auden (b. 1907)

QUESTIONS

1. Vocabulary: *aboriginal* (6), *unconditioned* (9), *fiat* (49). "S's with P's" (3) are logical symbols, standing for "Subjects with Predicates." *Transcendentals* (29) are a class of numbers used in modern mathematics that cannot be expressed by simple arithmetical definitions, as, for example, *pi* (3.14159 . . .). Why has Auden capitalized the word?

2. What states of society are contrasted in the poem? What is meant by "last night" and "tonight"? Discuss what is meant by each of the seven kingdoms. What does Caesar represent?

3. What is the poet's attitude toward the triumph of Caesar? Toward the idea of progress? What figurative device most characterizes the poem? In what lines is it most clearly apparent?

4. What elements of pattern has the poem? How is this pattern related to its structure? What is a fugue? How is this poem like a fugue? Why is it written for a chorus?

SPECTRUM

Brown from the sun's mid-afternoon caress,
And where not brown, white as a bridal dress,
And where not white, pink as an opened plum.

And where not pink, darkly mysterious,
And when observed, openly furious,
And then obscured, while the red blushes come.

William Dickey (b. 1928)

QUESTIONS

1. The situation described is not explicitly identified. What do the adjectives modify? Would the poem be better if it were clearer?

2. Describe the elements of pattern. What kind of rime is used in lines 4–5?

3. What applications has the title?

TWO JAPANESE HAIKU

The lightning flashes!
And slashing through the darkness,
A night-heron's screech.

A lightning gleam:
into darkness travels
a night heron's scream.

Matsuo Bashō (1644–1694)

The falling flower
I saw drift back to the branch
Was a butterfly.

Fallen flowers rise
back to the branch—I watch:
oh . . . butterflies!

Moritake (1452–1540)

QUESTION

The haiku, a Japanese form, consists of three lines with five, seven, and five syllables respectively. The translators of the left-hand versions above (Earl Miner and Babette Deutsch respectively) preserve this syllable count; the translator of the right-hand versions (Harold G. Henderson) seeks to preserve the sense of formal structure by making the first and last lines rime. Moritake's haiku, as Miss Deutsch points out, "refers to the Buddhist proverb that the fallen flower never returns to the branch; the broken mirror never again reflects." From these two examples, what would you say are the characteristics of effective haiku?

A CHRISTMAS TREE

Star,
If you are
A love compassionate,
You will walk with us this year.
We face a glacial distance, who are here
Huddld
At your feet.

William Burford (b. 1927)

QUESTION

Why do you think the author misspelled "huddled" in line 6?

all poems

Bad Poetry
and Good

The attempt to evaluate a poem should never be made before the poem is understood; and, unless you have developed the capacity to feel some poetry deeply, any judgments you make will be worthless. A person who likes no wines can hardly be a judge of them. The ability to make judgments, to discriminate between good and bad, great and good, good and half-good, is surely a primary object of all liberal education, and one's appreciation of poetry is incomplete unless it includes discrimination. Of the mass of verse that appears each year in print, as of all literature, most is "flat, stale, and unprofitable"; a very, very little is of any enduring value.

In judging a poem, as in judging any work of art, we need to ask three basic questions: (1) *What is its central purpose?* (2) *How fully has this purpose been accomplished?* (3) *How important is this purpose?* The first question we need to answer in order to understand the poem. The last two questions are those by which we evaluate it. The first of these measures the poem on a scale of perfection. The second measures it on a scale of significance. And, just as the area of a rectangle is determined by multiplying its measurements on two scales, breadth and height, so the greatness of a poem is determined by multiplying its measurements on two scales, perfection and significance. If the poem measures well on the first of these scales, we call it a good poem, at least of its kind. If it measures well on both scales, we call it a great poem.*

*As indicated in the footnote on page 25, some objection has been made to the use of the term "purpose" in literary criticism. For the two criteria suggested

257

The measurement of a poem is a much more complex process, of course, than is the measurement of a rectangle. It cannot be done as exactly. Agreement on the measurements will never be complete. Yet over a period of time the judgments of qualified readers* tend to coalesce: there comes to be more agreement than disagreement. There is almost universal agreement, for instance, that Shakespeare is the greatest of English poets. Although there might be sharp disagreements among qualified readers as to whether Donne or Keats is the superior poet, or Wordsworth or Chaucer, or Shelley or Pope, there is almost universal agreement among them that each of these is superior to Kipling or Longfellow. And there is almost universal agreement that Kipling and Longfellow are superior to James Whitcomb Riley and Edgar Guest.

But your problem is to be able to discriminate, not between already established reputations, but between poems—poems you have not seen before and of which, perhaps, you do not even know the author. Here, of course, you will not always be right—even the most qualified readers occasionally go badly astray—but you should, we hope, be able to make broad distinctions with a higher average of success than you could when you began this book. And, unless you allow yourself to petrify, your ability to do this should improve throughout your college years and beyond.

For answering the first of our evaluative questions, *How fully has the poem's purpose been accomplished?* there are no easy yardsticks that we can apply. We cannot ask, Is the poem melodious? Does it have smooth meter? Does it use good grammar? Does it contain figures of speech? Are the rimes perfect? Excellent poems exist without any of

---

above may be substituted these two: (1) How thoroughly are the materials of the poem integrated or unified? (2) How many and how diverse are the materials that it integrates? Thus a poem becomes successful in proportion to the tightness of its organization—that is, according to the degree to which all its elements work together and require each other to produce the total effect—and it becomes great in proportion to its scope—that is, according to the amount and diversity of the material it amalgamates into unity.

*Throughout this discussion the term "qualified reader" is of utmost importance. By a qualified reader we mean briefly a person with considerable experience of literature and considerable experience of life: a person of intelligence, sensitivity, and knowledge. Without these qualities a person is no more qualified to judge literature than would be a color-blind man to judge painting, or a tone-deaf man to judge music, or a man who had never seen a horse before to judge a horse.

these attributes. We can judge any element in a poem only as it contributes or fails to contribute to the achievement of the central purpose; and we can judge the total poem only as these elements work together to form an integrated whole. But we can at least attempt a few generalizations. In a perfect poem there are no excess words, no words that do not bear their full weight in contributing to the total meaning, and no words just to fill out the meter. Each word is the best word for expressing the total meaning: there are no inexact words forced by the rime scheme or the metrical pattern. The word order is the best order for expressing the author's total meaning; distortions or departures from normal order are for emphasis or some other meaningful purpose. The diction, the images, and the figures of speech are fresh, not trite (except, of course, when the poet uses trite language deliberately for purposes of irony). There are no clashes between the sound of the poem and its sense, or its form and its content; and in general the poet uses both sound and pattern in such a way as to support his meaning. The organization of the poem is the best possible organization: images and ideas are so effectively arranged that any rearrangement would be harmful to the poem. We will always remember, however, that a good poem may have flaws. We should never damn a poem for its flaws if these flaws are amply compensated for by positive excellence.

If a poem is to have true excellence, it must be in some sense a "new" poem; it must exact a fresh response from the qualified reader—make him respond in a new way. It will not be merely imitative of previous literature nor appeal to stock, preestablished ways of thinking and feeling that in some readers are automatically stimulated by words like *mother, baby, home, country, faith,* or *God,* as a coin put into a slot always gets an expected reaction.

And here, perhaps, may be discussed the kinds of poems that most frequently "fool" poor readers (and occasionally a few good ones) and achieve sometimes a tremendous popularity without winning the respect of most good readers. These poems are found pasted in great numbers in the scrapbooks of sweet old ladies and appear in anthologies entitled *Poems of Inspiration, Poems of Courage,* or *Heart-Throbs.* The people who write such poems and the people who like them are often the best of people, but they are not poets or lovers of poetry in any genuine sense. They are lovers of conventional ideas or sentiments or feelings, which they like to see expressed with the adornment of rime and meter, and which, when so expressed, they respond to in predictable ways.

Of the several varieties of inferior poetry, we shall concern ourselves with three: the sentimental, the rhetorical, and the purely didactic. All three are perhaps unduly dignified by the name of poetry. They might more aptly be described as verse.

SENTIMENTALITY is indulgence in emotion for its own sake, or expression of more emotion than an occasion warrants. A sentimental *person* is gushy, stirred to tears by trivial or inappropriate causes; he weeps at all weddings and all funerals; he is made ecstatic by manifestations of young love; he clips locks of hair, gilds baby shoes, and talks baby talk; he grows compassionate over hardened criminals when he hears of their being punished. His opposite is the callous or unfeeling person. The ideal is the person who responds sensitively on appropriate occasions and feels deeply on occasions that deserve deep feeling, but who has nevertheless a certain amount of emotional reserve, a certain command over his feelings. Sentimental *literature* is "tear-jerking" literature. It aims primarily at stimulating the emotions directly rather than at communicating experience truly and freshly; it depends on trite and well-tried formulas for exciting emotion; it revels in old oaken buckets, rocking chairs, mother love, and the pitter-patter of little feet; it oversimplifies; it is unfaithful to the full complexity of human experience. In our book the best example of sentimental verse is the first seven lines of the anonymous "Love" (page 176). If this verse had ended as it began, it would have been pure sentimentalism. The eighth line redeems it by making us realize that the writer is not serious and thus transfers the piece from the classification of sentimental verse to that of humorous verse. In fact, the writer is poking fun at sentimentality by showing that in its most maudlin form it is characteristic of drunks.

RHETORICAL poetry uses a language more glittering and high flown than its substance warrants. It offers a spurious vehemence of language—language without a corresponding reality of emotion or thought underneath. It is oratorical, overelegant, artificially eloquent. It is superficial and, again, often basically trite. It loves rolling phrases like "from the rocky coast of Maine to the sun-washed shores of California" and "our heroic dead" and "Old Glory." It deals in generalities. At its worst it is bombast. In this book an example is offered by the two lines quoted from the play-within-a-play in Shakespeare's *A Midsummer Night's Dream:*

> Whereat with blade, with bloody, blameful blade,
> He bravely broached his boiling bloody breast.

Another example may be found in the player's recitation in *Hamlet* (in Act II, scene 2):

> Out, out, thou strumpet Fortune! All you gods,
> In general synod take away her power,
> Break all the spokes and fellies from her wheel,
> And bowl the round nave down the hill of heaven
> As low as to the fiends!

DIDACTIC poetry has as a primary purpose to teach or preach. It is probable that all the very greatest poetry teaches in subtle ways, without being expressly didactic; and much expressly didactic poetry ranks high in poetic excellence: that is, it accomplishes its teaching without ceasing to be poetry. But when the didactic purpose supersedes the poetic purpose, when the poem communicates information or moral instruction only, then it ceases to be didactic poetry and becomes didactic verse. Such verse appeals to people who go to poetry primarily for noble thoughts or inspiring lessons and like them prettily expressed. It is recognizable often by the flatness of its diction, the poverty of its imagery and figurative language, its emphasis on moral platitudes, its lack of poetic freshness. It is either very trite or has little to distinguish it from informational prose except rime or meter. Tennyson's "The Oak" (page 204) is an excellent example of didactic *poetry*. The familiar couplet

> Early to bed and early to rise,
> Makes a man healthy, wealthy, and wise

is more aptly characterized as didactic *verse*.

Undoubtedly, so far in this chapter, we have spoken too categorically, have made our distinctions too sharp and definite. All poetic excellence is a matter of degree. There are no absolute lines between sentimentality and true emotion, artificial and genuine eloquence, didactic verse and didactic poetry. Though the difference between extreme examples is easy to recognize, subtler discriminations are harder to make. But a primary distinction between the educated man and the ignorant man is the ability to make value judgments.

A final caution to students. In making judgments on literature, always be honest. Do not pretend to like what you really do not like. Do not be afraid to admit a liking for what you do like. A genuine enthusiasm for the second-rate is much better than false enthusiasm or no enthusiasm at all. Be neither hasty nor timorous in making your judgments. When you have attentively read a poem and thoroughly considered it, decide what you think. Do not hedge, equivocate, or try to find out others' opinions before forming your own. Having formed an opinion and expressed it, do not allow it to petrify. Compare your opinion *then* with the opinions of others; allow yourself to change it when convinced of its error: in this way you learn. Honesty, courage, and humility are the necessary moral foundations for all genuine literary judgment.

In the poems for comparison in this chapter, the distinction to be made is not always between black and white; it may be between varying degrees of poetic merit.

EXERCISES

Poetry is not so much a thing as a quality; it exists in varying degrees in different specimens of language. Though we cannot always say definitely, "This is poetry; that is not," we can often say, "This is more poetical than that." Rank the following passages from most poetical to least poetical or not poetical at all.

1. Why should we be in such desperate haste to succeed and in such desperate enterprises? If a man does not keep pace with his companions, perhaps it is because he hears a different drummer. Let him step to the music which he hears, however measured or far away.

2. $(x - 12)(x - 2) = x^2 - 14x + 24$.

3. Thirty days hath September,
   April, June, and November.
   All the rest have thirty-one,
   Except February alone,
   To which we twenty-eight assign,
   Till leap year makes it twenty-nine.

4. "Meeting at Night" (page 55).

5. Thus, through the serene tranquillities of the tropical sea, among waves whose handclappings were suspended by exceeding rapture, Moby Dick moved on, still withholding from sight the full terrors of his submerged

trunk, entirely hiding the wrenched hideousness of his jaw. But soon the fore part of him slowly rose from the water; for an instant his whole marbleized body formed a high arch, like Virginia's Natural Bridge, and warningly waving his bannered flukes in the air, the grand god revealed himself, sounded, and went out of sight. Hoveringly halting, and dipping on the wing, the white sea fowls longingly lingered over the agitated pool that he left.

6. Nature in the abstract is the aggregate of the powers and properties of all things. Nature means the sum of all phenomena, together with the causes which produce them; including not only all that happens, but all that is capable of happening; the unused capabilities of causes being as much a part of the idea of Nature, as those which take effect.

SAY NOT THE STRUGGLE NOUGHT AVAILETH

Say not the struggle nought availeth,
   The labor and the wounds are vain,
The enemy faints not, nor faileth,
   And as things have been they remain.

If hopes were dupes, fears may be liars;   5
   It may be, in yon smoke concealed,
Your comrades chase e'en now the fliers,
   And, but for you, possess the field.

For while the tired waves, vainly breaking,
   Seem here no painful inch to gain,   10
Far back, through creeks and inlets making,
   Comes silent, flooding in, the main.

And not by eastern windows only,
   When daylight comes, comes in the light,
In front, the sun climbs slow, how slowly,   15
   But westward, look, the land is bright.

DON'T QUIT—FIGHT ONE MORE ROUND

When things go wrong, as they sometimes will,
When the road you're trudging seems all uphill,
When the funds are low and the debts are high
And you want to smile, but you have to sigh,

When care is pressing you down a bit,
Rest! if you must—but never quit.   5

Life is queer, with its twists and turns,
As every one of us sometimes learns,
And many a failure turns about
When he might have won if he'd stuck it out;   10
Stick to your task, though the pace seems slow—
You may succeed with one more blow.

Success is failure turned inside out—
The silver tint of the clouds of doubt—
And you never can tell how close you are,   15
It may be near when it seems afar;
So stick to the fight when you're hardest hit—
It's when things seem worst that *you mustn't quit.*

QUESTION

Which of the two poems above has more poetic merit? Discuss.

A PRAYER IN SPRING

Oh, give us pleasure in the flowers today;
And give us not to think so far away
As the uncertain harvest; keep us here
All simply in the springing of the year.

Oh, give us pleasure in the orchard white,   5
Like nothing else by day, like ghosts by night;
And make us happy in the happy bees,
The swarm dilating round the perfect trees.

And make us happy in the darting bird
That suddenly above the bees is heard,   10
The meteor that thrusts in with needle bill,
And off a blossom in mid air stands still.

For this is love and nothing else is love,
The which it is reserved for God above
To sanctify to what far ends He will,   15
But which it only needs that we fulfill.

PRAY IN MAY

Today the birds are singing and
The grass and leaves are green,
And all the gentle earth presents
A bright and sunny scene.
It is the merry month of May   5
When flowers bloom once more,
And there are hopes and happy dreams
And promises in store.
What time could be more wisely spent
Than this the first of May   10
To say that we are thankful for
Our blessings every day?
To give our gratitude to God
In humbleness and prayer
And offer deeds of charity   15
As incense in the air?
Then let us love our neighbor and
Our rich and fruitful sod,
And let us go to church today
And thank almighty God.   20

QUESTION

Which poem treats its subject with greater truth, freshness, and technical
skill?

LOITERING WITH A VACANT EYE

Loitering with a vacant eye
Along the Grecian gallery,
And brooding on my heavy ill,
I met a statue standing still.
Still in marble stone stood he,   5
And steadfastly he looked at me.
"Well met," I thought the look would say,
"We both were fashioned far away;
We neither knew, when we were young,
These Londoners we live among."   10

Still he stood and eyed me hard,
An earnest and a grave regard:
"What, lad, drooping with your lot?
I too would be where I am not.
I too survey that endless line   15
Of men whose thoughts are not as mine.
Years, ere you stood up from rest,
On my neck the collar prest;
Years, when you lay down your ill,
I shall stand and bear it still.   20
Courage, lad, 'tis not for long:
Stand, quit you like stone, be strong."
So I thought his look would say;
And light on me my trouble lay,
And I stept out in flesh and bone   25
Manful like the man of stone.

BE STRONG

Be strong!
We are not here to play,—to dream, to drift.
We have hard work to do and loads to lift.
Shun not the struggle,—face it: 'tis God's gift.

Be strong!   5
Say not the days are evil. Who's to blame?
And fold the hands and acquiesce,—O shame!
Stand up, speak out, and bravely, in God's name.

Be strong!
It matters not how deep intrenched the wrong,   10
How hard the battle goes, the day how long;
Faint not,—fight on! Tomorrow comes the song.

QUESTIONS

1. The "Grecian gallery" (2), in the first poem of this pair, is a room in the British Museum in London. Who is the speaker? Who is the speaker in the second poem?

2. Which is the superior poem? Discuss.

A POISON TREE

I was angry with my friend:
I told my wrath, my wrath did end.
I was angry with my foe:
I told it not, my wrath did grow.

And I watered it in fears,   5
Night and morning with my tears;
And I sunned it with smiles,
And with soft deceitful wiles.

And it grew both day and night
Till it bore an apple bright;   10
And my foe beheld it shine,
And he knew that it was mine,

And into my garden stole
When the night had veiled the pole:
In the morning glad I see   15
My foe outstretched beneath the tree.

THE MOST VITAL THING IN LIFE

When you feel like saying something
  That you know you will regret,
Or keenly feel an insult
  Not quite easy to forget,
That's the time to curb resentment   5
  And maintain a mental peace,
For when your mind is tranquil
  All your ill-thoughts simply cease.

It is easy to be angry
  When defrauded or defied,   10
To be peeved and disappointed
  If your wishes are denied;
But to win a worthwhile battle
  Over selfishness and spite,
You must learn to keep strict silence   15
  Though you know you're in the right.

So keep your mental balance
    When confronted by a foe,
Be it enemy in ambush
    Or some danger that you know.   20
If you are poised and tranquil
    When all around is strife,
Be assured that you have mastered
    The most vital thing in life.

QUESTION

Which poem has more poetic merit? Explain.

REVULSION

Though I waste watches framing words to fetter
Some unknown spirit to mine in clasp and kiss,
Out of the night there looms a sense 'twere better
To fail obtaining whom one fails to miss.

For winning love we win the risk of losing,   5
And losing love is as one's life were riven;
It cuts like contumely and keen ill-using
To cede what was superfluously given.

Let me then never feel the fateful thrilling
That devastates the love-worn wooer's frame,   10
The hot ado of fevered hopes, the chilling
That agonizes disappointed aim!
So may I live no junctive law fulfilling,
And my heart's table bear no woman's name.

NEUTRAL TONES

We stood by a pond that winter day,
And the sun was white, as though chidden of God,
And a few leaves lay on the starving sod;
    —They had fallen from an ash, and were gray.

Your eyes on me were as eyes that rove   5
Over tedious riddles of years ago;

And some words played between us to and fro
    On which lost the more by our love.

The smile on your mouth was the deadest thing
Alive enough to have strength to die;   10
And a grin of bitterness swept thereby
    Like an ominous bird a-wing. . . .

Since then, keen lessons that love deceives,
And wrings with wrong, have shaped to me
Your face, and the God-curst sun, and a tree,   15
    And a pond edged with grayish leaves.

QUESTION
Both poems, concerning the unhappiness of love, are by Thomas Hardy
(1840–1928). Which more surely gives him a respected place among English poets? Explain.*

TO MY SON

Do you know that your soul is of my soul such part
That you seem to be fibre and cord of my heart?
None other can pain me as you, dear, can do;
None other can please me or praise me as you.

Remember the world will be quick with its blame   5
If shadow or stain ever darken your name;
"Like mother like son" is a saying so true,
The world will judge largely of "Mother" by you.

Be yours then the task, if task it shall be,
To force the proud world to do homage to me;   10
Be sure it will say when its verdict you've won,
"She reaped as she sowed. Lo! this is her son."

ON THE BEACH AT FONTANA

Wind whines and whines the shingle, *Coarse rounded, material like gravel*
The crazy pierstakes groan;
A senile sea numbers each single
Slimesilvered stone.

*This pairing was suggested by Samuel Hynes, *The Pattern of Hardy's Poetry*
(Chapel Hill: University of North Carolina Press, 1961).

From whining wind and colder 5
Grey sea I wrap him warm
And touch his trembling fineboned shoulder
And boyish arm.

Around us fear, descending
Darkness of fear above 10
And in my heart how deep unending
Ache of love!

QUESTIONS

1. Vocabulary: *shingle* (1).
2. The first poem was written by a woman, the second by a man. Who is the speaker in each? Which is the better poem? Why?

LITTLE BOY BLUE

The little toy dog is covered with dust,
    But sturdy and staunch he stands;
And the little toy soldier is red with rust,
    And his musket moulds in his hands.
Time was when the little toy dog was new, 5
    And the soldier was passing fair;
And that was the time when our Little Boy Blue
    Kissed them and put them there.

"Now, don't you go till I come," he said,
    "And don't you make any noise!" 10
So, toddling off to his trundle-bed,
    He dreamt of the pretty toys;
And, as he was dreaming, an angel song
    Awakened our Little Boy Blue—
Oh! the years are many, the years are long, 15
    But the little toy friends are true!

Ay, faithful to Little Boy Blue they stand,
    Each in the same old place—
Awaiting the touch of a little hand,
    The smile of a little face; 20

And they wonder, as waiting the long years through
    In the dust of that little chair,
What has become of our Little Boy Blue,
    Since he kissed them and put them there.

THE TOYS

My little Son, who looked from thoughtful eyes
And moved and spoke in quiet grown-up wise,
Having my law the seventh time disobeyed,
I struck him, and dismissed
With hard words and unkissed,   5
His Mother, who was patient, being dead.
Then, fearing lest his grief should hinder sleep,
I visited his bed,
But found him slumbering deep,
With darkened eyelids, and their lashes yet   10
From his late sobbing wet.
And I, with moan,
Kissing away his tears, left others of my own;
For, on a table drawn beside his head,
He had put, within his reach,   15
A box of counters and a red-veined stone,
A piece of glass abraded by the beach,
And six or seven shells,
A bottle with bluebells,
And two French copper coins, ranged there with careful art,   20
To comfort his sad heart.
So when that night I prayed
To God, I wept, and said:
Ah, when at last we lie with trancèd breath,
Not vexing Thee in death,   25
And thou rememberest of what toys
We made our joys,
How weakly understood
Thy great commanded good,
Then, fatherly not less   30
Than I whom Thou hast moulded from the clay,
Thou'lt leave Thy wrath, and say,
"I will be sorry for their childishness."

One of these poems has an obvious appeal for the beginning reader. The
other is likely to have more meaning for the mature reader. Try to explain
in terms of sentimentality and honesty.

THE SEND–OFF

Down the close, darkening lanes they sang their way
To the siding-shed,
And lined the train with faces grimly gay.

Their breasts were stuck all white with wreath and spray
As men's are, dead.   5

Dull porters watched them, and a casual tramp
Stood staring hard,
Sorry to miss them from the upland camp.
Then, unmoved, signals nodded, and a lamp
Winked to the guard.   10

So secretly, like wrongs hushed-up, they went.
They were not ours:
We never heard to which front these were sent.

Nor there if they yet mock what women meant
Who gave them flowers.   15

Shall they return to beatings of great bells
In wild train-loads?
A few, a few, too few for drums and yells,
May creep back, silent, to village wells
Up half-known roads.   20

CHA TILL MACCRUIMEIN

The pipes in the street were playing bravely,
    The marching lads went by,
With merry hearts and voices singing
    My friends marched out to die;
But I was hearing a lonely pibroch   5
    Out of an older war,
"Farewell, farewell, farewell, MacCrimmon,
    MacCrimmon comes no more."

And every lad in his heart was dreaming
    Of honor and wealth to come,   10
And honor and noble pride were calling
    To the tune of the pipes and drum;
But I was hearing a woman singing
    On dark Dunvegan shore,
"In battle or peace, with wealth or honor,   15
    MacCrimmon comes no more."

And there in front of the men were marching,
    With feet that made no mark,
The grey old ghosts of the ancient fighters
    Come back again from the dark;   20
And in front of them all MacCrimmon piping
    A weary tune and sore,
"On the gathering day, for ever and ever,
    MacCrimmon comes no more."

QUESTIONS

1. Vocabulary: *pibroch* (5). *set of mournful variations for bagpipe*

2. The first poem was written by an English poet, the second by a Scottish; both poets were killed in World War I. "Cha Till Maccruimein" is Gaelic and means "MacCrimmon comes no more." The MacCrimmons were a famous race of hereditary pipers from the Isle of Skye. One of them, when his clan was about to leave on a dangerous expedition, composed a lament in which he accurately prophesied his own death in the coming fight. According to Sir Walter Scott, emigrants from the West Highlands and Western Isles usually left their native shore to the accompaniment of this strain. Compare these two poems as to subject and purpose. Taking into account their rhythm, imagery, freshness, and emotional content, decide which is the superior poem.*

THE LONG VOYAGE

Not that the pines were darker there,
nor mid-May dogwood brighter there,
nor swifts more swift in summer air;
    it was my own country,

*For this pairing I am indebted to Denys Thompson, *Reading and Discrimination*, rev. ed. (London: Chatto & Windus, 1954).

having its thunderclap of spring, 5
its long midsummer ripening,
its corn hoar-stiff at harvesting,
    almost like any country,

yet being mine; its face, its speech,
its hills bent low within my reach, 10
its river birch and upland beech
    were mine, of my own country.

Now the dark waters at the bow
fold back, like earth against the plow;
foam brightens like the dogwood now 15
    at home, in my own country.

BREATHES THERE THE MAN

Breathes there the man, with soul so dead,
Who never to himself hath said,
    This is my own, my native land!
Whose heart hath ne'er within him burned,
As home his footsteps he hath turned, 5
    From wandering on a foreign strand?
If such there breathe, go, mark him well;
For him no minstrel raptures swell;
High though his titles, proud his name,
Boundless his wealth as wish can claim— 10
Despite those titles, power, and pelf,
The wretch, concentered all in self,
Living, shall forfeit fair renown,
And, doubly dying, shall go down
To the evil dust from whence he sprung, 15
Unwept, unhonored, and unsung.

QUESTIONS

1. Which poem communicates the more genuine poetic emotion? Which is more rhetorical? Justify your answer.

2. Compare the first poem with "America for Me" (page 276). Which exhibits the greater maturity of attitude?

BOY–MAN

England's lads are miniature men
To start with, grammar in their shiny hats,
And serious: in America who knows when
Manhood begins? Presidents dance and hug
And while the kind King waves and gravely chats   5
America wets on England's old green rug.

The boy-man roars. Worry alone will give
This one the verisimilitude of age.
Those white teeth are his own, for he must live
Longer, grow taller than the Texas race.   10
Fresh are his eyes, his darkening skin the gauge
Of bloods that freely mix beneath his face.

He knows the application of the book
But not who wrote it; shuts it like a shot.
Rather than read he thinks that he will look,   15
Rather than look he thinks that he will talk,
Rather than talk he thinks that he will not
Bother at all; would rather ride than walk.

His means of conversation is the joke,
Humor his language underneath which lies   20
The undecoded dialect of the folk.
Abroad he scorns the foreigner: what's old
Is worn, what's different bad, what's odd unwise.
He gives off heat and is enraged by cold.

Charming, becoming to the suits he wears,   25
The boy-man, younger than his eldest son,
Inherits the state; upon his silver hairs
Time like a panama hat sits at a tilt
And smiles. To him the world has just begun
And every city waiting to be built.   30

Mister, remove your shoulder from the wheel
And say this prayer, "Increase my vitamins,
Make my decisions of the finest steel,
Pour motor oil upon my troubled spawn,
Forgive the Europeans for their sins,   35
Establish them, that values may go on."

state of having the appearance of truth or probable

1. Vocabulary: verisimilitúde (8), *spawn* (34).
2. What is the subject of the poem?
3. What is the tone—admiration? Mockery? Both?
4. Explain fully the figures of speech in 2, 6, 26, 28–29 and their appropriateness. What kind of irony appears in the last stanza?

AMERICA FOR ME

'Tis fine to see the Old World, and travel up and down
Among the famous palaces and cities of renown,
To admire the crumbly castles and the statues of the kings—
But now I think I've had enough of antiquated things.

    So it's home again, and home again, America for me!   5
    My heart is turning home again, and there I long to be,
    In the land of youth and freedom beyond the ocean bars,
    Where the air is full of sunlight and the flag is full of stars.

Oh, London is a man's town, there's power in the air;
And Paris is a woman's town, with flowers in her hair;   10
And it's sweet to dream in Venice, and it's great to study Rome;
But when it comes to living there is no place like home.

I like the German fir-woods, in green battalions drilled;
I like the gardens of Versailles with flashing fountains filled;
But, oh, to take your hand, my dear, and ramble for a day   15
In the friendly western woodlands where Nature has her way!

I know that Europe's wonderful, yet something seems to lack:
The Past is too much with her, and the people looking back.
But the glory of the Present is to make the Future free—
We love our land for what she is and what she is to be.   20

    Oh, it's home again, and home again, America for me!
    I want a ship that's westward bound to plow the rolling sea,
    To the blessèd Land of Room Enough beyond the ocean bars,
    Where the air is full of sunlight and the flag is full of stars.

1. In what respects do the attitudes expressed in this poem fit the characterization made in "Boy-Man"?
2. "America for Me" and "Boy-Man" were both written by Americans. Which is more worthy of prolonged consideration? Why?

Good Poetry
and Great

If a poem has successfully met the test in the question, *How fully has it accomplished its purpose?* we are ready to subject it to our second question, *How important is its purpose?*

Great poetry must, of course, be good poetry. Noble intent alone cannot redeem a work that does not measure high on the scale of accomplishment; otherwise the sentimental and purely didactic verse of much of the last chapter would stand with the world's masterpieces. But once a work has been judged as successful on the scale of execution, its final standing will depend on its significance of purpose.

Suppose, for instance, we consider three poems in our text: the limerick "There Was a Young Lady of Niger" (page 239), Browning's poem "Boot and Saddle" (page 227), and Shakespeare's sonnet "That Time of Year" (page 241). Each of these would probably be judged by competent critics as highly successful in accomplishing what it sets out to do. The limerick tells its little story without an unnecessary word, with no "wrong" word, with no distortion of normal sentence order forced by exigencies of meter or rime; the limerick form is ideally suited to the author's humorous purpose; and the manner in which the story is told, with its understatement, its neat shift in position of the lady and her smile, is economical and delicious. Yet we should hardly call this poetry at all: it does not really communicate experience, nor does it attempt to. It attempts merely to relate a brief anecdote humorously and effectively. Browning's poem, on the other hand, is poetry, and good poetry. It almost immediately catches us up in the breathless excitement of a spirited horseback ride to rescue a besieged castle. The vigorous language of the speaker briefly reveals a gallant and courageous man with a gallant and courageous wife. The rousing chorus shows that his comrades have not lost heart though the struggle is going against them. Yet this poem, good though it is, gives no profound insights into human nature or human experience. It engages our senses and our imagination, but it gives us little to think about, and, emotionally, it is superficially exciting rather than deeply moving. Shakespeare's sonnet takes us much closer to the core of human living and suffering and loving. Concerned as it is with the universal human tragedy of growing old, with approaching death, and with love, it "says" more than does either Browning's poem or the limerick; it communicates a richer experience; it successfully accomplishes a more significant purpose. Of the three poems it is the greatest. The discriminating reader will get from it a deeper enjoyment because he has been nourished as well as delighted.

Great poetry engages the whole man in his response—senses, imagination, emotion, intellect; it does not touch him merely on one or two sides of his nature. Great poetry seeks not merely to entertain the reader but to bring him, along with pure pleasure, fresh insights, or renewed insights, and important insights, into the nature of human experience. Great poetry, we might say, gives its reader a broader and deeper understanding of life, of his fellow men, and of himself, always with the qualification, of course, that the kind of insight literature gives is not necessarily the kind that can be summed up in a simple "lesson" or "moral." It is *knowledge—felt* knowledge, *new* knowledge—of the complexities of human nature and of the tragedies and sufferings, the excitements and joys, that characterize human experience.

Is Shakespeare's sonnet a *great* poem? It is, at least, a great *sonnet*. Greatness, like goodness, is relative. If we compare any of Shakespeare's sonnets with his greatest plays—*Macbeth, Othello, Hamlet, King Lear*—another big difference appears. What is undertaken and accomplished in these tragedies is enormously greater, more difficult, and more complex than could ever be undertaken or accomplished in a single sonnet. Greatness in literature, in fact, cannot be entirely dissociated from size. In literature, as in basketball and football, a good big man is better than a good little man. The greatness of a poem is in proportion to the range and depth and intensity of experience that it brings to us: its amount of life. Shakespeare's plays offer us a multiplicity of life and a depth of living that could never be compressed into the fourteen lines of a sonnet. They organize a greater complexity of life and experience into unity.

Yet, after all, we have provided no easy yardsticks or rule-of-thumb measures for literary judgment. There are no mechanical tests. The final measuring rod can be only the responsiveness, the maturity, the taste and discernment of the cultivated reader. Such taste and discernment are partly a native endowment, partly the product of maturity and experience, partly the achievement of conscious study, training, and intellectual effort. They cannot be achieved suddenly or quickly; they can never be achieved in perfection. The pull is a long pull and a hard pull. But success, even relative success, brings enormous rewards in enrichment and command of life.

Comparing brook to life that represents universal / that is running down & not being placed. / or eternity / setting: man & wife sitting beside brook.

WEST-RUNNING BROOK*

"Fred, where is north?"

"North? North is there, my love.
The brook runs west."

"West-running Brook then call it."
(West-running Brook men call it to this day.)
"What does it think it's doing running west
When all the other country brooks flow east
To reach the ocean? It must be the brook
Can trust itself to go by contraries
The way I can with you—and you with me—
Because we're—we're—I don't know what we are.
What are we?"

He's more philosophical & she's more practical & down to earth.

"Young or new?"

"We must be something.   10
We've said we two. Let's change that to we three.
As you and I are married to each other,
We'll both be married to the brook. We'll build
Our bridge across it, and the bridge shall be

*Mr. Frost recorded "West-Running Brook" (LP, Caedmon, TC 1060).

Our arm thrown over it asleep beside it.

Look, look, it's waving to us with a wave _____
To let us know it hears me."- *personification*

                    "Why, my dear,
That wave's been standing off this jut of shore—"
(The black stream, catching on a sunken rock,
Flung backward on itself in one white wave,   20
And the white water rode the black forever,
Not gaining but not losing, like a bird
White feathers from the struggle of whose breast
Flecked the dark stream and flecked the darker pool
Below the point, and were at last driven wrinkled   25
In a white scarf against the far shore alders.)
"That wave's been standing off this jut of shore
Ever since rivers, I was going to say,
Were made in heaven. It wasn't waved to us."

"It wasn't, yet it was. If not to you   30
It was to me—in an annunciation."

"Oh, if you take it off to lady-land,
As't were the country of the Amazons
We men must see you to the confines of
And leave you there, ourselves forbid to enter,—   35
It is your brook! I have no more to say."

"Yes, you have, too. Go on. You thought of something."

"Speaking of contraries, see how the brook
In that white wave runs counter to itself.
It is from that in water we were from   40
Long, long before we were from any creature.
Here we, in our impatience of the steps,
Get back to the beginning of beginnings,
The stream of everything that runs away.
Some say existence like a <u>Pirouot</u> *pen*   45
<u>And Pirouette</u>, forever in one place,
Stands still and dances, but it runs away,
It seriously, sadly, runs away
To fill the abyss' void with emptiness.
It flows beside us in this water brook,   50

But it flows over us. It flows between us
To separate us for a panic moment.
It flows between us, over us, and *with* us.
And it is time, strength, tone, light, life, and love—
And even substance lapsing unsubstantial;   55
The universal cataract of death
That spends to nothingness—and unresisted,
Save by some strange resistance in itself,
Not just a swerving, but a throwing back,
As if regret were in it and were sacred.   60
It has this throwing backward on itself
So that the fall of most of it is always
Raising a little, sending up a little.
Our life runs down in sending up the clock.
The brook runs down in sending up our life.   65
The sun runs down in sending up the brook.
And there is something sending up the sun.
It is this backward motion toward the source,
Against the stream, that most we see ourselves in,
The tribute of the current to the source.   70
It is from this in nature we are from.
It is most us."

        "Today will be the day
You said so."

        "No, today will be the day
You said the brook was called West-running Brook."

"Today will be the day of what we both said."   75

Robert Frost (1874–1963)

QUESTIONS   *an announcing*   *big women or female warriors*

1. Vocabulary: *annunciation* (31), *Amazons* (33). In *Pirouot* and
Pirouette (45–46) Frost is punning on *Pierrot* and *Pierette*, traditional
pantomime characters, and *pirouette*, a spin on one foot in ballet. How does
the pun serve the meaning?

2. In what section of the country is this poem set? How is the setting
important to the meaning?

3. Characterize the man and his wife. How are they alike? How different? What "contraries" do they exhibit in their conversation? How are these
harmonized?

281

4. According to the second law of thermodynamics, we live in a universe that is running down, in which usable energy is being exhausted. What symbol does Frost (or the husband) use for this notion? What counter-symbol does he set against it? In what does he find a source of meaning and value in existence?

5. Point out all the "contraries" in the poem. What function do they serve?

6. Using the criteria for literary greatness developed in this chapter, how would you rate this poem as compared with Alfred Noyes's "The Barrel-Organ" (page 210)? Why?

THE LOVE SONG OF J. ALFRED PRUFROCK*

S'io credesse che mia risposta fosse
A persona che mai tornasse al mondo,
Questa fiamma staria senza piu scosse.
Ma perciocche giammai di questo fondo
Non torno vivo alcun, s'i'odo il vero,
Senza tema d'infamia ti rispondo.

Let us go then, you and I,
When the evening is spread out against the sky
Like a patient etherized upon a table;
Let us go, through certain half-deserted streets,
The muttering retreats   5
Of restless nights in one-night cheap hotels
And sawdust restaurants with oyster-shells:
Streets that follow like a tedious argument
Of insidious intent
To lead you to an overwhelming question . . .   10
Oh, do not ask, "What is it?"
Let us go and make our visit.

In the room the women come and go
Talking of Michelangelo.

The yellow fog that rubs its back upon the window-panes,   15
The yellow smoke that rubs its muzzle on the window-panes
Licked its tongue into the corners of the evening,
Lingered upon the pools that stand in drains,

*Mr. Eliot recorded "The Love Song of J. Alfred Prufrock" (LP, Harvard Vocarium, L–6002; or LP, Caedmon, TC 1045).

Let fall upon its back the soot that falls from chimneys,
Slipped by the terrace, made a sudden leap, 20
And seeing that it was a soft October night,
Curled once about the house, and fell asleep.

   And indeed there will be time
For the yellow smoke that slides along the street,
Rubbing its back upon the window-panes; 25
There will be time, there will be time
To prepare a face to meet the faces that you meet;
There will be time to murder and create,
And time for all the works and days of hands
That lift and drop a question on your plate; 30
Time for you and time for me,
And time yet for a hundred indecisions,
And for a hundred visions and revisions,
Before the taking of a toast and tea.

   In the room the women come and go 35
Talking of Michelangelo.

   And indeed there will be time
To wonder, "Do I dare?" and, "Do I dare?"
Time to turn back and descend the stair,
With a bald spot in the middle of my hair— 40
[They will say: "How his hair is growing thin!"]
My morning coat, my collar mounting firmly to the chin,
My necktie rich and modest, but asserted by a simple pin—
[They will say: "But how his arms and legs are thin!"]
Do I dare 45
Disturb the universe?
In a minute there is time
For decisions and revisions which a minute will reverse.

   For I have known them all already, known them all:—
Have known the evenings, mornings, afternoons, 50
I have measured out my life with coffee spoons;
I know the voices dying with a dying fall
Beneath the music from a farther room.
   So how should I presume?

And I have known the eyes already, known them all— 55
The eyes that fix you in a formulated phrase,
And when I am formulated, sprawling on a pin,
When I am pinned and wriggling on the wall,
Then how should I begin
To spit out all the butt-ends of my days and ways? 60
And how should I presume?

And I have known the arms already, known them all—
Arms that are braceleted and white and bare
[But in the lamplight, downed with light brown hair!]
Is it perfume from a dress 65
That makes me so digress?
Arms that lie along a table, or wrap about a shawl.
And should I then presume?
And how should I begin?

. . . . . .

Shall I say, I have gone at dusk through narrow streets 70
And watched the smoke that rises from the pipes
Of lonely men in shirt-sleeves, leaning out of windows? . . .
Has lost identity so expresses yearning to go back to simpler time
I should have been a pair of ragged claws — Lobster or Crab
Scuttling across the floors of silent seas.

. . . . . .

And the afternoon, the evening, sleeps so peacefully! 75
Smoothed by long fingers,
Asleep . . . tired . . . or it malingers,
Stretched on the floor, here beside you and me.
Should I, after tea and cakes and ices,
Have the strength to force the moment to its crisis? 80
But though I have wept and fasted, wept and prayed,
Though I have seen my head [grown slightly bald] brought in
upon a platter,
I am no prophet—and here's no great matter;
I have seen the moment of my greatness flicker,
And I have seen the eternal Footman hold my coat, and snicker, 85
And in short, I was afraid.

And would it have been worth it, after all,
After the cups, the marmalade, the tea,

Among the porcelain, among some talk of you and me,
Would it have been worth while,   90
To have bitten off the matter with a smile,
To have squeezed the universe into a ball
To roll it toward some overwhelming question,
To say: "I am Lazarus, come from the dead,
Come back to tell you all, I shall tell you all"—   95
If one, settling a pillow by her head,
      Should say: "That is not what I meant at all.
      That is not it, at all."

      And would it have been worth it, after all,
Would it have been worth while,   100
After the sunsets and the dooryards and the sprinkled streets,
After the novels, after the teacups, after the skirts that trail
      along the floor—
And this, and so much more?—
It is impossible to say just what I mean!
But as if a magic lantern threw the nerves in patterns on a screen: 105
Would it have been worth while
If one, settling a pillow or throwing off a shawl,
And turning toward the window, should say:
      "That is not it at all,
      That is not what I meant, at all."   110

No! I am not Prince Hamlet, nor was meant to be; *represents traditional classic hero — Common man doesn't have the blood or far to fall so isn't tragic.*
Am an attendant lord, one that will do
To swell a progress, start a scene or two,
Advise the prince; no doubt, an easy tool,
Deferential, glad to be of use,   115
Politic, cautious, and meticulous;
Full of high sentence, but a bit obtuse;
At times, indeed, almost ridiculous—
Almost, at times, the Fool.

      I grow old . . . I grow old . . .   120
I shall wear the bottoms of my trousers rolled.°   cuffed

      Shall I part my hair behind? Do I dare to eat a peach?
I shall wear white flannel trousers, and walk upon the beach.
I have heard the mermaids singing, each to each.

I do not think that they will sing to me.

I have seen them riding seaward on the waves
Combing the white hair of the waves blown back
When the wind blows the water white and black.

We have lingered in the chambers of the sea
By sea-girls wreathed with seaweed red and brown
Till human voices wake us, and we drown. 130

T. S. Eliot (1888–1965)

QUESTIONS

1. Vocabulary: *insidious* (9), *Michelangelo* (14), *muzzle* (16), *malingers* (77), *progress* (113), *deferential* (115), *politic* (116), *meticulous* (116), *sentence* (117).

2. This poem may be for you the most difficult in the book, because it uses a "stream of consciousness" technique (that is, presents the apparently random thoughts going through a person's head within a certain time interval), in which the transitional links are psychological rather than logical, and also because it uses allusions you may be unfamiliar with. Even though you do not at first understand the poem in detail, you should be able to get from it a quite accurate picture of Prufrock's character and personality. What kind of person is he? (Answer this as fully as possible.) From what class of society is he? What one line especially well sums up the nature of his past life? A brief initial orientation may be helpful: Prufrock is apparently on his way, at the beginning of the poem, to a late afternoon tea, at which he wishes (or does he?) to make a declaration of love to some lady who will be present. The "you and I" of the first line are divided parts of Prufrock's own nature, for he is undergoing internal conflict. Does he make the declaration? Why not? Where does the climax of the poem come? If the first half of the poem (up to the climax) is devoted to Prufrock's effort to prepare himself psychologically to make the declaration (or to postpone such effort), what is the latter half (after the climax) devoted to?

3. There are a number of striking or unusual figures of speech in the poem. Most of them in some way reflect Prufrock's own nature or his desires or fears. From this point of view discuss lines 2–3; 15–22 and 75–78; 57–58; 73–74; and 124–31. What figure of speech is lines 73–74? In what respect is the title ironical?

4. The poem makes an extensive use of literary allusion. The Italian epigraph is a passage from Dante's *Inferno* in which a man in Hell tells a visitor that he would never tell his story if there were a chance that it would get back to living ears. In line 29 the phrase "works and days" is the title of

a long poem—a description of agricultural life and a call to toil—by the early Greek poet Hesiod. Line 52 echoes the opening speech of Shakespeare's *Twelfth Night*. The prophet of lines 81–83 is John the Baptist, whose head was delivered to Salome by Herod as a reward for her dancing (Matthew 14:1–11, and Oscar Wilde's play *Salome*). Line 92 echoes the closing six lines of Marvell's "To His Coy Mistress" (page 77). Lazarus (94-95) may be either the beggar Lazarus (of Luke 16) who was not permitted to return from the dead to warn the brothers of a rich man about Hell or the Lazarus (of John 11) whom Christ raised from death or both. Lines 111–19 allude to a number of characters from Shakespeare's *Hamlet*: Hamlet himself, the chamberlain Polonius, and various minor characters including probably Rosencrantz, Guildenstern, and Osric. "Full of high sentence" (117) echoes Chaucer's description of the Clerk of Oxford in the Prologue to *The Canterbury Tales*. Relate as many of these allusions as you can to the character of Prufrock. How is Prufrock particularly like Hamlet, and how is he unlike? Contrast Prufrock with the speaker in "To His Coy Mistress."

5. This poem and "West-running Brook" are dramatic in structure. One is a dialogue between two characters who speak in their own voices; the other is a highly allusive soliloquy or interior monologue. In what ways do their dramatic structures facilitate what they have to say?

6. This poem and Charlotte Mew's "The Changeling" (page 191) both focus on a conflict between two worlds—one real, the other unreal. Using the criteria for literary greatness developed in this chapter, how would you rate the two poems as compared to each other? Why?

Contrasting youth and age.

AMONG SCHOOL CHILDREN

I

I walk through the long schoolroom questioning;
A kind old nun in a white hood replies;
The children learn to cipher and to sing,
To study reading-books and history,
To cut and sew, be neat in everything   5
In the best modern way—the children's eyes
In momentary wonder stare upon
A sixty-year-old smiling public man.

II

I dream of a Ledaean body, bent
Above a sinking fire, a tale that she   10
Told of a harsh reproof, or trivial event

That changed some childish day to tragedy—
Told, and it seemed that our two natures blent
Into a sphere from youthful sympathy,
Or else, to alter Plato's parable,   15
Into the yolk and white of the one shell.

III

And thinking of that fit of grief or rage
I look upon one child or t'other there
And wonder if she stood so at that age—
For even daughters of the swan can share   20
Something of every paddler's heritage—
And had that color upon cheek or hair,
And thereupon my heart is driven wild:
She stands before me as a living child.

IV

Her present image floats into the mind—   25
Did Quattrocento finger fashion it
Hollow of cheek as though it drank the wind
And took a mess of shadows for its meat?
And I though never of Ledaean kind
Had pretty plumage once—enough of that,   30
Better to smile on all that smile, and show
There is a comfortable kind of old scarecrow.

V

What youthful mother, a shape upon her lap
Honey of generation had betrayed,
And that must sleep, shriek, struggle to escape   35
As recollection or the drug decide,
Would think her son, did she but see that shape
With sixty or more winters on its head,
A compensation for the pang of his birth,
Or the uncertainty of his setting forth?   40

VI

Plato thought nature but a spume that plays
Upon a ghostly paradigm of things;
Solider Aristotle played the taws
Upon the bottom of a king of kings;

> World-famous golden-thighed Pythagoras   45
> Fingered upon a fiddle-stick or strings
> What a star sang and careless Muses heard:
> Old clothes upon old sticks to scare a bird. *— image of scarecrow — thinks body & himself as no use & old.*
>
> ### VII
>
> Both nuns and mothers worship images,   *As opposed to*
> But those the candles light are not as those   *art & wisdom.*
> That animate a mother's reveries,
> But keep a marble or a bronze repose.
> And yet they too break hearts—O Presences
> That passion, piety or affection knows,
> And that all heavenly glory symbolize—   55
> O self-born mockers of man's enterprise;
>
> ### VIII
>
> *Immortality of art.*
>
> Labor is blossoming or dancing where
> The body is not bruised to pleasure soul,
> Nor beauty born out of its own despair,
> Nor blear-eyed wisdom out of midnight oil.   60
> O chestnut-tree, great-rooted blossomer,
> Are you the leaf, the blossom or the bole?
> O body swayed to music, O brightening glance,
> How can we know the dancer from the dance?

William Butler Yeats (1865–1939)

QUESTIONS

1. Vocabulary: *Quattrocento* (26) *15th century esp. w/ reference to Italian literature art*, *mess* (28) *food*, *spume* (41) *foam scum*, *paradigm* (42) *pattern or example*, *bole* (62) *— think of tree*.

2. William Butler Yeats was a senator of the Irish Free State from 1922 to 1928. This poem, written in 1926, arises out of a visit of inspection to an Irish school, probably Catholic since Ireland is primarily a Catholic country. In stanza II Yeats is thinking of the talented Maud Gonne, to whom he paid court so long and unsuccessfully (see "The Folly of Being Comforted," page 79). Plato (15), discussing love in the *Symposium*, represents male and female as having resulted from the division of an originally single being, round in shape, into two halves which are forever seeking to regain their original unity. What is "a Ledaean body" (9)? See line 20 and "Leda and the Swan" (page 140). What additional fairy-tale allusion is there in lines 20–21? What are the literal and symbolical implications of "bent" (9) and

of "a sinking fire" (10)? What is the "present image" of Maud Gonne (25–28)? What figure of speech is "Quattrocento finger" (26), and what historical persons might it refer to?

3. What is the meaning of lines 33–34—especially, why is the child "betrayed"? "Shape" (33) and "winters" (38) are both metonymies; what is their contribution? Why does Yeats use "winters" instead of, say, "springs"?

4. Plato (41) thought the visible world simply a pale reflection or copy of a divine and more real world of "forms" or "ideas." Aristotle (43), a more realistic philosopher, was tutor to the youthful Alexander the Great, whom he may have occasionally whipped with "taws" (a whip made of leather thongs). Pythagoras (45), a philosopher and mathematician, discovered the laws of vibrating strings upon which harmony is based, thus demonstrating a correspondence between music and mathematics; conceiving of the universe as mathematically ordered and therefore harmonious, he supposed that the planets in their courses must give off varying musical tones—"the music of the spheres." According to ancient legend, he had a golden hip or thigh. What do these philosophers have in common in Yeats's mind, and how does this stanza relate to stanzas IV and V?

5. What "images" are worshipped by nuns (49), and why are nuns mentioned here? What other kinds of "images" have been mentioned in the poem? What are the "Presences" of lines 53–54? Why do they mock "man's enterprise"?

6. What main contrasts have been made in the poem? How does stanza VIII bring together and comment on these contrasts? What two meanings has "Labor" (57)? What is Yeats's conclusion about the relationship of body and mind or body and soul, of the real and the ideal? What is symbolized by the blossoming chestnut tree and the dancing dancer? Why does Yeats use two symbols rather than just one?

7. Using the criteria for literary greatness developed in this chapter, how would you rate "Among School Children" as compared with Swinburne's "A Forsaken Garden" (page 183).

EXERCISES

In the following exercises, use both scales of poetic measurement—perfection and significance of accomplishment.

1. Which of the poems "Richard Cory" (page 45) and "The Rich Man" (page 47) is finer and why?

2. Considering such matters as economy and richness of poetic communication, inevitability of organization, and the complexity and maturity of the attitude or philosophy expressed, decide whether "Barter" (page 150) or "Stopping by Woods on a Snowy Evening" is the superior poem (page 150).

3. Which of the ballads "The Twa Corbies" (page 13) and "Edward" (page 250) is superior as judged by the power and complexity of its poetic achievement and the human significance of its result?

4. Rank the following short poems and explain the reasons for your ranking:
   a. "On a Dead Hostess" (page 107), "The Span of Life" (page 222).
   b. "Driving to Town Late to Mail a Letter" (page 63), "In the Garden" (page 147), "The Death of the Ball Turret Gunner" (page 323).
   c. "The Coming of Wisdom with Time" (page 167), "The Turtle" (page 178), "Splinter" (page 218).
   d. "The Sea-Gull" (page 69), "I May, I Might, I Must" (page 108), "Quatrain" (page 69).
   e. "There Is No Frigate Like a Book" (page 39), "The Sick Rose" (page 94), "Song: Hark, Hark!" (page 217).
   f. "Stars, I Have Seen Them Fall" (page 94), "Metrical Feet" (page 214), "Spectrum" (page 255).

5. "The Eagle" (page 5), "The Twa Corbies" (page 13), and "The Sea-Gull" (page 69) all deal with birds. Rank them on a scale of poetic worth.

6. The following poems are all on seasons of the year. Rank them on a scale of poetic accomplishment: "Winter" (page 6), "To Autumn" (page 62), "Spring" (page 11).

7. "The Man He Killed" (page 23) and "Naming of Parts" (page 47) both treat of the subject of war. Which is the superior poem?

8. The following poems all have a drinker as their subject. Rank them in order of excellence and support your ranking: "Was a Man" (page 12), "The Drinker" (page 328), "Mr. Flood's Party" (page 339).

9. "A Valediction: Forbidding Mourning" (page 76), "To Lucasta, Going to the Wars" (page 119), and "The 'Je Ne Sais Quoi'" (page 205) all in one way or another treat of the subject of love. Evaluate and rank them.

10. In this book you have read a number of poems by Robert Browning. Rank the following in order of their excellence and defend your ranking: "Meeting at Night" and "Parting at Morning" (considered as one poem) (pages 55 and 56), "My Star" (page 84), "My Last Duchess" (page 131), "Song" (page 152), "Boot and Saddle" (page 227).

11. Answer the preceding question with the following poems by Alfred, Lord Tennyson: "The Eagle" (page 5), "Ulysses" (page 96), "The De-

serted House" (page 106), "Crossing the Bar" (page 171), "The Oak" (page 204).

12. "The House on the Hill" (page 106) and "Mr. Flood's Party" (page 339) both evoke a sense of loneliness. Which more surely guarantees the poetic reputation of Edwin Arlington Robinson?

13. Herrick's "To the Virgins, to Make Much of Time" (page 91) and Marvell's "To His Coy Mistress" (page 77) are both *carpe diem* poems of acknowledged excellence. Which achieves the more complex unity?

14. Each of the following pairs is written by a single author. Pick the poem of each pair that you think represents the higher poetic accomplishment and explain why:
    a. "Hillside Thaw" (page 65), " 'Out, Out—' " (page 135).
    b. "On Moonlit Heath and Lonesome Bank" (page 58), "Oh Who Is That Young Sinner" (page 209).
    c. "When Adam Day by Day" (page 37), "Stars, I Have Seen Them Fall" (page 94).
    d. "To Autumn" (page 62), "Ode on a Grecian Urn" (page 323).
    e. "You, Andrew Marvell" (page 87), "Ars Poetica" (page 160).
    f. "There Is No Frigate Like a Book" (page 39), "Apparently with No Surpise" (page 164).
    g. "I Like to See It Lap the Miles" (page 228), "Because I Could Not Stop for Death" (page 309).
    h. "Winter" (page 6), "Spring" (page 11).
    i. "Yes; I Write Verses" (page 173), "To Age" (page 174).
    j. "The Margrave's Birthnight" (page 102), "The Bench of Boors" (page 233).
    k. "Had I the Choice" (page 215), "A Noiseless Patient Spider" (page 349).
    l. "The Folly of Being Comforted" (page 79), "Sailing to Byzantium" (page 359).
    m. "A Valediction: Forbidding Mourning" (page 76), "Song" (page 312).

PART TWO

Poems for
Further
Reading

MORNING SONG FROM "SENLIN"

It is morning, Senlin says, and in the morning
When the light drips through the shutters like the dew,
I arise, I face the sunrise,
And do the things my fathers learned to do.
Stars in the purple dusk above the rooftops   5
Pale in a saffron mist and seem to die,
And I myself on a swiftly tilting planet
Stand before a glass and tie my tie.

Vine leaves tap my window,
Dew-drops sing to the garden stones,   10
The robin chirps in the chinaberry tree
Repeating three clear tones.

It is morning. I stand by the mirror
And tie my tie once more.
While waves far off in a pale rose twilight   15
Crash on a coral shore.
I stand by a mirror and comb my hair:
How small and white my face!—
The green earth tilts through a sphere of air
And bathes in a flame of space.   20

There are houses hanging above the stars
And stars hung under a sea.
And a sun far off in a shell of silence
Dapples my walls for me.

It is morning, Senlin says, and in the morning   25
Should I not pause in the light to remember god?
Upright and firm I stand on a star unstable,
He is immense and lonely as a cloud.
I will dedicate this moment before my mirror
To him alone, for him I will comb my hair.   30
Accept these humble offerings, cloud of silence!
I will think of you as I descend the stair.

Vine leaves tap my window,
The snail-track shines on the stones,
Dew-drops flash from the chinaberry tree   35
Repeating two clear tones.

295

It is morning, I awake from a bed of silence,
Shining I rise from the starless waters of sleep.
The walls are about me still as in the evening,
I am the same, and the same name still I keep.   40
The earth revolves with me, yet makes no motion,
The stars pale silently in a coral sky.
In a whistling void I stand before my mirror,
Unconcerned, and tie my tie.

There are horses neighing on far-off hills   45
Tossing their long white manes,
And mountains flash in the rose-white dusk,
Their shoulders black with rains.
It is morning. I stand by the mirror
And surprise my soul once more;   50
The blue air rushes above my ceiling,
There are suns beneath my floor.

. . . It is morning, Senlin says, I ascend from darkness
And depart on the winds of space for I know not where,
My watch is wound, a key is in my pocket,   55
And the sky is darkened as I descend the stair.
There are shadows across the windows, clouds in heaven,
And a god among the stars; and I will go
Thinking of him as I might think of daybreak
And humming a tune I know.   60

Vine leaves tap at the window,
Dew-drops sing to the garden stones,
The robin chirps in the chinaberry tree
Repeating three clear tones.

Conrad Aiken (b. 1889)

A BOOKSHOP IDYLL

Between the *gardening* and the *cookery*
   Comes the brief *Poetry* shelf;
By the Nonesuch Donne, a thin anthology
   Offers itself.

Critical, and with nothing else to do,   5
   I scan the Contents page,

Relieved to find the names are mostly new;
    No one my age.

Like all strangers, they divide by sex:
    Landscape near Parma   10
Interests a man, so does *The Double Vortex*,
    So does *Rilke and Buddha*.

"I travel, you see," "I think" and "I can read"
    These titles seem to say;
But *I Remember You, Love is my Creed*,   15
    Poem for J.,

The ladies' choice, discountenance my patter
    For several seconds;
From somewhere in this (as in any) matter
    A moral beckons.   20

Should poets bicycle-pump the human heart
    Or squash it flat?
Man's love is of man's life a thing apart;
    Girls aren't like that.

We men have got love well weighed up; our stuff   25
    Can get by without it.
Women don't seem to think that's good enough;
    They write about it.

And the awful way their poems lay them open
    Just doesn't strike them.   30
Women are really much nicer than men:
    No wonder we like them.

Deciding this, we can forget those times
    We sat up half the night
Chock-full of love, crammed with bright thoughts, names, rhymes,   35
    And couldn't write.

Kingsley Amis (b. 1922)

Old Scottish Folk Ballad → just tells a story

SIR PATRICK SPENCE

4 speakers:
1) King
2) Knight
3) Sir Patrick
4) narrator – sailor

        The king sits in Dumferling toune,
          Drinking the blude-reid wine;

"O whar will I get guid sailor,
  To sail this schip of mine?"

Up and spak an eldern knicht,   5
  Sat at the kings richt kne:
"Sir Patrick Spence is the best sailor,
  That sails upon the se."

The king has written a braid letter,
  And signd it wi his hand,   10
And sent it to Sir Patrick Spence,
  Was walking on the sand.

The first line that Sir Patrick red,
  A loud lauch lauched he;
The next line that Sir Patrick red,   15
  The teir blinded his ee.

"O wha is this has don this deid,
  This ill deid don to me,
To send me out this time o' the yeir,
  To sail upon the se!   20

"Mak haste, mak haste, my mirry men all,
  Our guid schip sails the morne."
"O say no sae, my master deir,
  For I feir a deadlie storme.

"Late, late yestreen I saw the new moone,   25
  Wi the auld moone in hir arme,
And I feir, I feir, my deir master,
  That we will cum to harme."

Q our Scots nobles *sailors* wer richt laith - *right loathe*   29
  To weet thair cork-heild schoone;°   cork-heeled shoes
Bot lang owre a' the play wer playd, - *long before they finished.*
  Thair hats they swam aboone.

O lang, lang may thair ladies sit,
  Wi thair fans into their hand,
Or eir they se Sir Patrick Spence *is a noble.*   35
  Cum sailing to the land.

*If you are the best maybe called upon in crisis
and not make it thru it.*

O lang, lang may the ladies stand,
    Wi thair gold kems in thair hair,
Waiting for thair ain deir lords,
    For they'll se thame na mair.   40

Haf owre, haf owre, to Aberdour,
    It's fiftie fadom deip,
And thair lies guid Sir Patrick Spence,
    Wi the Scots lords at his feit.

Anonymous

DOVER BEACH

The sea is calm tonight,
The tide is full, the moon lies fair
Upon the straits;—on the French coast the light
Gleams and is gone; the cliffs of England stand,
Glimmering and vast, out in the tranquil bay.   5
Come to the window, sweet is the night-air!
Only, from the long line of spray
Where the sea meets the moon-blanched land,
Listen! you hear the grating roar
Of pebbles which the waves draw back, and fling,   10
At their return, up the high strand,
Begin, and cease, and then again begin,
With tremulous cadence slow, and bring
The eternal note of sadness in.

Sophocles long ago   15
Heard it on the Aegean, and it brought
Into his mind the turbid ebb and flow
Of human misery; we
Find also in the sound a thought,
Hearing it by this distant northern sea.   20

The Sea of Faith
Was once, too, at the full, and round earth's shore
Lay like the folds of a bright girdle furled,
But now I only hear
Its melancholy, long, withdrawing roar,   25
Retreating, to the breath

Of the night-wind, down the vast edges drear
And naked shingles° of the world.   pebbled beaches

Ah, love, let us be true
To one another! for the world, which seems   30
To lie before us like a land of dreams,
So various, so beautiful, so new,
Hath really neither joy, nor love, nor light,
Nor certitude, nor peace, nor help for pain;
And we are here as on a darkling plain   35
Swept with confused alarms of struggle and flight,
Where ignorant armies clash by night.

                                        Matthew Arnold (1822–1888)

SONG: OLD ADAM, THE CARRION CROW

Old Adam, the carrion crow,
    The old crow of Cairo;
He sat in the shower, and let it flow
    Under his tail and over his crest;
        And through every feather   5
        Leaked the wet weather;
    And the bough swung under his nest;
For his beak it was heavy with marrow.
        Is that the wind dying? O no;
        It's only two devils, that blow   10
        Through a murderer's bones, to and fro,
        In the ghosts' moonshine.

Ho! Eve, my grey carrion wife,
    When we have supped on kings' marrow,
Where shall we drink and make merry our life?   15
    Our nest it is Queen Cleopatra's skull,
        'Tis cloven and cracked,
        And battered and hacked,
    But with tears of blue eyes it is full;
    Let us drink then, my raven of Cairo!   20
        Is that the wind dying? O no;
        It's only two devils, that blow

Through a murderer's bones, to and fro,
In the ghosts' moonshine.

Thomas Lovell Beddoes (1803–1849)

THE DIVINE IMAGE

To Mercy, Pity, Peace, and Love
All pray in their distress;
And to these virtues of delight
Return their thankfulness.

For Mercy, Pity, Peace, and Love   5
Is God, our father dear;
And Mercy, Pity, Peace, and Love
Is Man, his child and care.

For Mercy has a human heart,
Pity, a human face,   10
And Love, the human form divine,
And Peace, the human dress.

Then every man, of every clime,
That prays in his distress,
Prays to the human form divine,   15
Love, Mercy, Pity, Peace.

And all must love the human form,
In heathen, turk, or jew;
Where Mercy, Love, and Pity dwell,
There God is dwelling too.   20

William Blake (1757–1827)

Fearful aspects of tiger, forest.

Considering dual nature of God. (like Dickinson)

✓ THE TIGER

- What made the immortal tiger - must also be immortal - suggests fierceness of God & also gentleness by creating lamb.

Tiger! Tiger! burning bright
In the forests of the night,
What immortal hand or eye
Could frame thy fearful symmetry?

In what distant deeps or skies   5
Burnt the fire of thine eyes?

301

On what wings dare he aspire?
What the hand dare seize the fire?

And what shoulder, and what art,
Could twist the sinews of thy heart?   10
And when thy heart began to beat,
What dread hand forged thy dread feet?

What the hammer? what the chain?
In what furnace was thy brain?
What the anvil? what dread grasp   15
Dare its deadly terrors clasp?

When the stars threw down their spears,
And watered heaven with their tears,
Did he smile his work to see?
Did he who made the Lamb make thee?   20

Tiger! Tiger! burning bright
In the forests of the night,
What immortal hand or eye,
Dare frame thy fearful symmetry?

William Blake (1757–1827)

SO WE'LL GO NO MORE A-ROVING

So we'll go no more a-roving
    So late into the night,
Though the heart be still as loving,
    And the moon be still as bright.

For the sword outwears its sheath,   *compare body & soul*
    And the soul wears out the breast,
And the heart must pause to breathe,
    And Love itself have rest.

Though the night was made for loving,
    And the day returns too soon,   10
Yet we'll go no more a-roving
    By the light of the moon.   *inconsistant it is a reflection of*
                                                    sun.
        George Gordon, Lord Byron (1788–1824)

They'll enjoy
spiritual love in
death & forget
physical love on
earth.

NO PLATONIC LOVE

Tell me no more of minds embracing minds,
   And hearts exchanged for hearts;
That spirits spirits meet, as winds do winds,
   And mix their subt'lest parts;
That two unbodied essences may kiss,   5
And then like angels, twist and feel one bliss.

I was that silly thing that once was wrought
   To practise this thin love:
I climbed from sex to soul, from soul to thought;
   But thinking there to move,   10
Headlong I rolled from thought to soul, and then
From soul I lighted at the sex again.

As some strict down-looked men pretend to fast,
   Who yet in closets eat;
So lovers who profess they spirits taste,   15
   Feed yet on grosser meat;
I know they boast they souls to souls convey,
Howe'er they meet, the body is the way.

Come, I will undeceive thee, they that tread
   Those vain aerial ways,   20
Are like young heirs and alchemists misled
   To waste their wealth and days,
For searching thus to be forever rich,
They only find a medicine for the itch.

William Cartwright (1611–1643)

THE LATEST DECALOGUE

Thou shalt have one God only; who
Would be at the expense of two?
No graven images may be
Worshipped, except the currency.
Swear not at all; for, for thy curse   5
Thine enemy is none the worse.
At church on Sunday to attend
Will serve to keep the world thy friend.

Honor thy parents; that is, all
From whom advancement may befall.   10
Thou shalt not kill; but need'st not strive
Officiously to keep alive.
Do not adultery commit;
Advantage rarely comes of it.
Thou shalt not steal: an empty feat,   15
When it's so lucrative to cheat.
Bear not false witness; let the lie
Have time on its own wings to fly.
Thou shalt not covet, but tradition
Approves all forms of competition.   20

Arthur Hugh Clough (1819–1861)

KUBLA KHAN

*Believed wrote during a pain
dream cause he was addicted, but had sickness maybe*

In Xanadu did Kubla Khan
A stately pleasure-dome decree:
Where Alph, the sacred river, ran
Through caverns measureless to man
    Down to a sunless sea.   5
*supposed to be
best cause wrote
after dream*
So twice five miles of fertile ground
With walls and towers were girdled round:
And here were *freedom & religious activities* gardens bright with sinuous rills, *natures uneasy*
Where blossomed many an incense-bearing tree;
And here were forests ancient as the hills,   10
Enfolding sunny spots of greenery.

*interrupted &
forgot what dreamt*
But oh! that deep romantic chasm which slanted
Down the green hill athwart a cedarn cover!
A savage place! as holy and enchanted
As e'er beneath a waning moon was haunted   15
By woman wailing for her demon-lover!
And from this chasm, with ceaseless turmoil seething,
As if this earth in fast thick pants were breathing,
A mighty fountain momently was forced:
Amid whose swift half-intermitted burst   20
*Symbolizes
power of
man.*
Huge fragments vaulted like rebounding hail,
Or chaffy grain beneath the thresher's flail:
And 'mid these dancing rocks at once and ever

It flung up momently the sacred river.

romantic unity Five miles meandering with a mazy motion   25
Through wood and dale the sacred river ran,
Then reached the caverns measureless to man,
And sank in tumult to a lifeless ocean:
And 'mid this tumult Kubla heard from far
Ancestral voices prophesying war!   30
    The shadow of the dome of pleasure
    Floated midway on the waves;
    Where was heard the mingled measure
    From the fountain and the caves.
It was a miracle of rare device,   35
A sunny pleasure-dome with caves of ice!

A damsel with a dulcimer
In a vision once I saw:
It was an Abyssinian maid,
And on her dulcimer she played,   40
Singing of Mount Abora.
Could I revive within me
Her symphony and song,
To such a deep delight, 'twould win me,
That with music loud and long,   45
supposed to be word. I would build that dome in air,
That sunny dome! those caves of ice!
And all who heard should see them there,
And all should cry, Beware! Beware!
His flashing eyes, his floating hair!   50
Weave a circle round him thrice,   *criticizing*
And close your eyes with holy dread,   *him for taking this*
For he on honey-dew hath fed,   *drug)*
And drunk the milk of Paradise.

Samuel Taylor Coleridge (1772–1834)

INCIDENT

Once riding in old Baltimore
    Heart-filled, head-filled with glee,
I saw a Baltimorean
    Keep looking straight at me.

Now I was eight and very small,
    And he was no whit bigger,
And so I smiled, but he poked out   5
    His tongue, and called me, "Nigger."

I saw the whole of Baltimore
    From May until December;   10
Of all the things that happened there
    That's all that I remember.

Countée Cullen (1903–1946)

THE LISTENERS

spirits represent the past — silent
and things that can't be replaced.
Can't communicate with past cause can't relive.

"Is there anybody there?" said the Traveller, *represents every man*
    Knocking on the moonlit door;
And his horse in the silence champed the grasses
    Of the forest's ferny floor:
And a bird flew up out of the turret,   5
    Above the Traveller's head:
And he smote upon the door again a second time;
    "Is there anybody there?" he said.

man is calling out to the past for answers but the past can't answer cause can't relive

But no one descended to the Traveller;
    No head from the leaf-fringed sill   10
Leaned over and looked into his grey eyes,
    Where he stood perplexed and still. — *confused*
But only a host of phantom listeners   *represents the unknown*
    That dwelt in the lone house then
Stood listening in the quiet of the moonlight   15
    To that voice from the world of men:
Stood thronging the faint moonbeams on the dark stair,
    That goes down to the empty hall,
Hearkening in an air stirred and shaken
    By the lonely Traveller's call.
And he felt in his heart their strangeness,   20
    Their stillness answering his cry,   *feels there's a mysteriousness that will never be uncovered*
While his horse moved, cropping the dark turf,
    'Neath the starred and leafy sky;
For he suddenly smote on the door, even   25
    Louder, and lifted his head:—

"Tell them I came, and no one answered,
   That I kept my word," he said.
Never the least stir made the listeners,
   Though every word he spake   30
Fell echoing through the shadowiness of the still house
   From the one man left awake:
Ay, they heard his foot upon the stirrup,
   And the sound of iron on stone,
And how the silence surged softly backward,   35
   When the plunging hoofs were gone.

                         Walter de la Mare (1873–1956)

Past can never be awaken uncovered or relived.

THE BEE

To the football coaches of Clemson College, 1942

One dot
Grainily shifting   we at roadside and
The smallest wings coming   along the rail fence out
Of the woods   one dot   of all that green. It now
Becomes flesh-crawling   then the quite still   5
Of stinging. I must live faster for my terrified
Small son   it is on him. Has come. Clings.

Old wingback, come
To life. If your knee action is high
Enough, the fat may fall in time   God damn   10
You, Dickey, *dig*   this is your last time to cut
And run   but you must give it everything you have
Left, for screaming near your screaming child is the sheer
Murder of California traffic: some bee hangs driving

Your child   15
Blindly onto the highway. Get there however
Is still possible. Long live what I badly did
At Clemson   and all of my clumsiest drives
For the ball   all of my trying to turn
The corner downfield   and my spindling explosions   20
Through the five-hole over tackle. O backfield

Coach Shag Norton,
Tell me as you never yet have told me

To get the lead out   scream whatever will get
The slow-motion of middle age off me   I cannot   25
Make it this way   I will have to leave
My feet   they are gone   I have him where
He lives   and down we go singing with screams into

The dirt,
Son-screams of fathers   screams of dead coaches turning   30
To approval   and from between us the bee rises screaming
With flight . grainily shifting   riding the rail fence
Back into the woods   traffic blasting past us
Unchanged, nothing heard through the air-
conditioning glass   we lying at roadside full   35

Of the forearm prints
Of roadrocks   strawberries on our elbows as from
Scrimmage with the varsity   now we can get
Up   stand   turn away from the highway   look straight
Into trees. See, there is nothing coming out   no   40
Smallest wing   no shift of a flight-grain   nothing
Nothing. Let us go in, son, and listen

For some tobacco-
mumbling voice in the branches   to say "That's
a little better,"   to our lives still hanging   45
By a hair. There is nothing to stop us   we can go
Deep   deeper   into elms, and listen to traffic die
Roaring, like a football crowd from which we have
Vanished. Dead coaches live in the air, son   live

In the ear   50
Like fathers, and *urge*   and *urge*. They want you better
Than you are. When needed, they rise and curse you   they scream
When something must be saved. Here, under this tree,
We can sit down. You can sleep, and I can try
To give back what I have earned by keeping us   55
Alive, and safe from bees: the smile of some kind

Of savior—
Of touchdowns, of fumbles, battles,
Lives. Let me sit here with you, son
As on the bench, while the first string takes back   60

Over, far away   and say with my silentest tongue, with the man-
creating bruises of my arms   with a live leaf a quick
Dead hand on my shoulder, "Coach Norton, I am your boy."

James Dickey (b. 1923)

BECAUSE I COULD NOT STOP FOR DEATH

Because I could not stop for <u>Death</u>,— *personified as a carriage driver.*
He kindly stopped for me;
The <u>carriage</u> held but just ourselves   *hearse*
And Immortality.

We slowly drove; he knew no haste,   5
And I had put away
My labor and my leisure too,
For his civility.

We passed the school, where children strove,
At recess, in the ring,   10
We passed the fields of <u>gazing grain</u>,— *symbol of maturity (time of harvest)*   *reliving the past*
We passed the <u>setting sun</u>.— *end of life*

Or rather, he passed us;
The dews drew quivering and chill;
For only gossamer, <u>my gown</u>;— *a woman personae* 15
My tippet, only tulle.

We paused before a house that seemed
A swelling of the ground;
The roof was scarcely visible.
The cornice, in the ground.   20

Since then, 'tis centuries, and yet
Feels shorter than the day
I first surmised the horses' heads
Were toward eternity.

Emily Dickinson (1830–1886)

MY LIFE HAD STOOD, A LOADED GUN

My life had stood, a loaded gun,
In corners, till a day

309

The owner passed, identified,
And carried me away.

And now we roam in sovereign woods,   5
And now we hunt the doe,
And every time I speak for him,
The mountains straight reply.

And do I smile, such cordial light
Upon the valley glow,   10
It is as a Vesuvian face
Had let its pleasure through.

And when at night, our good day done,
I guard my master's head,
'Tis better than the eider-duck's   15
Deep pillow, to have shared.

To foe of his I'm deadly foe:
None stir the second time
On whom I lay a yellow eye
Or an emphatic thumb.   20

Though I than he may longer live,
He longer must than I,
For I have but the power to kill,
Without the power to die.

Emily Dickinson (1830–1886)

THE GOOD-MORROW

I wonder, by my troth, what thou and I
Did till we loved? were we not weaned till then,
But sucked on country pleasures, childishly?
Or snorted we in the seven sleepers' den?
'Twas so; but this, all pleasures fancies be.   5
If ever any beauty I did see,
Which I desired, and got, 'twas but a dream of thee.

And now good-morrow to our waking souls,
Which watch not one another out of fear;

THE GOOD-MORROW.   4. *seven sleepers' den*: a cave where, according to Christian
legend, seven youths escaped persecution and slept for two centuries.

For love all love of other sights controls,   10
And makes one little room an everywhere.
Let sea-discoverers to new worlds have gone;
Let maps to other,° worlds on worlds have shown;   others
Let us possess one world; each hath one, and is one.

My face in thine eye, thine in mine appears,   15
And true plain hearts do in the faces rest;
Where can we find two better hemispheres
Without sharp north, without declining west?
Whatever dies was not mixed equally;
If our two loves be one, or thou and I   20
Love so alike that none can slacken, none can die.

John Donne (1572–1631)

THE SUN RISING

Busy old fool, unruly Sun,
    Why dost thou thus
Through windows and through curtains call on us?
Must to thy motions lovers' seasons run?
        Saucy pedantic wretch, go chide   5
        Late schoolboys and sour prentices,
    Go tell court-huntsmen that the king will ride,
    Call country ants to harvest offices;
Love, all alike, no season knows, nor clime,
Nor hours, days, months, which are the rags of time.   10

        Thy beams so reverend and strong
        Why shouldst thou think?
I could eclipse and cloud them with a wink,
But that I would not lose her sight so long;
        If her eyes have not blinded thine,   15
        Look, and tomorrow late tell me,
    Whether both th' Indias of spice and mine
    Be where thou left'st them, or lie here with me.
Ask for those kings whom thou saw'st yesterday,
And thou shalt hear, "All here in one bed lay."   20
        She's all states, and all princes I;
        Nothing else is.

Princes do but play us; compared to this,
All honor's mimic, all wealth alchemy.
      Thou, Sun, art half as happy as we,   25
      In that the world's contracted thus;
      Thine age asks ease, and since thy duties be
      To warm the world, that's done in warming us.
Shine here to us, and thou art everywhere;
This bed thy center is, these walls thy sphere.   30

John Donne (1572–1631)

SONG: GO AND CATCH A FALLING STAR

Faithfulness of Women.

Go and catch a falling star, —*impossible to humans*
      Get with child a mandrake root,—
Tell me where all past years are,
      Or who cleft the devil's foot,
Teach me to hear mermaids singing, —*no proof there are mermaids* 5
      Or to keep off envy's stinging,
            And find
            What wind
Serves to advance an honest mind.

If thou be'st born to strange sights,   10
      Things invisible to see,
Ride ten thousand days and nights,
      Till age snow white hairs on thee,
Thou, when thou return'st, wilt tell me
      All strange wonders that befell thee,   15
            And swear
            No where
Lives a woman true and fair.

If thou find'st one, let me know;
      Such a pilgrimage were sweet.   20
Yet do not; I would not go,
      Though at next door we might meet.

SONG.   2. *mandrake*: supposed to resemble a human being because of its forked
root.

Though she were true when you met her,
    And last till you write your letter,
        Yet she   25
        Will be
False, ere I come, to two or three.

✓ **VERGISSMEINICHT** – *forget me not*

Three weeks gone and the combatants gone,
returning over the nightmare ground – *imagery*
we found the place again, and found
the soldier sprawling in the sun.

The frowning barrel of his gun   5
overshadowing. As we came on
that day, he hit my tank with one
like the entry of a demon.

Look. Here in the gunpit spoil
the dishonored picture of his girl   10
who has put: *Steffi.° Vergissmeinicht*   a girl's name
in a copybook gothic script.

We see him almost with content
abased, and seeming to have paid
and mocked at by his own equipment   15
that's hard and good when he's decayed.

But she would weep to see to-day
how on his skin the swart flies move;
the dust upon the paper eye
and the burst stomach like a cave.   20

For here the lover and killer are mingled
who had one body and one heart.
And death who had the soldier singled
has done the lover mortal hurt.

Keith Douglas (1920–1944)

VERGISSMEINICHT. The German title means "Forget me not." The author, an
English poet, fought with a tank battalion in World War II and was killed in the
invasion of Normandy.

MARY HYNES

(After the Irish of Raftery)

That Sunday, on my oath, the rain was a heavy overcoat
On a poor poet, and when the rain began
In fleeces of water to buckleap like a goat
I was only a walking penance reaching Kiltartan;
And there, so suddenly that my cold spine   5
Broke out on the arch of my back in a rainbow,
This woman surged out of the day with so much sunlight
I was nailed there like a scarecrow,

But I found my tongue and the breath to balance it
And I said: "If I bow to you with this hump of rain   10
I'll fall on my collarbone, but look, I'll chance it,
And after falling, bow again."
She laughed, ah, she was gracious, and softly said to me,
"For all your lovely talking I go marketing with an ass,
I'm no hill-queen, alas, or Ireland, that grass widow,   15
So hurry on, sweet Raftery, or you'll keep me late for Mass!"

The parish priest has blamed me for missing second Mass
And the bell talking on the rope of the steeple,
But the tonsure of the poet is the bright crash
Of love that blinds the irons on his belfry;   20
Were I making an Aisling I'd tell the tale of her hair,

MARY HYNES. Raftery (1784?–1835) was a famous itinerant Irish bardic poet,
and Mary Hynes was the peasant girl whom he made famous in his verse. The
present poem, while not a translation of any Raftery poem, does depend on a
sense of Raftery as a folk figure, as well as on a mixture of Irish and classical
mythology. An account of Raftery and Mary Hynes is given in W. B. Yeats's
essay "Dust Hath Closed Helen's Eye" from *The Celtic Twilight*, reprinted in
Mythologies. 4. *Kiltartan*, 33. *Ballylea*, 66. *Loughrea*: Ballylea is a group of
houses in the barony of Kiltartan in County Galway, Ireland. Loughrea is a
nearby town. 19. *crash*: a coarse, heavy linen fabric; also a brilliant reddish-yellow
color. 20. *his belfry*: the priest's. 21. *Aisling*: an old name for Ireland; a vision
of a maiden, usually Ireland personified. 53. *Boccaccio*: the fourteenth-century
Italian author, humanist, and poet whose endlessly imitated *Decameron* includes
many well-known love stories. 54. *Ovid*: Roman poet of the first century B.C.,
famous and infamous for his sensuous and ironic poetry of love, e.g. *Amores* and
Ars Amatoria. 59. *Herod's hussy*: Salome. See Note in question 4, "The Love
Song of J. Alfred Prufrock" (page 287). 67. *Helen*: Helen of Troy. 72. *Shank's
mare*: one's own legs. 82. *haggard*: an enclosure of stacked grain. 86. *delph*: china.

But now I've grown careful of my listeners
So I pass over one long day and the rainy air
Where we sheltered in whispers.

When we left the dark evening at last outside her door,   25
She lighted a lamp though a gaming company
Could have sighted each trump by the light of her unshawled poll,
And indeed she welcomed me
With a big quart bottle and I mooned there over glasses
Till she took that bird, the phoenix, from the spit;   30
And "Raftery," says she, "a feast is no bad dowry,
Sit down now and taste it!"

If I praised Ballylea before it was only for the mountains
Where I broke horses and ran wild,
And not for its seven crooked smoky houses   35
Where seven crones are tied
All day to the listening top of a half door,
And nothing to be heard or seen
But the drowsy dropping of water
And a gander on the green.   40

But, Boys! I was blind as a kitten till last Sunday.
This town is earth's very navel!
Seven palaces are thatched there of a Monday,
And O the seven queens whose pale
Proud faces with their seven glimmering sisters,   45
The Pleiads, light the evening where they stroll,
And one can find the well by their wet footprints,
And make one's soul;

For Mary Hynes, rising, gathers up there
Her ripening body from all the love stories;   50
And, rinsing herself at morning, shakes her hair
And stirs the old gay books in libraries;
And what shall I do with sweet Boccaccio?
And shall I send Ovid back to school again
With a new headline for his copybook,   55
And a new pain?

Like a nun she will play you a sweet tune on a spinet,
And from such grasshopper music leap

Like Herod's hussy who fancied a saint's head
For grace after meat;   60
Yet she'll peg out a line of clothes on a windy morning
And by noonday put them ironed in the chest,
And you'll swear by her white fingers she does nothing
But take her fill of rest.

And I'll wager now that my song is ended,   65
Loughrea, that old dead city where the weavers
Have pined at the mouldering looms since Helen broke the thread,
Will be piled again with silver fleeces:
O the new coats and big horses! The raving and the ribbons!
And Ballylea in hubbub and uproar!   70
And may Raftery be dead if he's not there to ruffle it
On his own mare, Shank's mare, that never needs a spur!

But ah, Sweet Light, though your face coins
My heart's very metals, isn't it folly without a pardon
For Raftery to sing so that men, east and west, come   75
Spying on your vegetable garden?
We could be so quiet in your chimney corner—
Yet how could a poet hold you any more than the sun,
Burning in the big bright hazy heart of harvest,
Could be tied in a henrun?   80

Bless your poet then and let him go!
He'll never stack a haggard with his breath:
His thatch of words will not keep rain or snow
Out of the house, or keep back death.
But Raftery, rising, curses as he sees you   85
Stir the fire and wash delph,
That he was bred a poet whose selfish trade it is
To keep no beauty to himself.

Padraic Fallon (b. 1906)

√ THE SILKEN TENT — *to describe woman*

She is as in a field a silken tent
At midday when a sunny summer breeze

THE SILKEN TENT. This poem was recorded by Mr. Frost (LP, Yale Series of
Recorded Poets, YP 320).

Has dried the dew and all its ropes relent,
So that in guys it gently sways at ease,
And its supporting central cedar pole,   5
That is its pinnacle to heavenward
And signifies the sureness of the soul,
Seems to owe naught to any single cord,
But strictly held by none, is loosely bound
By countless silken ties of love and thought   10
To everything on earth the compass round,
And only by one's going slightly taut
In the capriciousness of summer air
Is of the slightest bondage made aware.

Robert Frost (1874–1963)

REDEMPTION

Having been tenant long to a rich Lord,
  Not thriving, I resolvèd to be bold,
  And make a suit unto him, to afford
A new small-rented lease and cancel the old.
In heaven at his manor I him sought: 5
  They told me there that he was lately gone
  About some land which he had dearly bought
Long since on earth, to take possession.
I straight returned, and knowing his great birth,
  Sought him accordingly in great resorts;   10
  In cities, theaters, gardens, parks, and courts:
At length I heard a ragged noise and mirth
  Of thieves and murderers; there I him espied,
  Who straight, "Your suit is granted," said, and died.

George Herbert (1593–1633)

CORINNA'S GOING A-MAYING

Get up, get up, for shame, the blooming morn
Upon her wings presents the god unshorn.
  See how Aurora throws her fair
  Fresh-quilted colors through the air!

Get up, sweet slug-a-bed, and see 5
The dew bespangling herb and tree.
Each flower has wept, and bowed toward the East,
Above an hour since; yet you not dressed,
 Nay! not so much as out of bed?
 When all the birds have matins said, 10
 And sung their thankful hymns: 'tis sin,
 Nay, profanation, to keep in;
Whenas a thousand virgins on this day
Spring, sooner than the lark, to fetch in May.

Rise, and put on your foliage, and be seen 15
To come forth, like the spring-time, fresh and green,
 And sweet as Flora. Take no care
 For jewels for your gown or hair;
 Fear not, the leaves will strew
 Gems in abundance upon you; 20
Besides, the childhood of the day has kept,
Against you come, some orient pearls unwept;
 Come, and receive them while the light
 Hangs on the dew-locks of the night:
 And Titan on the eastern hill 25
 Retires himself, or else stands still
Till you come forth. Wash, dress, be brief in praying:
Few beads are best, when once we go a-Maying.

Come, my Corinna, come; and, coming, mark
How each field turns a street, each street a park 30
 Made green, and trimmed with trees; see how
 Devotion gives each house a bough
 Or branch; each porch, each door, ere this,
 An ark, a tabernacle is,
Made up of white-thorn neatly interwove; 35
As if here were those cooler shades of love.
 Can such delights be in the street,
 And open fields, and we not see't?
 Come, we'll abroad; and let's obey
 The proclamation made for May: 40
And sin no more, as we have done, by staying;
But, my Corinna, come, let's go a-Maying.

There's not a budding boy or girl this day
But is got up, and gone to bring in May.
    A deal of youth, ere this, is come   45
    Back, and with white-thorn laden home.
    Some have dispatched their cakes and cream,
    Before that we have left to dream;
And some have wept, and wooed, and plighted troth,
And chose their priest, ere we can cast off sloth;   50
    Many a green-gown has been given;
    Many a kiss, both odd and even:
    Many a glance too has been sent
    From out the eye, love's firmament;
Many a jest told of the keys betraying   55
This night, and locks picked, yet we're not a-Maying.

Come, let us go while we are in our prime;
And take the harmless folly of the time.
    We shall grow old apace and die
    Before we know our liberty.   60
    Our life is short, and our days run
    As fast away as does the sun;
And as a vapor, or a drop of rain,
Once lost, can ne'er be found again: 64
    So when or° you or I are made   either
    A fable, song, or fleeting shade,
    All love, all liking, all delight
    Lies drowned with us in endless night.
Then while time serves, and we are but decaying,
Come, my Corinna, come, let's go a-Maying.   70

Robert Herrick (1591–1674)

EVE

Relates what happened in the Garden of Eden

    Eve, with her basket, was
    Deep in the bells and grass,
    Wading in bells and grass
    Up to her knees,
    Picking a dish of sweet   5
    Berries and plums to eat,

Down in the bells and grass
Under the trees.

Mute as a mouse in a
Corner the cobra lay,   10
Curled round a bough of the
Cinnamon tall. . . .
Now to get even and
Humble proud heaven and
Now was the moment or   15
Never at all.

"Eva!" Each syllable
Light as a flower fell,
"Eva!" he whispered the
Wondering maid,   20
Soft as a bubble sung
Out of a linnet's lung,
Soft and most silverly
"Eva!" he said.

Picture that orchard sprite,   25
Eve, with her body white,
Supple and smooth to her
Slim finger tips,
Wondering, listening,
Listening, wondering,   30
Eve with a berry
Half-way to her lips.

Oh had our ~~simple Eve~~ *simple-minded* *couldst see false front.*
Seen through the make-believe!
Had she but known the   35
Pretender he was!
Out of the boughs he came,
Whispering still her name,
Tumbling in twenty rings
Into the grass.   40

Here was the strangest pair
In the world anywhere,
Eve in the bells and grass

Kneeling, and he
Telling his story low. . . .   45
Singing birds saw them go
Down the dark path to
The Blasphemous Tree.

Oh, what a clatter when
Titmouse and Jenny Wren   50
Saw him successful and
Taking his leave!
How the birds rated him,
How they all hated him! *- Devil, Satan disguised*
How they all pitied *God made him crawl*   55
Poor motherless Eve! *belly rest of life.*

Picture her crying
Outside in the lane,
Eve, with no dish of sweet
Berries and plums to eat,   60
Haunting the gate of the
Orchard in vain. . . .
Picture the lewd delight
Under the hill tonight— *In hell they're celebrating*
"Eva!" the toast goes round *Satan's success.*   65
"Eva!" again.

Narrative poem.

                              Ralph Hodgson (1872–1962)

AGONY COLUMN

Sir George and Lady Cepheus of Upper Slaughter
Desire to announce to family and friends
That the death has been arranged of their only daughter
Andromeda, aged twenty—Sir George intends

To avoid undesirable pomp and ostentation: 5
A simple ceremony, a quiet funeral feast
And the usual speeches; a train will leave the station
For the Virgin's Rock at four. No flowers by Request!

Owing to the informal nature of the occasion
Guests are requested to wear ordinary dress.   10

It is hoped that, in view of Sir George's official station
The event will be treated discreetly by the press.

In accord with religious custom and public duty,
The populace is expected to maintain order and quiet;
But, because of her daughter's quite exceptional beauty   15
And numerous suitors, to discourage scandal or riot,

Lady Cepheus wishes it to be distinctly stated
That any attempt at rescue has been banned;
Offenders will be summarily emasculated;
Heroes are warned: the police have the matter in hand.   20

As the victim is to be chained wearing only her skin,
The volunteer armorers will be blinded at once.
On the following morning her lovers and next-of-kin
May assist in gathering any remaining bones.

A. D. Hope (b. 1907)

BREDON HILL

In summertime on Bredon
   The bells they sound so clear;
Round both the shires they ring them
   In steeples far and near,
   A happy noise to hear.   5

Here of a Sunday morning
   My love and I would lie,
And see the coloured counties,
   And hear the larks so high
   About us in the sky.   10

The bells would ring to call her
   In valleys miles away:
"Come all to church, good people;
   Good people, come and pray."
   But here my love would stay.   15

And I would turn and answer
   Among the springing thyme,

"Oh, peal upon our wedding,
  And we will hear the chime,
And come to church in time." 20

But when the snows at Christmas
  On Bredon top were strown,
My love rose up so early
  And stole out unbeknown
And went to church alone. 25

They tolled the one bell only,
  Groom there was none to see,
The mourners followed after,
  And so to church went she,
And would not wait for me. 30

The bells they sound on Bredon,
  And still the steeples hum.
"Come all to church, good people,"—
  Oh, noisy bells, be dumb;
I hear you, I will come. 35

A. E. Housman (1859–1936)

THE DEATH OF THE BALL TURRET GUNNER

From my mother's sleep I fell into the State,
And I hunched in its belly till my wet fur froze.
Six miles from earth, loosed from its dream of life,
I woke to black flak and the nightmare fighters.
When I died they washed me out of the turret with a hose.

Randall Jarrell (1914–1965)

ODE ON A GRECIAN URN

Thou still unravished bride of quietness,
  Thou foster-child of silence and slow time,

ODE ON A GRECIAN URN. 49–50. In the 1820 edition of Keats's poems the words
"Beauty is truth, truth beauty" were enclosed in quotation marks. Critics have dis-
agreed as to whether only this statement is uttered by the Urn, with the remainder
of the poem spoken *to* the Urn (or the figures on the Urn) by the speaker of the
poem; or whether the entire last two lines are spoken by the Urn.

Sylvan historian, who canst thus express
  A flowery tale more sweetly than our rhyme:
What leaf-fringed legend haunts about thy shape   5
  Of deities or mortals, or of both,
    In Tempe or the dales of Arcady?
  What men or gods are these? What maidens loth?
What mad pursuit? What struggle to escape?
    What pipes and timbrels? What wild ecstasy?   10

Heard melodies are sweet, but those unheard
  Are sweeter; therefore, ye soft pipes, play on;
Not to the sensual ear, but, more endeared,
  Pipe to the spirit ditties of no tone:
Fair youth, beneath the trees, thou canst not leave   15
  Thy song, nor ever can those trees be bare;
    Bold Lover, never, never canst thou kiss,
Though winning near the goal—yet, do not grieve;
  She cannot fade, though thou hast not thy bliss,
    For ever wilt thou love, and she be fair!   20

Ah, happy, happy boughs! that cannot shed
  Your leaves, nor ever bid the Spring adieu;
And, happy melodist, unwearied,
  For ever piping songs for ever new;
More happy love! more happy, happy love!   25
  For ever warm and still to be enjoyed,
    For ever panting and for ever young;
All breathing human passion far above,
  That leaves a heart high-sorrowful and cloyed,
    A burning forehead, and a parching tongue.   30

Who are these coming to the sacrifice?
  To what green altar, O mysterious priest,
Lead'st thou that heifer lowing at the skies,
  And all her silken flanks with garlands drest?
What little town by river or sea shore,   35
  Or mountain-built with peaceful citadel,
    Is emptied of its folk, this pious morn?
And, little town, thy streets for evermore
  Will silent be; and not a soul to tell
    Why thou art desolate, can e'er return.   40

O Attic shape! Fair attitude! with brede
   Of marble men and maidens overwrought,
With forest branches and the trodden weed;
   Thou, silent form, dost tease us out of thought
As doth eternity: Cold Pastoral!   45
   When old age shall this generation waste,
     Thou shalt remain, in midst of other woe
   Than ours, a friend to man, to whom thou say'st,
<u>Beauty is truth, truth beauty,—that is all</u>
   <u>Ye know on earth, and all ye need to know.</u>   50

Keats stops time. The urn is peaceful and everlasting.
Celebrating the permanence of art.

John Keats (1795–1821)

ODE ON MELANCHOLY

No, no, go not to Lethe, neither twist
   Wolf's-bane,° tight-rooted, for its poisonous wine;   poisonous plant
Nor suffer thy pale forehead to be kissed
   By nightshade,° ruby grape of Proserpine;   poisonous plant
Make not your rosary of yew°-berries,   tree of mourning
   Nor let the beetle, nor the death-moth be   6
     Your mournful Psyche, nor the downy owl
A partner in your sorrow's mysteries;°   religious rites
   For shade to shade will come too drowsily,
     And drown the wakeful anguish of the soul.   10

But when the melancholy fit shall fall
   Sudden from heaven like a weeping cloud,
That fosters the droop-headed flowers all,
   And hides the green hill in an April shroud;
Then glut thy sorrow on a morning rose,   15
   Or on the rainbow of the salt sand-wave,
     Or on the wealth of globed peonies;
Or if thy mistress some rich anger shows,
   Emprison her soft hand, and let her rave,
     And feed deep, deep upon her peerless eyes.   20

ODE ON MELANCHOLY. 1. *Lethe:* river in the Greek Hades that caused forgetful-ness. 4. *Proserpine:* queen of Hades. 6. *death-moth:* moth with skull-like mark-ings. 7. *Psyche:* the soul, symbolized sometimes by a butterfly, sometimes by a beautiful maiden beloved of Cupid (desire).

She dwells with Beauty—Beauty that must die;
   And Joy, whose hand is ever at his lips
Bidding adieu; and aching Pleasure nigh,
   Turning to Poison while the bee-mouth sips:
Ay, in the very temple of Delight   25
   Veiled Melancholy has her sovran shrine,
      Though seen of none save him whose strenuous tongue
   Can burst Joy's grape against his palate fine;
His soul shall taste the sadness of her might,
   And be among her cloudy trophies hung.   30

John Keats (1795–1821)

CHURCH GOING

Once I am sure there's nothing going on
I step inside, letting the door thud shut.
Another church: matting, seats, and stone,
And little books; sprawlings of flowers, cut
For Sunday, brownish now; some brass and stuff   5
Up at the holy end; the small neat organ;
And a tense, musty, unignorable silence,
Brewed God knows how long. Hatless, I take off
My cycle-clips in awkward reverence,

Move forward, run my hand around the font.   10
From where I stand, the roof looks almost new—
Cleaned, or restored? Someone would know: I don't.
Mounting the lectern, I peruse a few
Hectoring large-scale verses, and pronounce
"Here endeth" much more loudly than I'd meant.   15
The echoes snigger briefly. Back at the door
I sign the book, donate an Irish sixpence,
Reflect the place was not worth stopping for.

Yet stop I did: in fact I often do,
And always end much at a loss like this,   20
Wondering what to look for; wondering, too,
When churches fall completely out of use
What we shall turn them into, if we shall keep
A few cathedrals chronically on show,

Their parchment, plate and pyx in locked cases, 25
And let the rest rent-free to rain and sheep.
Shall we avoid them as unlucky places?

Or, after dark, will dubious women come
To make their children touch a particular stone;
Pick simples for a cancer; or on some 30
Advised night see walking a dead one?
Power of some sort or other will go on
In games, in riddles, seemingly at random;
But superstition, like belief, must die,
And what remains when disbelief has gone? 35
Grass, weedy pavement, brambles, buttress, sky,

A shape less recognizable each week,
A purpose more obscure. I wonder who
Will be the last, the very last, to seek
This place for what it was; one of the crew 40
That tap and jot and know what rood-lofts were?
Some ruin-bibber, randy° for antique,   wild, lustful
Or Christmas-addict, counting on a whiff
Of gown-and-bands and organ-pipes and myrrh?
Or will he be my representative, 45

Bored, uninformed, knowing the ghostly silt
Dispersed, yet tending to this cross of ground
Through suburb scrub because it held unspilt
So long and equably what since is found
Only in separation—marriage, and birth, 50
And death, and thoughts of these—for whom was built
This special shell? For though I've no idea
What this accoutred frowsty barn is worth,
It pleases me to stand in silence here;

A serious house on serious earth it is, 55
In whose blent air all our compulsions meet,
Are recognized, and robed as destinies.
And that much never can be obsolete,
Since someone will forever be surprising
A hunger in himself to be more serious, 60
And gravitating with it to this ground,

Which, he once heard, was proper to grow wise in,
If only that so many dead lie round.

Philip Larkin (b. 1922)

CITY LIFE

When I am in a great city, I know that I despair.
I know there is no hope for us, death waits, it is useless to care.
For oh the poor people, that are flesh of my flesh,
I, that am flesh of their flesh,
when I see the iron hooked into their faces   5
their poor, their fearful faces
I scream in my soul, for I know I cannot
take the iron hooks out of their faces, that make them so drawn,
nor cut the invisible wires of steel that pull them
back and forth, to work,   10
back and forth to work,
like fearful and corpse-like fishes hooked and being played
by some malignant fisherman on an unseen shore
where he does not choose to land them yet, hooked fishes of
    the factory world.

D. H. Lawrence (1885–1930)

THE DRINKER

The man is killing time—there's nothing else.
No help now from the fifth of Bourbon
chucked helter-skelter into the river,
even its cork sucked under.

Stubbed before-breakfast cigarettes   5
burn bull's-eyes on the bedside table;
a plastic tumbler of alka seltzer
champagnes in the bathroom.

No help from his body, the whale's
warm-hearted blubber, foundering down   10
leagues of ocean, gasping whiteness.
The barbed hooks fester. The lines snap tight.

When he looks for neighbors, their names blur in the window,
his distracted eye sees only glass sky.
His despair has the galvanized color 15
of the mop and water in the galvanized bucket.

Once she was close to him
as water to the dead metal.
He looks at her engagements inked on her calendar.
A list of indictments. 20
At the numbers in her thumbed black telephone book.
A quiver full of arrows.

Her absence hisses like steam,
the pipes sing . . .
even corroded metal somehow functions. 25
He snores in his iron lung,

and hears the voice of Eve,
beseeching freedom from the Garden's
perfect and ponderous bubble. No voice
outsings the serpent's flawed, euphoric hiss. 30

The cheese wilts in the rat-trap,
the milk turns to junket in the cornflakes bowl,
car keys and razor blades
shine in an ashtray.

Is he killing time? Out on the street, 35
two cops on horseback clop through the April rain
to check the parking meter violations—
their oilskins yellow as forsythia.

Robert Lowell (b. 1917)

LUCIFER IN STARLIGHT

On a starred night Prince Lucifer uprose.
  Tired of his dark dominion swung the fiend
  Above the rolling ball in cloud part screened,
Where sinners hugged the specter of repose.
Poor prey to his hot fit of pride were those. 5
  And now upon his western wing he leaned,
  Now his huge bulk o'er Afric's sands careened,

Now the black planet shadowed Arctic snows.
Soaring through wider zones that pricked his scars   9
   With memory of the old revolt from Awe,°   Satan's rebellion
He reached a middle height, and at the stars,   against God
Which are the brain of heaven, he looked, and sank.
Around the ancient track marched, rank on rank,
   The army of unalterable law.

George Meredith (1828–1909)

ON THE LATE MASSACRE IN PIEMONT

Avenge, O Lord, thy slaughtered saints, whose bones
   Lie scattered on the Alpine mountains cold,
   Even them who kept thy truth so pure of old
   When all our fathers worshiped stocks and stones,
Forget not; in thy book record their groans   5
   Who were thy sheep, and in their ancient fold
   Slain by the bloody Piemontese that rolled
   Mother with infant down the rocks. Their moans
The vales redoubled to the hills, and they
   To heaven. Their martyred blood and ashes sow   10
   O'er all the Italian fields, where still doth sway
The triple tyrant, that from these may grow
   A hundredfold, who, having learnt thy way,
   Early may fly the Babylonian woe.

John Milton (1608–1674)

ON THE LATE MASSACRE IN PIEMONT. This poem has for its background the
bitter religious struggles between Protestants and Roman Catholics during the late
Reformation. When, in 1655, the soldiers of an Italian Catholic duke massacred
a group of Waldensian Protestants in Piedmont (in Northern Italy), Milton, a
Puritan poet, wrote this sonnet. 4. *stocks and stones:* wooden and stone images
in English churches before England turned Protestant. 12. *triple tyrant:* the
pope, who wore a triple crown. 14. *Babylonian:* Babylon in the Bible is associated with idolatry, pagan luxury, and abuse of power.

A CARRIAGE FROM SWEDEN

They say there is a sweeter air
　　　　where it was made, than we have here;
　　　　a Hamlet's castle atmosphere.
At all events there is in Brooklyn
something that makes me feel at home.　　　　　　　5

No one may see this put-away
　　　　museum-piece, this country cart
　　　　that inner happiness made art;
and yet, in this city of freckled
integrity it is a vein　　　　　　　　　　　　　10

of resined straightness from north-wind
　　　　hardened Sweden's once-opposed-to-
　　　　compromise archipelago
of rocks. Washington and Gustavus
Adolphus, forgive our decay.　　　　　　　　　15

Seats, dashboard and sides of smooth gourd-
　　　　rind texture, a flowered step, swan-
　　　　dart brake, and swirling crustacean-
tailed equine amphibious creatures
that garnish the axle-tree! What　　　　　　　20

a fine thing! What unannoying
　　　　romance! And how beautiful, she
　　　　with the natural stoop of the
snowy egret, grey-eyed and straight-haired,
for whom it should come to the door,—　　　　25

of whom it reminds me. The split
　　　　pine fair hair, steady gannet-clear
　　　　eyes and the pine-needled-path deer-
swift step; that is Sweden, land of the
free and the soil for a spruce-tree—　　　　　30

A CARRIAGE FROM SWEDEN.　14–15. *Gustavus Adolphus:* Swedish king and military hero (1594–1632).　35. *Denmark's sanctuaried Jews:* Many Jewish refugees
fled to Sweden after the German invasion of Denmark in World War II.　52.
Dalen light-house: Gustaf Dalén, Swedish scientist, won a Nobel Prize in 1912
chiefly for his invention of an automatic regulator, responsive to the sun's rays,
for turning on and off the gas lights used in marine buoys and beacons and in
railway signals.

vertical though a seedling—all
    needles: from a green trunk, green shelf
    on shelf fanning out by itself.
The deft white-stockinged dance in thick-soled
shoes! Denmark's sanctuaried Jews!   35

The puzzle-jugs and hand-spun rugs,
    the root-legged kracken° shaped like dogs,   wooden
    the hanging buttons and the frogs   stools
that edge the Sunday jackets! Sweden,
you have a runner called the Deer, who   40

when he's won a race, likes to run
    more; you have the sun-right gable-
    ends due east and west, the table
spread as for a banquet; and the put-
in twin vest-pleats with a fish-fin   45

effect when you need none. Sweden,
    what makes the people dress that way
    and those who see you wish to stay?
The runner, not too tired to run more
at the end of the race? And that   50

cart, dolphin-graceful? A Dalen
    light-house, self-lit?—responsive and
    responsible. I understand;
it's not pine-needle-paths that give spring
when they're run on, it's a Sweden   55

of moated white castles,—the bed
    of white flowers densely grown in an S
    meaning Sweden and stalwartness,
skill, and a surface that says
Made in Sweden: carts are my trade.   60

Marianne Moore (b. 1887)

THE HORSES

Barely a twelvemonth after
The seven days war that put the world to sleep,
Late in the evening the strange horses came.

By then we had made our covenant with silence,
But in the first few days it was so still   5
We listened to our breathing and were afraid.
On the second day
The radios failed; we turned the knobs; no answer.
On the third day a warship passed us, heading north,
Dead bodies piled on the deck. On the sixth day   10
A plane plunged over us into the sea. Thereafter
Nothing. The radios dumb;
And still they stand in corners of our kitchens,
And stand, perhaps, turned on, in a million rooms
All over the world. But now if they should speak,   15
If on a sudden they should speak again,
If on the stroke of noon a voice should speak,
- We would not listen, we would not let it bring
That old bad world that swallowed its children quick
At one great gulp. We would not have it again.   20
Sometimes we think of the nations lying asleep,
Curled blindly in impenetrable sorrow,
And then the thought confounds us with its strangeness.

The tractors lie about our fields; at evening
They look like dank sea-monsters couched and waiting.   25
We leave them where they are and let them rust:
"They'll moulder away and be like other loam."
We make our oxen drag our rusty ploughs,
Long laid aside. We have gone back
Far past our fathers' land.

          And then, that evening   30
Late in the summer the strange horses came.
We heard a distant tapping on the road,
A deepening drumming; it stopped, went on again
And at the corner changed to hollow thunder.
We saw the heads   35
Like a wild wave charging and were afraid.
We had sold our horses in our fathers' time
To buy new tractors. Now they were strange to us
As fabulous steeds set on an ancient shield
Or illustrations in a book of knights.   40

We did not dare go near them. Yet they waited,
Stubborn and shy, as if they had been sent
By an old command to find our whereabouts
And that long-lost archaic companionship.
In the first moment we had never a thought   45
That they were creatures to be owned and used.
Among them were some half-a-dozen colts
Dropped in some wilderness of the broken world,
Yet new as if they had come from their own Eden.
Since then they have pulled our ploughs and borne our loads,   50
But that free servitude still can pierce our hearts.
Our life is changed; their coming our beginning.

Edwin Muir (1887–1959)

SPRING

Spring, the sweet Spring, is the year's pleasant king;
Then blooms each thing, then maids dance in a ring,
Cold doth not sting, the pretty birds do sing—
   Cuckoo, jug-jug, pu-we, to-witta-woo!

The palm and may make country houses gay,   5
Lambs frisk and play, the shepherds pipe all day,
And we hear aye birds tune this merry lay—
   Cuckoo, jug-jug, pu-we, to-witta-woo!

The fields breathe sweet, the daisies kiss our feet,
Young lovers meet, old wives a-sunning sit,   10
In every street these tunes our ears do greet—
   Cuckoo, jug-jug, pu-we, to-witta-woo!
      Spring! the sweet Spring!

Thomas Nashe (1567–1601)

LOVE POEM

My clumsiest dear, whose hands shipwreck vases,
At whose quick touch all glasses chip and ring,
Whose palms are bulls in china, burs in linen,
And have no cunning with any soft thing

Except all ill-at-ease fidgeting people: 5
The refugee uncertain at the door
You make at home; deftly you steady
The drunk clambering on his undulant floor.

Unpredictable dear, the taxi drivers' terror,
Shrinking from far headlights pale as a dime   10
Yet leaping before red apoplectic streetcars—
Misfit in any space. And never on time.

A wrench in clocks and the solar system. Only
With words and people and love you move at ease.
In traffic of wit expertly manoeuvre   15
And keep us, all devotion, at your knees.

Forgetting your coffee spreading on our flannel,
Your lipstick grinning on our coat,
So gayly in love's unbreakable heaven
Our souls on glory of spilt bourbon float.   20

Be with me, darling, early and late. Smash glasses—
I will study wry music for your sake.
For should your hands drop white and empty
All the toys of the world would break.

John Frederick Nims (b. 1914)

EPISTLE TO A YOUNG LADY, ON HER LEAVING THE TOWN AFTER THE CORONATION

As some fond virgin, whom her mother's care
Drags from the town to wholesome country air,
Just when she learns to roll a melting eye,
And hear a spark,° yet think no danger nigh—   beau
From the dear man unwilling she must sever,   5
Yet takes one kiss before she parts forever—
Thus from the world fair Zephalinda flew,
Saw others happy, and with sighs withdrew;

EPISTLE TO A YOUNG LADY. The young lady, whom Pope here calls *Zephalinda* (7), was in actuality his good friend Teresa Blount, and *Parthenia* (46) was his even better friend, her younger sister, Martha. *Your slave* (41) is Poe himself, and *Gay* (47) is the poet John Gay, also a good friend of Pope's. The coronation was that of George I in 1714.

Not that their pleasures caused her discontent:
She sighed not that they stayed, but that she went.   10
　　She went—to plain-work and to purling brooks,
Old-fashioned halls, dull aunts, and croaking rooks;
She went from opera, park, assembly, play,
To morning walks, and prayers three hours a day;   14
To part her time 'twixt reading and bohea,°   black tea
To muse, and spill her solitary tea;
Or o'er cold coffee trifle with the spoon,
Count the slow clock, and dine exact at noon;
Divert her eyes with pictures in the fire,
Hum half a tune, tell stories to the squire;   20
Up to her godly garret after seven,
There starve and pray, for that's the way to heaven.
　　Some squire, perhaps, you take delight to rack,
Whose game is "whisk,"° whose treat a toast in sack;   whist
Who visits with a gun, presents you birds,   25
Then gives a smacking buss, and cries, "No words!"
Or with his hound comes hollowing from the stable,
Makes love with nods, and knees beneath a table;
Whose laughs are hearty, though his jests are coarse,
And loves you best of all things—but his horse.   30
　　In some fair evening, on your elbow laid,
You dream of triumphs in the rural shade;
In pensive thought recall the fancied scene,
See coronations rise on every green:
Before you pass the imaginary sights   35
Of Lords, and Earls, and Dukes, and gartered Knights,
While the spread fan o'ershades your closing eyes,
Then gives one flirt, and all the vision flies.
Thus vanish sceptres, coronets, and balls,
And leave you in lone woods, or empty walls!   40
　　So when your slave, at some dear idle time
(Not plagued with headaches, or the want of rhyme)
Stands in the streets, abstracted from the crew,
And while he seems to study, thinks of you;
Just when his fancy paints your sprightly eyes,   45
Or sees the blush of soft Parthenia rise,
Gay pats my shoulder, and you vanish quite,
Streets, chairs,° and coxcombs rush upon my sight.   sedan chairs

Vexed to be still in town, I knit my brow,
Look sour, and hum a tune—as you may now.   50

                                        Alexander Pope (1688–1744)

CAPTAIN CARPENTER

*Comment of human
nature*

Captain Carpenter rose up in his prime
Put on his pistols and went riding out
But had got wellnigh nowhere at that time   *Liked to talk to people*
Till he fell in with ladies in a rout.

It was a pretty lady and all her train   5
That played with him so sweetly but before
An hour she'd taken a sword with all her main
And twined him of his nose for evermore.

Captain Carpenter mounted up one day
And rode straightway into a stranger rogue   10
That looked unchristian but be that as may
The Captain did not wait upon prologue.

But drew upon him out of his great heart
The other swung against him with a club
And cracked his two legs at the shinny part   15
And let him roll and stick like any tub.

Captain Carpenter rode many a time
From male and female took he sundry harms
He met the wife of Satan crying "I'm
The she-wolf bids you shall bear no more arms."   20

Their strokes and counters whistled in the wind
I wish he had delivered half his blows   *he was reasoning*
But where she should have made off like a hind *by logic & he*
The bitch bit off his arms at the elbows.   *was using physical*
                                            clause, he should
And Captain Carpenter parted with his ears *have won.*
To a black devil that used him in this wise
O Jesus ere his threescore and ten years
Another had plucked out his sweet blue eyes.

CAPTAIN CARPENTER. Mr. Ransom recorded this poem (LP, Yale, YP 306; or
LP, Library of Congress, PL 20).

Captain Carpenter got up on his roan
And sallied from the gate in hell's despite   30
I heard him asking in the grimmest tone
If any enemy yet there was to fight?

"To any adversary it is fame
If he risk to be wounded by my tongue
Or burnt in two beneath my red heart's flame   35
Such are the perils he is cast among.

"But if he can he has a pretty choice
From an anatomy with little to lose
Whether he cut my tongue and take my voice
Or whether it be my round red heart he choose."   40

It was the neatest knave that ever was seen
Stepping in perfume from his lady's bower
Who at this word put in his merry mien
And fell on Captain Carpenter like a tower.

I would not knock old fellows in the dust   45
But there lay Captain Carpenter on his back
His weapons were the old heart in his bust
And a blade shook between rotten teeth alack.

The rogue in scarlet and grey soon knew his mind
He wished to get his trophy and depart   50
With gentle apology and touch refined
He pierced him and produced the Captain's heart.

God's mercy rest on Captain Carpenter now
I thought him Sirs an honest gentleman
Citizen husband soldier and scholar enow   55
Let jangling kites eat of him if they can.

But God's deep curses follow after those
That shore him of his goodly nose and ears
His legs and strong arms at the two elbows
And eyes that had not watered seventy years.   60

The curse of hell upon the sleek upstart
That got the Captain finally on his back

And took the red red vitals of his heart
And made the kites to whet their beaks clack clack.

John Crowe Ransom (b. 1888)

PIAZZA PIECE

—I am a gentleman in a dustcoat trying
To make you hear. Your ears are soft and small
And listen to an old man not at all,
They want the young men's whispering and sighing.
But see the roses on your trellis dying   5
And hear the spectral singing of the moon;
For I must have my lovely lady soon,
I am a gentleman in a dustcoat trying.

—I am a lady young in beauty waiting
Until my truelove comes, and then we kiss.   10
But what grey man among the vines is this
Whose words are dry and faint as in a dream?
Back from my trellis, Sir, before I scream!
I am a lady young in beauty waiting.

John Crowe Ransom (b. 1888)

√ MR. FLOOD'S PARTY - *autobiographical*

Old Eben Flood, climbing alone one night
Over the hill between the town below
And the forsaken upland hermitage
That held as much as he should ever know
On earth again of home, paused warily.   5
The road was his with not a native near;
And Eben, having leisure, said aloud,
For no man else in Tilbury Town to hear:

PIAZZA PIECE.   Mr. Ransom recorded this poem (LP, Yale, YP 306).
MR. FLOOD'S PARTY.   11. *bird*: Mr. Flood is quoting from *The Rubáiyát of Omar Khayyám*, "The bird Time . . . is on the wing."   20. *Roland*: hero of the French epic poem *The Song of Roland*. He died fighting a rearguard action for Charlemagne against the Moors in Spain; before his death he sounded a call for help on his famous horn, but the king's army arrived too late.

"Well, Mr. Flood, we have the harvest moon
Again, and we may not have many more;   10
The bird is on the wing, the poet says,
And you and I have said it here before.
Drink to the bird." He raised up to the light
The jug that he had gone so far to fill,
And answered huskily: "Well, Mr. Flood,   15
Since you propose it, I believe I will."

Alone, as if enduring to the end
A valiant armor of scarred hopes outworn,
He stood there in the middle of the road
Like Roland's ghost winding a silent horn.   20
Below him, in the town among the trees,
Where friends of other days had honored him,
A phantom salutation of the dead
Rang thinly till old Eben's eyes were dim.

Then, as a mother lays her sleeping child   25
Down tenderly, fearing it may awake,
He set the jug down slowly at his feet
With trembling care, knowing that most things break;
And only when assured that on firm earth
It stood, as the uncertain lives of men   30
Assuredly did not, he paced away,
And with his hand extended paused again:

"Well, Mr. Flood, we have not met like this
In a long time; and many a change has come
To both of us, I fear, since last it was   35
We had a drop together. Welcome home!"
Convivially returning with himself,
Again he raised the jug up to the light;
And with an acquiescent quaver said:
"Well, Mr. Flood, if you insist, I might.   40

"Only a very little, Mr. Flood—
For auld lang syne. No more, sir; that will do."
So, for the time, apparently it did,
And Eben evidently thought so too;
For soon amid the silver loneliness   45

His life is ebbing away
Or passing away.

Of night he lifted up his voice and sang,
Secure, with only two moons listening, - *seeing double*
Until the whole harmonious landscape rang—

Nothing to do except grew old & die.

"For auld lang syne." The weary throat gave out,
The last word wavered, and the song was done.   50
He raised again the jug regretfully
And shook his head, and was again alone.
There was not much that was ahead of him,
And there was nothing in the town below—

Either dead or gone away.

Where strangers would have shut the many doors   55
That many friends had opened long ago.

                        Edwin Arlington Robinson (1869–1935)
                                    He drank

I KNEW A WOMAN

I knew a woman, lovely in her bones,
When small birds sighed, she would sigh back at them;
Ah, when she moved, she moved more ways than one:
The shapes a bright container can contain!
Of her choice virtues only gods should speak,   5
Or English poets who grew up on Greek
(I'd have them sing in chorus, cheek to cheek).

How well her wishes went! She stroked my chin,
She taught me Turn, and Counter-turn, and Stand;
She taught me Touch, that undulant white skin;   10
I nibbled meekly from her proffered hand;
She was the sickle; I, poor I, the rake,
Coming behind her for her pretty sake
(But what prodigious mowing we did make).

Love likes a gander, and adores a goose: 15
Her full lips pursed, the errant note to seize;
She played it quick, she played it light and loose;
My eyes, they dazzled at her flowing knees;
Her several parts could keep a pure repose,
Or one hip quiver with a mobile nose   20
(She moved in circles, and those circles moved).

I KNEW A WOMAN. Mr. Roethke recorded this poem (LP, Folkways, FL 9736).

Let seed be grass, and grass turn into hay:
I'm martyr to a motion not my own;
What's freedom for? To know eternity.
I swear she cast a shadow white as stone.   25
But who would count eternity in days?
These old bones live to learn her wanton ways:
(I measure time by how a body sways).

Theodore Roethke (1908–1963)

FEAR NO MORE

Fear no more the heat o' the sun,
   Nor the furious winter's rages;
Thou thy worldly task hast done,
   Home art gone, and ta'en thy wages.
Golden lads and girls all must,   5
As chimney-sweepers, come to dust.

Fear no more the frown o' the great;
   Thou art past the tyrant's stroke;
Care no more to clothe and eat;
   To thee the reed is as the oak.   10
The scepter, learning, physic,° must   **art of healing**
All follow this, and come to dust.

Fear no more the lightning-flash,
   Nor the all-dreaded thunder-stone;°   **thunderbolt**
Fear not slander, censure rash;   15
   Thou hast finished joy and moan.
All lovers young, all lovers must
Consign to thee,° and come to dust.   **yield to your condition**

William Shakespeare (1564–1616)

LET ME NOT TO THE MARRIAGE OF TRUE MINDS—*friendship*

Sonnet

Let me not to the marriage of true minds   *[faithful]*
Admit impediments. Love is not love
Which alters when it alteration finds,   *love is change*
Or bends with the remover to remove.
O no! it is an ever-fixèd mark   *metaphor*   5

That looks on tempests and is never shaken;
It is the star to every wandering bark,
Whose worth's unknown, although his height be taken.
Love's not Time's fool, though rosy lips and cheeks
Within his bending sickle's compass come;
Love alters not with his brief hours and weeks,
But bears it out even to the edge of doom.
  If this be error and upon me proved,
  I never writ, nor no man ever loved.

William Shakespeare (1564–1616)

MY MISTRESS' EYES ARE NOTHING LIKE THE SUN

My mistress' eyes are nothing like the sun;
Coral is far more red than her lips' red:
If snow be white, why then her breasts are dun;
If hairs be wires, black wires grow on her head.   4
I have seen roses damasked,° red and white,   of different colors
But no such roses see I in her cheeks;
And in some perfumes is there more delight
Than in the breath that from my mistress reeks.
I love to hear her speak, yet well I know
That music hath a far more pleasing sound: 10
I grant I never saw a goddess go,—
My mistress, when she walks, treads on the ground.
  And yet, by heaven, I think my love as rare
  As any she belied with false compare.

William Shakespeare (1564–1616)

SINCE BRASS, NOR STONE, NOR EARTH

Since brass, nor stone, nor earth, nor boundless sea,
But sad mortality o'er-sways their power,
How with this rage shall beauty hold a plea,
Whose action is no stronger than a flower?
O, how shall summer's honey breath hold out   5
Against the wrackful siege of battering days,
When rocks impregnable are not so stout,
Nor gates of steel so strong, but Time decays?

O fearful meditation! where, alack,
Shall Time's best jewel from Time's chest lie hid? 10
Or what strong hand can hold his swift foot back?
Or who his spoil of beauty can forbid?
   O, none, unless this miracle have might,
   That in black ink my love may still shine bright.

William Shakespeare (1564–1616)

THE GLORIES OF OUR BLOOD AND STATE

The glories of our blood and state
   Are shadows, not substantial things;
There is no armor against fate;
   Death lays his icy hand on kings:
      Scepter and crown 5
      Must tumble down,
And in the dust be equal made
With the poor crooked scythe and spade.

Some men with swords may reap the field,
   And plant fresh laurels where they kill; 10
But their strong nerves at last must yield;
   They tame but one another still:
      Early or late,
      They stoop to fate,
And must give up their murmuring breath, 15
When they, pale captives, creep to death.

The garlands wither on your brow,
   Then boast no more your mighty deeds;
Upon death's purple altar now,
   See where the victor-victim bleeds: 20
      Your heads must come
      To the cold tomb;
Only the actions of the just
Smell sweet and blossom in their dust.

James Shirley (1596–1666)

SONG

Sweet beast, I have gone prowling,
   a proud rejected man
who lived along the edges
   catch as catch can;
in darkness and in hedges   5
   I sang my sour tone
and all my love was howling
   conspicuously alone.

I curled and slept all day
   or nursed my bloodless wounds   10
until the squares were silent
   where I could make tunes
singular and violent.
   Then, sure as hearers came
I crept and flinched away.   15
   And, girl, you've done the same.

A stray from my own type,
   led along by blindness,
my love was near to spoiled
   and curdled all my kindness.   20
I find no kin, no child;
   only the weasel's ilk.
Sweet beast, cat of my own stripe,
   come and take my milk.

W. D. Snodgrass (b. 1926)

AT THE UN–NATIONAL MONUMENT
ALONG THE CANADIAN BORDER

This is the field where the battle did not happen,
where the unknown soldier did not die.
This is the field where grass joined hands,
where no monument stands,
and the only heroic thing is the sky.   5

Birds fly here without any sound,
unfolding their wings across the open.

SONG. Mr. Snodgrass recorded this poem (LP, Library of Congress, PL 29).

No people killed—or were killed—on this ground
hallowed by neglect and an air so tame
that people celebrate it by forgetting its name.   10

William Stafford (b. 1914)

A GLASS OF BEER

The lanky hank of a she in the inn over there
Nearly killed me for asking the loan of a glass of beer;
May the devil grip the whey-faced slut by the hair,
And beat bad manners out of her skin for a year.

That parboiled ape, with the toughest jaw you will see   5
On virtue's path, and a voice that would rasp the dead,
Came roaring and raging the minute she looked at me,
And threw me out of the house on the back of my head!

If I asked her master he'd give me a cask a day;
But she, with the beer at hand, not a gill would arrange!   10
May she marry a ghost and bear him a kitten, and may
The High King of Glory permit her to get the mange.

James Stephens (1882–1950)

A HIGH-TONED OLD CHRISTIAN WOMAN

Poetry is the supreme fiction, madame.
Take the moral law and make a nave of it
And from the nave build haunted heaven. Thus,
The conscience is converted into palms,
Like windy citherns hankering for hymns.   5
We agree in principle. That's clear. But take
The opposing law and make a peristyle,
And from the peristyle project a masque
Beyond the planets. Thus, our bawdiness,
Unpurged by epitaph, indulged at last,   10
Is equally converted into palms,
Squiggling like saxophones. And palm for palm,
Madame, we are where we began. Allow,
Therefore, that in the planetary scene

A GLASS OF BEER.   Mr. Stephens recorded this poem (LP, Spoken Arts, 744).

Your disaffected flagellants, well-stuffed,   15
Smacking their muzzy bellies in parade,
Proud of such novelties of the sublime,
Such tink and tank and tunk-a-tunk-tunk,
May, merely may, madame, whip from themselves
A jovial hullabaloo among the spheres.   20
This will make widows wince. But fictive things
Wink as they will. Wink most when widows wince.

Wallace Stevens (1879–1955)

THE SNOW MAN

One must have a mind of winter
To regard the frost and the boughs
Of the pine-trees crusted with snow;

And have been cold a long time
To behold the junipers shagged with ice,   5
The spruces rough in the distant glitter

Of the January sun; and not to think   *Contrast between natural world & human world*
Of any misery in the sound of the wind,
In the sound of a few leaves,

Which is the sound of the land   10
Full of the same wind
That is blowing in the same bare place

For the listener, *human* who listens in the snow,
And, nothing himself, beholds
Nothing that is not there and the nothing that is. *limits of human mind* 15

Wallace Stevens (1879–1955)

A SATIRICAL ELEGY
ON THE DEATH OF A LATE FAMOUS GENERAL

treate satire of Duke of Marlborough that died yr. before

His Grace! impossible! what dead!
Of old age too, and in his bed!
And could that Mighty Warrior fall?
And so inglorious, after all!
Well, since he's gone, no matter how,   5

347

The last loud trump must wake him now:
And, trust me, as the noise grows stronger,
He'd wish to sleep a little longer.
And could he be indeed so old
As by the newspapers we're told?   10
Threescore, I think, is pretty high;
'Twas time in conscience he should die.
This world he cumbered long enough;
He burnt his candle to the snuff; *lived as long as could*
And that's the reason, some folks think,   15
He left behind so great a s - - - k.
Behold his funeral appears,
Nor widow's sighs, nor orphan's tears,
Wont at such times each heart to pierce,
Attend the progress of his hearse.   20
But what of that, his friends may say,
He had those honors in his day.
True to his profit and his pride,
He made them weep before he died.

  Come hither, all ye empty things— *warning others that*
Ye bubbles raised by breath of Kings— *they'll be forgotten.*
Who float upon the tide of state,
Come hither, and behold your fate.
Let pride be taught by this rebuke
How very mean a thing's a Duke: 30
From all his ill-got honors flung,
Turned to that dirt from whence he sprung.

Attack public personages.

                          Jonathan Swift (1667–1745)

DO NOT GO GENTLE INTO THAT GOOD NIGHT

Do not go gentle into that good night,
Old age should burn and rave at close of day;
Rage, rage against the dying of the light.

Though wise men at their end know dark is right,
Because their words had forked no lightning they   5
Do not go gentle into that good night.

DO NOT GO GENTLE INTO THAT GOOD NIGHT.   Mr. Thomas recorded this poem
(LP, Caedmon, TC 1002, or TC 2014).

Good men, the last wave by, crying how bright
Their frail deeds might have danced in a green bay,
Rage, rage against the dying of the light.

Wild men who caught and sang the sun in flight,   10
And learn, too late, they grieved it on its way,
Do not go gentle into that good night.

Grave men, near death, who see with blinding sight
Blind eyes could blaze like meteors and be gay,
Rage, rage against the dying of the light.   15

And you, my father, there on the sad height,
Curse, bless, me now with your fierce tears, I pray.
Do not go gentle into that good night.
Rage, rage against the dying of the light.

Dylan Thomas (1914–1953)

A NOISELESS PATIENT SPIDER

A noiseless patient spider,
I marked where on a little promontory it stood isolated,
Marked how to explore the vacant vast surrounding,
It launched forth filament, filament, filament, out of itself,
Ever unreeling them, ever tirelessly speeding them.   5

And you O my soul where you stand,
Surrounded, detached, in measureless oceans of space,
Ceaselessly musing, venturing, throwing, seeking the spheres to connect
    them,
Till the bridge you will need be formed, till the ductile anchor hold,
Till the gossamer thread you fling catch somewhere, O my soul.   10

Walt Whitman (1819–1892)

THERE WAS A CHILD WENT FORTH

There was a child went forth every day,
And the first object he looked upon, that object he became,
And that object became part of him for the day or a certain part of the day,
Or for many years or stretching cycles of years.
The early lilacs became part of this child,   5

And grass and white and red morning-glories, and white and red clover, and
    the song of the phoebe-bird,
And the Third-month lambs and the sow's pink-faint litter, and the mare's
    foal and the cow's calf,
And the noisy brood of the barnyard or by the mire of the pond-side,
And the fish suspending themselves so curiously below there, and the beau-
    tiful curious liquid,
And the water-plants with their graceful flat heads, all became part of
    him.   10

The field-sprouts of Fourth-month and Fifth-month became part of him,
Winter-grain sprouts and those of the light-yellow corn, and the esculent roots
    of the garden,
And the apple-trees covered with blossoms and the fruit afterward, and wood-
    berries, and the commonest weeds by the road,
And the old drunkard staggering home from the outhouse of the tavern
    whence he had lately risen,
And the schoolmistress that passed on her way to the school,   15
And the friendly boys that passed, and the quarrelsome boys,
And the tidy and fresh-cheeked girls, and the barefoot negro boy and girl,
And all the changes of city and country wherever he went.

His own parents, he that had fathered him and she that had conceived him
    in her womb and birthed him,
They gave this child more of themselves than that,   20
They gave him afterward every day, they became part of him.

The mother at home quietly placing the dishes on the supper-table,
The mother with mild words, clean her cap and gown, a wholesome odor
    falling off her person and clothes as she walks by,
The father, strong, self-sufficient, manly, mean, angered, unjust,
The blow, the quick loud word, the tight bargain, the crafty lure,   25
The family usages, the language, the company, the furniture, the yearning
    and swelling heart,
Affection that will not be gainsayed, the sense of what is real, the thought
    if after all it should prove unreal,
The doubts of day-time and the doubts of night-time, the curious whether
    and how,
Whether that which appears so is so, or is it all flashes and specks?
Men and women crowding fast in the streets, if they are not flashes and
    specks what are they?   30

The streets themselves and the façades of houses, and goods in the windows,
Vehicles, teams, the heavy-planked wharves, the huge crossing at the ferries,
The village on the highland seen from afar at sunset, the river between,
Shadows, aureola and mist, the light falling on roofs and gables of white
    or brown two miles off,
The schooner near by sleepily dropping down the tide, the little boat slack-
    towed astern,   35
The hurrying tumbling waves, quick-broken crests, slapping,
The strata of colored clouds, the long bar of maroon-tint away solitary by
    itself, the spread of purity it lies motionless in,
The horizon's edge, the flying sea-crow, the fragrance of salt marsh and shore
    mud,
These became part of that child who went forth every day, and who now
    goes, and will always go forth every day.

Walt Whitman (1819–1892)

A BAROQUE WALL-FOUNTAIN IN THE VILLA SCIARRA

    Under the bronze crown
Too big for the head of the stone cherub whose feet
    A serpent has begun to eat,
Sweet water brims a cockle and braids down

    Past spattered mosses, breaks   5
On the tipped edge of a second shell, and fills
    The massive third below. It spills
In threads then from the scalloped rim, and makes

    A scrim or summery tent
For a faun-ménage and their familiar goose.   10
    Happy in all that ragged, loose
Collapse of water, its effortless descent

    And flatteries of spray,
The stocky god upholds the shell with ease,

A BAROQUE WALL-FOUNTAIN IN THE VILLA SCIARRA. Mr. Wilbur recorded this
poem (LP, Spoken Arts, 747). The Villa Sciarra is in Rome, as is St. Peter's
Cathedral (31). 20. *saecular*: a variant spelling of *secular* that here gathers in
the sense of *saeculum*, a period of long duration, an age. 30. *Maderna*: Italian
architect (1556–1629). 43. *areté*: a Greek word meaning roughly "virtue" (Wilbur's note). 52. *Francis*: St. Francis of Assisi.

Watching, about his shaggy knees,   15
The goatish innocence of his babes at play;

    His fauness all the while
Leans forward, slightly, into a clambering mesh
    Of water-lights, her sparkling flesh
In a saecular ecstasy, her blinded smile   20

    Bent on the sand floor
Of the trefoil pool, where ripple-shadows come
    And go in swift reticulum,
More addling to the eye than wine, and more

    Interminable to thought   25
Than pleasure's calculus. Yet since this all
    Is pleasure, flash, and waterfall,
Must it not be too simple? Are we not

    More intricately expressed
In the plain fountains that Maderna set   30
    Before St. Peter's—the main jet
Struggling aloft until it seems at rest

    In the act of rising, until
The very wish of water is reversed,
    That heaviness borne up to burst   35
In a clear, high, cavorting head, to fill

    With blaze, and then in gauze
Delays, in a gnatlike shimmering, in a fine
    Illumined version of itself, decline,
And patter on the stones its own applause?   40

    If that is what men are
Or should be, if those water-saints display
    The pattern of our areté,
What of these showered fauns in their bizarre,

    Spangled, and plunging house?   45
They are at rest in fulness of desire
    For what is given, they do not tire
Of the smart of the sun, the pleasant water-douse

    And riddled pool below,
Reproving our disgust and our ennui   50

With humble insatiety.
Francis, perhaps, who lay in sister snow

Before the wealthy gate
Freezing and praising, might have seen in this
No trifle, but a shade of bliss—   55
That land of tolerable flowers, that state

As near and far as grass
Where eyes become the sunlight, and the hand
Is worthy of water: the dreamt land
Toward which all hungers leap, all pleasures pass.   60

Richard Wilbur (b. 1921)

THIS IS JUST TO SAY

I have eaten
the plums
that were in
the icebox

and which   5
you were probably
saving
for breakfast

Forgive me
they were delicious   10
so sweet
and so cold

William Carlos Williams (1883–1963)

THE SOLITARY REAPER

Behold her, single in the field,
Yon solitary Highland lass!
Reaping and singing by herself;
Stop here, or gently pass!

THE SOLITARY REAPER.   2. *Highland:* Scottish upland. The girl is singing in the Highland language, a form of Gaelic, quite different from English.   16. *Hebrides:* islands off northwest tip of Scotland.

Alone she cuts and binds the grain,   5
And sings a melancholy strain;
O listen! for the vale profound
Is overflowing with the sound.

No nightingale did ever chaunt
More welcome notes to weary bands   10
Of travellers in some shady haunt
Among Arabian sands.
A voice so thrilling ne'er was heard
In springtime from the cuckoo-bird,
Breaking the silence of the seas   15
Among the farthest Hebrides.

Will no one tell me what she sings?—
Perhaps the plaintive numbers° flow   measures
For old, unhappy, far-off things,
And battles long ago.   20
Or is it some more humble lay,°   song
Familiar matter of today?
Some natural sorrow, loss, or pain,
That has been, and may be again?

Whate'er the theme, the maiden sang   25
As if her song could have no ending;
I saw her singing at her work,
And o'er the sickle bending—
I listened, motionless and still;
And, as I mounted up the hill,   30
The music in my heart I bore
Long after it was heard no more.

William Wordsworth (1770–1850)

STRANGE FITS OF PASSION

Strange fits° of passion have I known: whims
And I will dare to tell,
But in the Lover's ear alone,
What once to me befell.

When she I love looked every day   5
Fresh as a rose in June,

I to her cottage bent my way,
Beneath an evening-moon.

Upon the moon I fixed my eye,
All over the wide lea;   10
With quickening pace my horse drew nigh
Those paths so dear to me.

And now we reached the orchard-plot;
And, as we climbed the hill,   14
The sinking moon to Lucy's cot°   cottage
Came near, and nearer still.

In one of those sweet dreams I slept,
Kind Nature's gentlest boon!
And all the while my eyes I kept
On the descending moon.   20

My horse moved on; hoof after hoof
He raised, and never stopped:
When down behind the cottage roof,
At once, the bright moon dropped.   24

What fond° and wayward thoughts will slide   foolish
Into a Lover's head!
"O mercy!" to myself I cried,
"If Lucy should be dead!"

William Wordsworth (1770–1850)

THEY FLEE FROM ME

They flee from me that sometime did me seek,
  With naked foot stalking in my chamber.
I have seen them gentle, tame, and meek,
  That now are wild, and do not remember
  That sometime they put themselves in danger   5
To take bread at my hand; and now they range,
Busily seeking with a continual change.

Thanked be fortune, it hath been otherwise
  Twenty times better; but once, in special,

THEY FLEE FROM ME. 20. *kindëly*: kindly. In addition to its modern meaning, it
means *typically*, according to her type or kind.

355

In thin array, after a pleasant guise,
    When her loose gown from her shoulders did fall,
    And she me caught in her arms long and small.
Therewith all sweetly did me kiss,
And softly said, "Dear heart, how like you this?"

It was no dream: I lay broad waking.   15
    But all is turned, thorough° my gentleness,   through
Into a strange fashion of forsaking;
    And I have leave to go of° her goodness,   because of
    And she also to use newfangleness.
But since that I so kindëly am served,   20
I would fain know what she hath deserved.

Sir Thomas Wyatt (1503?–1542)

A PRAYER FOR MY DAUGHTER

Once more the storm is howling, and half hid
Under this cradle-hood and coverlid
My child sleeps on. There is no obstacle
But Gregory's wood and one bare hill
Whereby the haystack- and roof-levelling wind,   5
Bred on the Atlantic, can be stayed;
And for an hour I have walked and prayed
Because of the great gloom that is in my mind.

I have walked and prayed for this young child an hour
And heard the sea-wind scream upon the tower,   10
And under the arches of the bridge, and scream
In the elms above the flooded stream;
Imagining in excited reverie

A PRAYER FOR MY DAUGHTER. 10, 14. *tower, future years:* When Yeats wrote this poem he lived in an old tower near the west coast of Ireland. It was a time of civil strife, and Yeats foresaw worse times coming. 25–26. Helen of Troy found life dull as the wife of Menelaus, was later given trouble by Paris, who abducted her to Troy, precipitating the Trojan War. 27. *great Queen:* Aphrodite, goddess of beauty, born full-grown out of the ocean, chose for her husband the lame and ill-favored Hephaestos, god of the forge. 32. *Horn of Plenty:* the cornucopia, which poured out to its recipient anything he desired. 59–64: *loveliest woman born:* Maud Gonne, whom Yeats wooed unsuccessfully (see "The Folly of Being Comforted," question 1, page 79, and "Among School Children," question 2, page 289, became a speaker for political and nationalistic causes.

That the future years had come,
Dancing to a frenzied drum, 15
Out of the murderous innocence of the sea.

May she be granted beauty and yet not
Beauty to make a stranger's eye distraught,
Or hers before a looking-glass, for such,
Being made beautiful overmuch, 20
Consider beauty a sufficient end,
Lose natural kindness and maybe
The heart-revealing intimacy
That chooses right, and never find a friend.

Helen being chosen found life flat and dull 25
And later had much trouble from a fool,
While that great Queen, that rose out of the spray,
Being fatherless could have her way
Yet chose a bandy-leggèd smith for man.
It's certain that fine women eat 30
A crazy salad with their meat
Whereby the Horn of Plenty is undone.

In courtesy I'd have her chiefly learned;
Hearts are not had as a gift but hearts are earned
By those that are not entirely beautiful; 35
Yet many, that have played the fool
For beauty's very self, has charm made wise,
And many a poor man that has roved,
Loved and thought himself beloved,
From a glad kindness cannot take his eyes. 40

May she become a flourishing hidden tree
That all her thoughts may like the linnet be,
And have no business but dispensing round
Their magnanimities of sound,
Nor but in merriment begin a chase, 45
Nor but in merriment a quarrel.
O may she live like some green laurel
Rooted in one dear perpetual place.

My mind, because the minds that I have loved,
The sort of beauty that I have approved, 50
Prosper but little, has dried up of late,

Yet knows that to be choked with hate
May well be of all evil chances chief.
If there's no hatred in a mind
Assault and battery of the wind   55
Can never tear the linnet from the leaf.

An intellectual hatred is the worst,
So let her think opinions are accursed.
Have I not seen the loveliest woman born
Out of the mouth of Plenty's horn,   60
Because of her opinionated mind
Barter that horn and every good
By quiet natures understood
For an old bellows full of angry wind?

Considering that, all hatred driven hence,   65
The soul recovers radical innocence
And learns at last that it is self-delighting,
Self-appeasing, self-affrighting,
And that its own sweet will is Heaven's will;
She can, though every face should scowl   70
And every windy quarter howl
Or every bellows burst, be happy still.

And may her bridegroom bring her to a house
Where all's accustomed, ceremonious;
For arrogance and hatred are the wares   75
Peddled in the thoroughfares.
How but in custom and in ceremony
Are innocence and beauty born?
Ceremony's a name for the rich horn,
And custom for the spreading laurel tree.   80

William Butler Yeats (1865–1939)

Comparing Byzantium to the modern world.

SAILING TO BYZANTIUM — *eastern half of Roman empire that tried to preserve the Roman culture!*

I

<u>That is no country for old men</u>. The young
In one another's arms, birds in the trees

358   POEMS FOR FURTHER READING

I stanza — Yeats creates an image of natural reproduction or the cycle of life.

—Those dying generations—at their song,
The salmon-falls, the mackerel-crowded seas,
Fish, flesh, or fowl, commend all summer long   5
Whatever is begotten, born, and dies.
Caught in that sensual music all neglect *what He admires the most in*
Monuments of unageing intellect. *Byzantium — the unaging intellect.*

II

An aged man is but a paltry thing, *The only thing an old man has left*
metaphor A tattered coat upon a stick, unless *that is essential & living is his soul.*
Soul clap its hands and sing, and louder sing *He used his soul to balance his*
For every tatter in its mortal dress, *decaying body. An old man*
Nor is there singing school but studying *can give nutritions by going*
Monuments of its own magnificence; *to Byzantium.*
And therefore I have sailed the seas and come   15
To the holy city of Byzantium.

It addresses the Saints.

III

O sages standing in God's holy fire *(spirit) He is looking at a picture of God*
ibi As in the gold mosaic of a wall, *with Saints around him.*
Come from the holy fire, perne in a gyre, *He is about spin in spiralling or*
And be the singing-masters of my soul. *to die and anyone-shaped flight*
Consume my heart away; sick with desire *that art has caused his*   21
And fastened to a dying animal *soul to awaken.*
It knows not what it is; and gather me *Spiral is ever ending, intellect &*
Into the artifice of eternity. *mystic*

Symbolizes eternity.

IV

Once out of nature I shall never take *Compares his life to art. He*
My bodily form from any natural thing, *wishes himself out of nature &*
But such a form as Grecian goldsmiths make *wishes to be turned into art. He*
Of hammered gold and gold enamelling *wants the required to take him*
to purity to become art.

SAILING TO BYZANTIUM. *Byzantium:* Ancient eastern capital of the Holy Roman
Empire; here symbolically a holy city of the imagination. 1. *That:* Ireland, or
the ordinary sensual world. 27–31. *such . . . Byzantium:* The Byzantine Emperor
Theophilus had made for himself mechanical golden birds which sang upon the
branches of a golden tree.

359

To keep a drowsy Emperor awake;
Or set upon a golden bough to sing   30
To lords and ladies of Byzantium
Of what is past, or passing, or to come.

[handwritten: Timelessness — idea of art which]
[handwritten: Yeats believes that art can   symbolizes classless beauty of a]
[handwritten: bring man immortality. Only in art does man remain]
[handwritten: immortal. The only part of an individual that lives forever is his]
[handwritten: ideas & art.]

William Butler Yeats (1865–1939)

FROM SATIRE ON WOMEN

Lavinia is polite, but not profane,°   irreligious
To church as constant as to Drury Lane.
She decently, in form, pays Heaven its due,
And makes a civil visit to her pew.
Her lifted fan, to give a solemn air,   5
Conceals her face, which passes for a prayer;
Curtsies to curtsies, then, with grace succeed,
Not one the fair omits, but at the creed.
Or if she joins the service, 'tis to speak;
Through dreadful silence the pent heart might break;   10
Untaught to bear it, women talk away
To God himself, and fondly think they pray.
But sweet their accent, and their air refined;
For they're before their Maker,—and mankind.
When ladies once are proud of praying well,   15
Satan himself will toll the parish bell.

Edward Young (1683–1765)

SATIRE ON WOMEN. 1. *Drury Lane:* A fashionable London theater.

[handwritten: paltry — trivial, inferior, or trashy]
[handwritten: artifice — guile, trickery]
[handwritten: sages — people distinguished for wisdom (as a profound philosopher)]
[handwritten: or mature & venerable man sound in judgment.]

Index of Authors, Titles, and First Lines

Authors' names appear in capitals, titles of poems in italics, and first lines of poems in roman type. Numbers in roman type indicate the page of the selection, and italic numbers indicate discussion of the poem.

Index of Topics

371

Rhythm 195, 202
Rime 180
Rime scheme 239
Run-on line 203

Sarcasm 113
Satire 113
Scansion 197–201
Sentimentality 260
Sestet 240
Simile 65
Single rime 190
Sonnet 240–43
Spondee 197
Stanza 197, 237–38
Stanzaic form 237

Symbol 82–90
Synecdoche 69–70

Tetrameter 197
Theme 28
Tone 162–66
Total meaning 148–49
Trimeter 197
Triple meter 197
Triple rime 190
Trochaic foot 197

Understatement 111

Verbal irony 113–15
Verse 195
Villanelle 243